ORLAND PARK PUBLIC LIBRARY

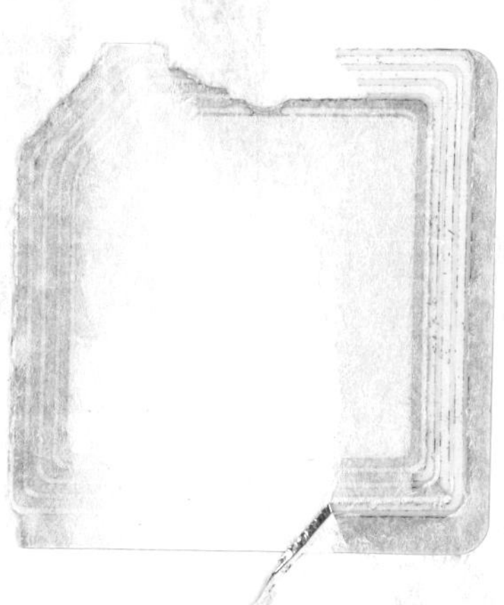

A Woman's Place. . .

CONTENTS

Acknowledgments ix
Foreword by the Honorable Barbara Jordan x
Preface xiii

Prologue 1

1. A Collision of Opportunity:
How We Got Here 9

2. Excuse Me, Miss, but Are You a Member?:
The Male Culture of the Capitol 40

3. Chicks in Congress:
What We Bring as Women 63

4. Women's Business:
How We Approach the Issues 88

5. You Can Run but You Can't Hyde:
The Hyde Amendment Vote 111

6. Legislating Dignity:
Minority Women 135

7. For Whom the Bells Toll:
Juggling Job and Family 151

8. Shattering the Glass Ceiling:
How Far Can We Go? 178

9. 218:
The Vote 191

Epilogue:
Our Legacy to Our Children 210

The Freshmen Women 215

ACKNOWLEDGMENTS

To the women of the freshman class—and the men behind them—a special thanks for helping me with this book and for your strength and support; and to the senior women in the House for paving the way.

To Hillary Rodham Clinton, for finding the time to share her insights.

To Barbara Jordan, for realizing the importance of this book.

To Paul Mahon, who has always been there for me, and who, with utmost good humor, can see the light—and can always distinguish the light and the heat.

To my friends Nancy Chasen and Don Spero, for putting up with me.

To Roberta McLean, who kept the lid on while I worked all hours of the day and night.

To Barbara Feinman, who put her heart into this effort like no one else.

Finally, to Jane Cavolina Meara, whose enthusiasm and dedication never wavered. It was her energy, and that of Crown's staff, that guided us through this project.

FOREWORD

By the Honorable Barbara Jordan

You've done it. Well done. You, the voters, have cast your ballots and in a single election have sent more women to Congress to represent your districts and your country than in any election ever before. And *you've* done it, too: You, the twenty-four new women representatives have really done it. You started shaking things up right from the start and show no signs of stopping. Good for you. Good for us. It's about time.

We can now say to the country that its elected representatives are finally becoming more representative. It happened in a big way on a wonderful night in November in the Year of the Woman. Congress, you can be sure, will never be the same. Nor will we.

My Year of the Woman was 1973, when a newly drawn Houston district sent me to Capitol Hill as the first black woman representative from the Deep South. I had served in the Texas senate for six years with thirty other senators and, despite its large size and diversity, we managed to get some good things done for the state. Then I got to Washington and found that my 434 close colleagues were engaged in what seemed to me to be divisive partisan maneuverings on every issue, no matter how trivial. The fulfillment of my dream to serve in national politics became at first a daunting challenge. I worked hard to understand the myriad of complex issues and to learn how things got done, reconciling my personal feelings with the positions of my party and the interests of my constituents. This was a new, unreal world to me, not only in the way the House of Representatives operated, but also in the very way it looked.

It sure didn't resemble the way I looked. And with only fifteen other women in the House—a whopping 3.5 percent of the body—

we sure didn't resemble the way the country looked. I worried about how our few voices would get heard on the important issues that meant something to us and to women nationwide.

I had sworn in my oath of office to uphold the Constitution of the United States. Yet even as I became one of its chosen defenders, I again felt excluded from its promising embrace. The Constitution opens eloquently enough with its sweeping proclamation, "We the people . . ." But for many years I had been certain that George Washington, James Madison, Benjamin Franklin, and the other draftsmen had left me out, both as a black and as a woman, by mistake and in ignorance. With the ratification of constitutional amendments and remedial decisions by the courts over the years, I came to feel that I really was included in "We the people."

When I came to Washington and took the oath of office, I felt excluded from the assurances of the Constitution, because women lacked representation in Congress itself, the most important place to be represented. Despite the evolution of women's political power since the passage of the Nineteenth Amendment, the fact remained that there were only sixteen of us in 1973. Although the number of women legislators nationwide has increased with each successive election, women remain woefully underrepresented.

At the very least, women should speak for the issues that uniquely belong to women. The new women representatives have created the opportunity to vault the impediments of congressional fears, failures, and fatigue and advance *our* legislative agenda. I had the misfortune to be in Congress when the Hyde Amendment was introduced and passed in 1977. I even served with Henry Hyde on the House Judiciary Committee. He pursued his legislation with an unusual enthusiasm and stridency that was as shocking as it was eye-opening to me. I used all my influence with the Texas delegation to get these representatives to vote against the Hyde Amendment. On one occasion, Texas representative and Majority Leader Jim Wright was on the floor during a Hyde Amendment vote. I noticed that he was about to cast his vote in support of the legislation. I took his hand and talked to him about it and eventually changed his vote. Although I was discouraged to see legislation pass which was sponsored by men and designed to limit women's freedom, I was pleased to help Jim Wright switch his influential vote. And yet, sixteen years later, the Hyde Amendment, incredibly, is still being flaunted by men over the desires of the women it tyrannizes.

When I saw the blow dealt to women by the Senate Judiciary Committee during the Clarence Thomas confirmation hearings, I knew that the Year of the Woman—the long-awaited, long-discussed, long-overdue Year of the Woman—was coming. The Committee's behavior was outrageous, a great disservice to the country. I knew at the conclusion of the hearings that this moment would be a rallying point to reenergize women all over the country to get involved in politics.

And so they did, and we did, voting in twenty-four new women. Well done. They face many of the same obstacles and frustrations I faced twenty years ago, but now we have so many more of them to overcome these barriers together. We now are in our strongest position to tell the men what's what and who's who. And they know it. There has been great movement since the elections of 1992 and there is an increasing awareness that we need to make Congress into the representative body that it should be, reflecting the true, vibrant diversity of our country. We were fifteen in 1973 and it's taken twenty years to triple that number to forty-eight. Sure, it has been too long, but we'll take it and we'll keep doubling, tripling, and growing until we at least achieve the 52 percent of the population that we are.

Things are changing and they are changing fast. Get active in politics wherever you are at whatever level you choose. Get out there and do what you are able to put more of us where we need to be. We will not rest until more women speak for the needs, worries, and interests of women.

It's about time.

PREFACE

I can remember standing on the stage at the Democratic National Convention, with all the women running for office that year, and thinking what an incredible experience it was and how incredible it was just for me to be there and be a part of all that was occurring.

But I was also thinking about what Barbara Jordan had said in the keynote address the night before, that it was so important that women enter the halls and councils of power. I was remembering how powerful those words were, coming from the granddaughter of a slave, when considered next to the words of Thomas Jefferson, a slave owner, and how the Jeffersonian notion that all men are created equal (if you are white, male, and a landowner) made Barbara Jordan's message really come into focus. It was then that I realized how truly important it was that women make it to Congress in numbers that count.

I decided to write this book shortly after I arrived in Washington in December of 1992. Once I got here and began to get my bearings, it sunk in just how few women have entered these imposing halls and how this void has historically molded the legislation that has been churned out over the years.

Our class was elected in what was dubbed the Year of the Woman—a campaign cycle like no other, a time in which record numbers of women from all different walks of life had the chutzpah, the campaign money, and the community support to run for office. Some people said we couldn't do it, that we weren't ready, but nonetheless, twenty-four of us beat the odds and woke up on November 5 transformed into congresswomen-elect of the United States House of Representatives. (There were twenty-nine women in the 102d Congress, including Eleanor Holmes Norton, the delegate representing the District of Columbia; twenty-four of them returned.) But the grand total of 48 women equals only 11 percent of the 435 members, and you don't need to be a census taker to know those numbers bear no relation to the true profile of America.

Yet still, it's a notable increase, so much so that I felt compelled to chronicle this historical sea change in our country's most important and visible institution. I am a chronicler by training and profession—and by inclination—and as I sit in a congressional committee hearing or at a joint session of Congress with the President, I find myself taking notes and writing questions to myself in the margin, much the way I did during my twenty-five years in broadcast news.

The same impulse was behind the writing of my first book, *They Came to Stay,* which was about the adoption of my first two children. At age twenty-eight, I became the first single woman in the United States to adopt a foreign child. Lee Heh came from Korea to the United States in 1970, and then Holly, from Vietnam, in 1974. I wanted to make sure that there was some sort of written record of their first six years, before we came into one another's lives. I hoped to document the process of single-parent adoption for others who might choose to do the same—and especially for Lee Heh and Holly. It was important to me to do this before the details were obscured by time.

Seventeen years later, I had the same sensation in Washington as the 103d Congress began to unfold. I was anxious to get it all down on paper before memories grew foggy and uncertain.

This book, if it accomplishes what I set out to do, will tell people why it was so important for us to get here and what it is really like to be a woman in Congress. The freshmen women were true collaborators in that they gave generously of their time and of themselves, sharing their stories about how they got here, why they came, and what challenges they encountered once they arrived. You'll see us through the first eight months, from finding our way around the maze of the Capitol to voting on major legislative issues. The women, both freshmen and senior members, spoke candidly about the obstacles they faced, about coming to understand just how things work, about learning to use the system without becoming subverted by it, and about reshaping the rules of the game to include women and their concerns. First Lady Hillary Rodham Clinton generously took the time to sit down with me and discuss the changing role of women in government. As chief architect of our nation's health care–reform package, the First Lady is more directly involved in policymaking than any of her predecessors.

■ ■ ■

As a reporter for NBC and its owned and operated stations, the stories that I enjoyed covering the most were the ones that had an effect on people's lives, on subjects such as adoption, child and sexual abuse, and homelessness. But after spending half my life asking questions, sitting on the other side of the desk armed with notepad and tape recorder, I decided I was dissatisfied with the answers I was getting, singularly unimpressed with the progress our lawmakers were making in so many areas vitally important to our nation—particularly concerning women, children, and the disenfranchised. Issues such as education, joblessness, and health care may not be the "sexy" ones, but they're the ones that matter most to me. These are the issues that made me get out of the bleachers and onto the playing field.

Back in December of 1991, when I was first approached by a small group of Montgomery County Democratic women to consider making a bid for the seat, I was, in a word, skeptical. But the specter of that all-white, all-male Senate Judiciary panel conducting the Anita Hill–Clarence Thomas hearings—an image that has since haunted the collective female American psyche—enraged me. And as if that wasn't enough, there was the fact that in Pennsylvania's 204-year history, my state had sent a mere 3 women to Congress, all of whom had succeeded their husbands after their deaths. I looked around, saw no other woman declaring her candidacy, and said to myself, "If I'm not going to do it, who is?" And I thought of how many times I had told my kids, "You have to be prepared to lose before you can win."

■ ■ ■

Getting here is only half the magic act; the task at hand is to carve out our own place. Some of our male colleagues, uncomfortable with change, have had trouble with our presence. My colleague

Oklahoma Congressman James Inhofe, for instance, publicly referred to me as "that three M girl," eight months into the job. Referring to me at age fifty-one as a "girl" is inaccurate, demeaning, and pathetically behind the times. I took pity on my out-of-touch colleague and pulled him aside to let him know it's time to thaw out, that the ice age is over. He still didn't get it. And so, Congressman Inhofe, I hope you'll take the time to read chapter 2. It might illuminate for you what your two daughters are up against in a world like ours.

With each passing day, I realize how much we have to learn about one another, that this is a kind of joint educational journey. We have so far to go in regard to true equity; at times, it seems easier to work on the obvious problems, such as comparable wages and funding for women's health care, than to work on the conflicts that manifest themselves on a personal level.

My husband and best friend, Ed Mezvinsky, is a former Iowa congressman. I have kidded him that his voting record in regard to gender issues was really terrific but that he didn't always personally live the changes he tried to implement. This topic would typically surface when we were loading up the kids for a vacation (Ed's four daughters from a previous marriage, two adopted children, three children for whom we are legal guardians, and two biological kids make for a pretty lively crowd). I'd say to Ed, "There are thirteen of us going on this vacation. I've been responsible for twelve of us." So maybe it's time to rethink the way we've been taught to do things so that we can teach our children how to live their lives in a more balanced way. I believe that one of the differences between the sexes is that women tend to be nurturers, and in that role, it is natural to be more cognizant of fundamental rights and individuality. More and more men these days are taking on that role, and we need to encourage this in our fathers, husbands, and brothers so that they, in turn, will teach their sons.

I hope this book will be read by women and men alike—and by young girls who are trying to figure out what kind of lives they are going to lead and what their choices really are. When I was growing up, it never, *ever* occurred to me that a political career was an option; there were remarkably few female role models in government.

And so these collected impressions are meant for the next generation. I hope that if you are a young woman reading this book, you will see yourself in these pages, that among this diverse group of intensely committed women you will hear a voice that inspires you, and that you will not feel left out of the equation, as young women of my generation did.

I want to add here that it's not that I believe women are inherently better or worse—we are different—or that we should single-handedly be running the show. On the contrary, I love and respect my husband and sons, and I count among my favorite colleagues many terrific congress*men.* The point is that we *all* have something to bring to the conversation—each in our own way.

Those of us who came in with the Year of the Woman owe a huge debt to the congresswomen who preceded us. I, as one of the few women here with no previous official political experience, have particular reason to be grateful to my more politically seasoned colleagues—for their generosity of spirit, wisdom, and counsel.

When we first arrived, we wanted to add our energy and commitment to the fight that had already been waged. We very quickly agreed on four issues that were a priority for all twenty-four women of the 103d Congress. However, we knew we were not mavericks on these issues.

California congresswoman Nancy Pelosi, who had been serving since 1988, gently reminded us that there had already been a lot of blood shed on the floor of the House, that we were entering the war midbattle. I appreciated her honesty, and knowing that we were the new kids on the block, I felt it important that no one mistake our enthusiasm for arrogance. We knew full well that we were here because others had paved the way for us, and none of us presumed to think otherwise. Our biggest hope was that our sheer numbers would make a difference in the lives of those who had served before us, as well as in the lives of those who would come after, and that someday our daughters could look to the nation's capital and see something that wasn't there before—a woman's place.

MARJORIE MARGOLIES-MEZVINSKY
Narberth, Pennsylvania
March 1994

A Woman's Place . . .

Prologue

Carrie Meek had seen a lot in her sixty-seven years. And a lot of what she had seen was about change—social change, political change, economic change. The daughter of sharecroppers, the granddaughter of slaves, the newly elected Democratic congresswoman had grown up just two miles from the Florida state capitol. As a young girl, she was prohibited from entering the building because of the color of her skin. More than fifty years later, not only would she enter that same building but she would be one of the most powerful and revered lawmakers to grace its halls, first as a member of the state house and then of its senate.

And now, here she was, a member of the United States House of Representatives, in office only six months, and she had to endure this pathetic disgrace—this national display of racism and sexism for all the American public to tune into on C-SPAN. What she was witnessing, the drama that was unfolding before her very eyes, was enough to make her sick. In fact, it was enough to make her cry, and cry she did. But these tears were not tears of fear. These were tears of anger, and she was not embarrassed by them. Oh no, the only people who should have been embarrassed were her white male colleagues who were orchestrating this archaic concert of ill will.

It was Wednesday, June 30, a hot, muggy Washington morning, and the issue up for debate on the House floor was the Hyde Amendment, a restriction on the use of Medicaid funds for abortions. Since 1977, Henry Hyde, a well-respected Republican member from Illinois, had successfully blocked the expenditure of federal money for this purpose. The only exceptions his amendment allowed for were cases in which the mother's life was in danger. And here he was, back again, trying to shepherd through a revised version of his amendment.

His new version broadened the exceptions to include rape and incest, but for pro-choice legislators, this was sorely inadequate, to say the least. The Hyde Amendment had to go; it was one in a series of steps that needed to be taken to undo the damage of the Reagan-Bush era regarding abortion policy. Although there was finally a pro-choice President in the White House, it did not mean—as abortion rights groups had hoped—that there would be consensus on their issue. Sure, the Year of the Woman had reaped the symbolically significant gain in female congressional membership from twenty-eight to forty-eight, but that was nowhere near enough to ensure the passage of the Freedom of Choice Act (FOCA)—a bill that would bar states from restricting a woman's right to an abortion except in limited circumstances. (Although most of the newly elected twenty-four congresswomen and twenty-four senior female members were pro-choice, some of them came from districts where their constituents did not want their tax dollars paying for poor women's abortions. When pressure was brought to bear on them by their fellow congresswomen, they argued that the Hyde funding issue was a separate one from the FOCA issue, that being pro-choice didn't automatically mean you were willing to force constituents to pay for other people's abortions.)

And so here we were, the pro-choice women and the pro-life men, duking it out, and it wasn't pretty. In fact, it was downright ridiculous. The scene resembled a bad high school dance, with all the girls huddled in one corner and all the boys in another, each camp eyeing the other warily.

It became an exercise in frustration and anguish for the women, one in which knowledge of arcane parliamentary procedure became key to winning the day.

The first obstacle we faced was when eighty-three-year-old Kentucky Democrat William Natcher, the chairman of the powerful House Appropriations Committee, worked out a deal with the House leadership that allowed Henry Hyde to present his amendment. The amendment was to be attached to the fiscal 1994 spending bill for the departments of Labor, Health and Human Services, and Education, as it was each year. Now Henry Hyde was free to bring the politics of abortion to the floor.

Maria Cantwell, a thirty-five-year-old freshman Democrat from Washington State, was positioned by one of the doors. She had been given a list of colleagues to work. But as members rolled by her and she tried to enlist their aid, she was rebuffed. "Uh-huh, well, I can't help you out," she was told by one after the other. Maria stood there, stunned. All the dialoguing, all the friendships she had worked so hard to build over the last few months were just deteriorating before her very eyes. Maria, usually even-keeled, was shocked.

She is the kind of woman who is good at getting along well with her male colleagues. Back home, she had served in the state house, where she often ventured to a place her distaff colleagues hesitated to enter—the men's lounge. She'd sit there and watch basketball with the guys, hooting and hollering right alongside them. But here, things are different.

■ ■ ■

Meanwhile, on the floor, the debating had begun. As Maria watched the Republicans perform their pirouettes of parliamentary procedure across the House floor, it underscored for her the fact that while the women had come a long way, they still had a long ways to go.

Henry Hyde, a friendly, cordial, white-haired, rather portly man, who looked more like a small-town baker than a big-time congressman, was in top form. "Now, my colleagues, the French have a marvelous gift for phrasemaking, and one of their marvelous phrases is *cri di coeur,* a cry of the heart, and there are two cries of the heart in every human being's life. The very first cry of the heart occurs in the womb, and if my colleagues have ever looked at a sonogram picture of a little baby in the womb, they would know that this is when the first *cri di coeur* occurs: I want to be born. It is a reflection of instincts, the urge to survive. It is inaudible, but it is there: I want to be born.

"And the second cry of the heart is at the end of our lives. It is the last thing we say: I don't want to die, I don't want to die. . . . Humanity asks an anguished question, and it asks it many, many times. It asks it a million and a half times in our country to the unborn:

"To be or not to be?

"That is Hamlet's great question, and we answer it, not to be, when we perform an abortion. We ask it a million and a half times a year. . . ."

New York Democratic congresswoman Nita Lowey, the chairwoman of the Pro-Choice Task Force, had been in Congress since 1989, and she knew we were in trouble. Things weren't going the way we had planned. After consulting with pro-choice male members of the Appropriations Committee, the women members had come up with a strategy of using procedural maneuvers to prevent Henry Hyde from speaking. But they hadn't figured that William Natcher, one of their own, would help the Republicans get the amendment onto the floor for discussion. Although Natcher wasn't pro-choice, he was a Democrat and you could usually count on him to vote with his party on procedural votes. Now we were going to have to figure out something else, and we were going to have to figure fast. Nita Lowey rose to speak.

"Mr. Chairman, we heard from my good friend, the gentleman from Illinois, about listening to the cry of the heart, and I ask my friends, let us listen to the cry of the heart, let us put a human face on the Hyde Amendment, and let us think very carefully. . . .

"For far too long, women's health-care needs have been neglected . . . our work will not be complete if we fail to affirm the medical significance of American women to make their own reproductive health-care decisions."

Cynthia McKinney, a young black Democratic congresswoman from Georgia who represents Atlanta suburbs and parts of Augusta and Savannah, listened intently as the debate ensued. Anger welled up inside her. Finally, she grabbed a pen and paper, and while her colleagues grew hotter under the collar, she scribbled furiously, expressing the cry that was in *her* heart.

Cynthia indicated that she had something to say and the floor was yielded to her by Pat Schroeder. She rose for her turn, walking forcefully to the well. A beautiful woman with delicately plaited hair, huge dark eyes, and usually an even bigger smile, Cynthia looked very solemn at the moment. Divorced, the mother of a seven-year-old son, this thirty-eight-year-old woman knew that the issue of choice was an important one to her constituency and to herself.

"Mr. Chairman, for far too many women in this country, the legal right to choose is meaningless because they have had no practical access to the full range of reproductive services. The real choice for low-income women becomes carrying their pregnancy to term or finding alternative funding, that is, for rent, for food, or clothing, or money for unsafe and sometimes self-induced abortions," declared Cynthia, her clear, strong voice filling the hall, the resonance of her controlled fury reverberating against the walls of the House chamber. This was the same voice that, whenever she was a little down, would sweetly sing along with her Ray Charles recording of "Georgia on My Mind." She knew that there were people back home who needed this funding. She wasn't about to lose this one, at least not without a fight.

"During the past sixteen years of the Hyde Amendment the unintended pregnancies have not gone away. All available data confirms that what Henry Hyde has succeeded in doing has been to create devastating consequences in the lives of low-income women. The Hyde Amendment is nothing but a discriminatory policy against poor women who happen to be disproportionately black. By denying poor women abortion services while at the same time paying for childbirth and sterilization, the federal government is practicing discriminatory policies," said Cynthia, taking a breath, looking up from her paper.

"Mr. Chairman, this is about equity and fairness for all women, and quite frankly, I have just about had it with my colleagues who vote against people of color, against the poor, and vote against women."

Cynthia sat down. The other black women nodded and gave her signs of support. Carrie Meek, who thought of Cynthia as a daughter, was proud of the way she handled herself with grace and dignity.

Karen Shepherd, a pro-choice freshman Democrat from Utah, was overwhelmed and dismayed by the emotional bubble that had formed around the group of women with whom she was sitting. Quietly, she slipped from her seat and walked to the back of the room, where she stayed to watch the scene play itself out. What appalled her most was how vulnerable she realized the Democrats were, as a party, to clever people like Henry Hyde who knew how to tap into racism and divide the members.

"Mr. Chairman, I believe strongly in a woman's right to choose. The right to choose is meaningless without the means to choose," Carolyn Maloney, a freshman from New York, said. "But even to my colleagues who do not believe in a woman's right to choose, this is not the way to make policy on this important issue."

As the pro-choice members took turns making their pleas, Henry Hyde got back up to speak. "I want to say to my friends on the other side, especially those that debated opposite my position, that I am sincerely glad they were born and they avoided being aborted. I am delighted they are here. They have added to the civilization we live in.

"About those people that say the poor are discriminated against, you know what we do? We tell poor people, 'You can't have a job, you can't have a good education, you can't have a decent place to live. . . . I'll tell you what we'll do, we'll give you a free abortion because there are too many of you people, and we want to kind of refine, refine the breed. . . .' "

Some of the women began to hiss.

"And I tell you, if you read the literature, that is what is said, and that is what is done," Henry Hyde continued. "The poor children—"

"Mr. Chairman, will the gentleman yield?" Cardiss Collins, a black Democratic congresswoman also from Illinois, sharply demanded.

"I do not have the time," Henry Hyde replied.

"I am offended by that kind of debate," Cardiss shouted, rising to her feet and hurrying to a microphone.

"I'm going to direct my friend to a few ministers who will tell her just what goes on in her community," Henry Hyde countered.

Cardiss, infuriated, demanded that Henry Hyde's words be expunged from the record. A contingent of black congresswomen had joined Cardiss at the microphone. For a few moments, it seemed as though all hell had broken loose. Instead of the floor of the House of Representatives, the place had taken on the frenzy of Wall Street's trading floor, people waving their arms, pointing fingers, and yelling.

Carrie Meek, for one, was fuming. How dare any white male tell us what goes on in our damn communities? she thought. The condescension, the patronizing manner, was more than she could stand. She turned to me and said, "Just let me at him. I'll get him by the you-know-whats."

David Obey, a Democrat from Wisconsin who had been serving in Congress for more than two decades, had an alternative amendment of his own. But when he requested a turn to speak, Corrine Brown, a black Democratic freshman from Florida, said, "I object."

"Shut up!" Obey growled.

This started another round of fire. Nothing could save the situation now.

Finally, the vote was taken and the bill went through, with the Hyde Amendment intact. One by one, we left the floor, feeling like second-class citizens.

When we returned to our offices, the reality of the situation began to sink in. One woman told another, "I feel like we were raped on the House floor today." Some blamed the leadership, whom they felt hadn't done enough to protect their position. Others blamed the parliamentarian, who they felt stacked the deck in favor of the Hyde supporters. And some blamed themselves—for not being better versed in parliamentary procedure.

"I'm not sure a lot of women are willing to lower their ethical standards to fight the battle," observed Democratic freshman Karan English. "You know we want to maintain our dignity. At the same time, we want to win. Well, there's a lot of people on the other side that don't give a hoot about dignity or ethics or facts."

Outside the Capitol, Pat Schroeder, among others, faced the press. She had been fighting these battles for nearly twenty years now, and in the beginning she was practically alone. When the new class arrived, with a record number of women, they brought with them hope and energy and the promise of a new era.

When asked to characterize what had just happened inside the Capitol, Pat looked the camera squarely in the lens and delivered her verdict. "The Year of the Woman," said the congressional doyenne, "just went down the chute."

■ ■ ■

As painful as the Hyde Amendment episode was for the women, it served a critical purpose: It defined for them how far they'd come, how far they still needed to go, and exactly where they stood among their colleagues. This point was driven home best by Congressman George Miller, who turned to freshman Anna Eshoo during the debate and said, "Look around, because everybody just changed today. It will never be the same."

CHAPTER ONE

A Collision of Opportunity: How We Got There

When Deborah Pryce told her mother and father she had decided to resign from her judgeship on the Franklin County Municipal Court in order to run for the open seat in Ohio's Fifteenth Congressional District, a thick veil of silence draped itself over the room. Deborah waited nervously for someone to say something, anything. Finally, to break the silence, Deborah leaned forward.

"Mom, what do you think?"

Her mother, all choked up, appeared reluctant to speak her mind. After a moment, she responded to the news her eldest daughter had just delivered. "How can you leave that job? You love your job on the bench. How can you leave it to go to that sleazy place?"

Deborah felt as if she had been punched in the stomach. Her mother, her role model, a woman who had had a career when few did, didn't think her daughter should do this.

Deborah's mother and father were both pharmacists and had worked alongside each other in a family business while they raised four girls and a boy. Deborah's mom was the kind of woman who taught her daughters to believe in themselves, to know in their hearts that they could accomplish whatever it was they set their sights upon. Sure, it wasn't the traditional Ozzie and Harriet family scenario around the Pryce house when they were growing up. Rather, it was grab what you could out of the refrigerator and pick up after yourself. It was, "I'll try not to forget to pick you up after swimming lessons. If I get off from work in time, I'll be there; if not, just hang out on the front steps and I'll be there shortly." The kids were used to seeing their mom in a white pharmacist uniform, not an apron.

Even though her mother couldn't endorse her daughter's decision, Deborah had to follow her heart, and her heart said to run. It was too good an opportunity to pass up. For one, the seat was open, as a result of incumbent Chalmers Wylie stepping out of the race ten days before the filing deadline. After twenty-six years in the seat, he suddenly decided to pull out, even after the district had been redrawn with him in mind. Congressman Wylie had been one of the members whose name appeared on the notorious list of House bank offenders, with 515 overdrafts. He contended that the bank scandal did not cause him to drop out. Whatever the reason, the seat was open and Deborah wanted to go for it.

Deborah's mother was right about her daughter loving her job as a judge; in fact, she'd recently been elected to serve another six years. It was a good, secure position, not one to be discarded on a whim. Deborah, torn between the comfortable known and the exciting unknown, sat down with a piece of paper and made a list of the pros and cons.

After careful deliberation, the pros won. "I think the thing that finally decided it for me was that if I got this seat, it would really raise the consciousness level of my community about women and their involvement in politics, and everything else in life," says Deborah in retrospect. But settling the decision of whether to run was only the first step in an uphill journey. And it was perhaps steeper for a Republican woman candidate than for her Democratic counterparts. "I didn't feel a whole groundswell of support from women, necessarily, in an organized way. But I did feel it out and about, on parade routes. I would just get so many thumbs-up and 'Thata girl!' 'Do it!'

your call. I've been sitting here waiting for the press to call. Don't you want my endorsement?"

"Yes! I do! I just needed to confirm that you actually called. In fact, we'll have a press release out within the hour." So Karan called the campaign crew and reported, "Goldwater is at this number, will take press calls, and he's endorsing me."

Karan, who had been up about seven points before the Goldwater endorsement, won by a twelve-point margin. To this day, she believes Goldwater was very influential with the moderate Republican vote. Goldwater endorsed Karan because, while he didn't necessarily agree with her on every issue, she'd been in Arizona politics for more than a decade and she was an Arizonan, by God. In addition, Karan was pro-choice, as was Goldwater, whose late wife had been a highly respected pro-choice activist.

Also, he had been very unhappy about the fact that Doug Wead was going around identifying himself as a "Goldwater Republican," when in fact he was a carpetbagger who had moved to the state only two years before he put in his bid for office. As his name suggested, he was just shooting up all over the state, invasively setting down roots in every little nook and cranny, moving five times within the state in the preceding year to make sure he ended up in Arizona's newly redrawn Sixth Congressional District.

Karan regards Goldwater as key to her political shaping. "One of the reasons that he has become so influential to me is because I am so proud of his endorsement. I think about him when I vote." She admires Goldwater for having adhered to his convictions, even when he knew it could hamstring his political legacy. "He has been criticized from that day. They were going to change the name of the Republican party building, which is named after him."

Karan looks back on her race with gratitude to Goldwater, as well as appreciation for the unique variety of factors that created the Year of the Woman. "The choice issue was one. The fact that we redistricted and there were open seats all over this country gave women an opportunity that they wouldn't have had had they run against incumbents. There was a series of events . . . and other women's organizations having come to maturity, developed to a level where they were providing the same kinds of support teams that men have known for a long time. So there was a kind of collision of opportunity, a kind of chemical reaction."

The Anita Hill hearings fired Karan up. "I was very angry when I was watching the hearings, for a lot of different reasons. . . . You know, it just amazed me that we have people in Congress who didn't understand the issue enough to let it elevate to that level. That was just a disgusting display; it should never have happened. It was nothing to do with whether or not you agree with her or with him; it should never have happened. Had one of those guys been sensitive to the differences between men and women—just the difference!—then it would not have happened."

■ ■ ■

Clear across the country, in Brooklyn, New York, another woman was making one of the hardest decisions of her life, trying to decide whether or not to run for public office. The summer and fall of 1991 had been extremely difficult for Nydia Velazquez, then thirty-eight years old. Her mother, back in Puerto Rico, was quite ill, her brother was struggling with a drug problem, and Nydia herself was exhausted and emotionally drained. She had always given a lot of herself and she was beginning to feel, just lately, that she wasn't getting enough back. Around this time, a group of people in her community came to her with an idea. They told her they wanted her to run for Congress in the newly drawn Hispanic-majority Twelfth Congressional District. If she won, she would be the first Puerto Rican woman in Congress. Nydia was used to being first. She was already the first Hispanic woman to serve on the New York City Council, a seat she held from 1984 to 1986. And she was the first person in her family to earn a high school diploma.

It had been her lifelong dream to help the Puerto Rican community, to give them the voice that she felt they needed so desperately and deserved perhaps even more. Going to Congress would be a sure way to do that. But the depression that had been building for months hit its crescendo. "I just reached this point where I thought, Hey, this is not worth it."

And then Nydia did the unthinkable. She tried to end her own life, to stifle the pain, disappointment, and frustration that had somehow enveloped her and was squeezing the hope and strength out of her. "I reached this moment in my life when I couldn't realize that I was ill, that I needed professional help. . . . After it happened, when I woke up in the hospital, I realized that I was still alive. The first thought that came into my mind was, God wants me here, and he wants me here for a reason. And that day when I woke up, I knew that I was coming here, that I was coming to Congress."

But even though Nydia was able to recover her physical and emotional strength quickly, she had a long battle in front of her. She won the Democratic primary, beating out five contenders, one of whom was nine-term incumbent Stephen Solarz. Solarz's district had been dismantled and he had decided to throw his hat in the ring in the newly drawn Twelfth District. While critics labeled him a well-financed outsider who couldn't understand the needs of the Hispanic community, there were those who predicted that Solarz would benefit from the divisive Hispanic community, which seemed unable to back one candidate.

The only advantage that Solarz had, in Nydia's opinion, was that he had so much money to spend on the campaign. When Nydia didn't have the money to run an ad, she would pick up the paper and there would be Solarz smiling back at her. When she woke in the morning and switched on the radio, there would be Solarz's voice filling her bedroom. And when she turned on the television in the evening to watch the news, there would be Solarz staring back at her. But instead of overwhelming her, his ubiquitousness fired her up.

"It made me stronger to get out there earlier in the morning and hit the streets and the subways and the senior citizens' centers," she says. "I think fighting poverty gives you so much strength, and that is what people like Stephen Solarz did not understand. He thought that he would intimidate me, that he would destroy me. But I knew that this fight was going to be fought in the street, not on TV or radio or in the newspaper. Newspapers do not vote; TV does not vote. Let's take the message onto the street, to the people who have not been represented before."

And so Nydia and her grassroots efforts prevailed. She won the primary, and it seemed like it would be smooth sailing against her Republican opponent, Angel Diaz, in the general election. After all, the district was nearly 75 percent Democratic.

But then hospital records of her suicide attempt were anonymously, cruelly, faxed to the media and Nydia was forced to discuss publicly an extremely personal experience. At a news conference, she said, "It was a sad and painful experience for me—and one I thought was now in the past."

Clearly, the voters agreed that this low point in her life was not relevant to the election at hand. Nydia had been right, of course, that televisions and newspapers don't vote—people do. So the people elected her, with 77 percent of the vote, and Señorita Smith was on her way to Washington.

■ ■ ■

Of the twenty-four freshmen women, only two of us, both Democrats, got here by beating out incumbents in the general election: Carolyn Maloney, from New York, and Pat Danner, from Missouri. In addition, Nydia Velazquez and Blanche Lambert, from Arkansas, beat out Democrat incumbents in their primaries.

"I think that in the women's movement we're seeing a progression," says Carolyn Maloney. "If you go back and look at most women, the first women who were elected to Congress took the seats of their husbands, then women elected to Congress took open seats, and now women are beginning to beat incumbents."

But beating an incumbent isn't easy. Carolyn had a rough ride. She was turned down by organizations that help raise money so that women can run for Congress because they didn't perceive her to be a good bet.

The leading fund-raising organization is EMILY's List, which stands for "early money is like yeast (it makes the dough rise)." It was founded to help women raise the money that men have traditionally raised from business and industry connections. EMILY's List is for pro-choice female Democrats and backs only the most promising candidates. Although they've been tremendously successful, raising several million dollars in the last campaign cycle, they still feel they can't afford to risk money on potential losers.

When I first went to EMILY's List, they turned me down, too. They said, "You're not a terrible candidate; it's just that you can't win." But then when the numbers started to come in and they saw that I had a chance, they decided to back me. But I won by only 1,373 votes, and their endorsement and that of other funding groups helped me every step of the way. So did the tenacity of my finance director, Linda August, who never took no for an answer. But it was so close, even up to the last minute, that my opponent's staff was already hunting for Washington apartments.

Another factor that made Carolyn's race tough was that she was running against Bill Green, who had already served seven terms and had proven himself to be one of the more sympathetic Republicans in the House with regard to women's issues. However, Carolyn did garner the enthusiastic support of the local chapters of the National Women's Political Caucus, Business & Professional Women, and the National Organization of Women (NOW). But only NOW came out in support of Carolyn on the national level; most of the other national organizations assumed she couldn't overcome Green's fund-raising prowess, name recognition, and impressive record of having previously beaten strong Democratic candidates such as Bella Abzug.

This did not dissuade Carolyn from continuing her race; she had never been a quitter and wasn't about to become one now. "I think that's one reason I beat Green. I just said, 'I'm not going to give up. I'm going to win.' "

In one of the biggest upsets in the country, she won with an ultimate margin of nearly five thousand votes, despite the fact that Bill Green spent $1.14 million to Carolyn's $277,000. "More than anything else, people told me that I couldn't win because of his fund-raising advantage," Carolyn says.

"After I won, he demanded a recount, even though there was a four-thousand-vote margin. He got his recount and I ended up with almost a thousand votes more!" Carolyn shakes her thick mane of blond hair as she remembers this.

It's clear that Carolyn, a former New York City Council member, is more comfortable doing than reflecting. When asked where she got the chutzpah to wage such a tough race, if she's been a fighter since she was a child, she shrugs dismissively. "I don't know how others see me. What was it that Robert Burns said? 'Oh, for the gift of God to see ourselves as others see us.' I do know that I've always been a hard worker, especially for things I really believe in."

■ ■ ■

Another candidate who was no stranger to adversity was Democrat Lynn Woolsey. She knew two years before California congresswoman Barbara Boxer started running for the Senate that her House seat would become available. Barbara had brought a group of people to her home whom she thought might realistically consider running. This group, both men and women, had been her supporters, and Barbara had had her eye on them. She wanted to give them an early heads up. That afternoon, the lights went on for Lynn and she realized this could be her opportunity. She had dreamed of running for Congress but would never have tried to run against Barbara.

All along, Barbara had been sponsoring "Women Making History" luncheons that Lynn attended with friends. The others would say, "Oh, isn't this great, but I can't imagine doing that." But of course, Lynn could imagine it, and she told them so. "That's exactly what I want to be doing." And they responded, "You're crazy."

But Lynn wasn't scared off. She'd waged bigger wars, beaten the odds before. When she was twenty-nine, she'd divorced her husband, a stockbroker, and was left with a nearly blank résumé and a family to feed and clothe.

In the fall of 1992, while Lynn was on the campaign trail, weeks before the general election, she told a backyard gathering in Petaluma how her life had taken a different course from the one she had imagined it would. "I didn't plan on being a career woman or a politician. My plans were to marry and raise children. But my marriage didn't work out . . . and I was faced with some harsh realities, three small children, and no means of support."

Woolsey explained how she had landed a job that paid a pathetically inadequate salary and how she was forced to rely on welfare and food stamps to feed her children. She had to sell her house and trade in her new station wagon for a very used Volkswagen Bug. It wasn't until she remarried that she was able to give up government assistance. At age forty-two, she completed her college degree, then started her own employment agency, and in 1984 she was elected to the Petaluma City Council.

But those three years on public assistance left an indelible mark on her spirit and formed the priorities she would ultimately define for herself as a politician. Not long after Woolsey started to serve in Washington, she returned home to northern California for a town hall meeting with a group of social service agencies, arranged by the Sonoma County Task Force on the Homeless. "You hired me because I think you know I've walked your talk," she told the crowd. They nodded their heads; they clapped their hands. That's exactly why they had voted for her. Lynn was grateful that they believed in her and she would never forget how hard it had been back when she was struggling just to feed her kids. But as hard as her own personal experiences had been, she knew that she was one of the lucky ones, even when she had had to get public assistance. "I always knew in my head how lucky I was because I was educated, I could speak English, and I was assertive. It never left me that I was so much more fortunate than most mothers on welfare," Lynn says forcefully, her silver-gray, shoulder-length bobbed hair bouncing around as she moves her head. "It was, Oh my God, if it was this hard for me, imagine! That's why it never left me. It was never, Oh my God, I made it. Why can't you?"

Lynn knew that women had sent her to Washington, and she was glad. But she also knew that it wasn't enough, that the Year of the Woman needed to become the Decade of the Woman, the Century of the Woman.

"Anita Hill helped me get here," Lynn says firmly. "For most

Americans, the Clarence Thomas hearings brought into focus how underrepresented women are here in their government. But forty-eight women is not representative; there's not nearly enough of us."

■ ■ ■

Some of the women already serving in Congress were angry, plenty angry, when the news first broke that there was a woman who claimed to have been sexually harassed by Supreme Court Justice nominee Clarence Thomas and that there weren't going to be additional hearings to look into the charges. One of those particularly ticked off was Representative Rosa DeLauro, a Democrat from Connecticut, who had been elected to Congress in 1990.

"When the news came forward that there were charges of sexual harassment over that weekend, and when we went back into session on that Tuesday, a number of us decided that we would do what we call the 'one-minutes,' where you get up [on the House floor] and speak." There were a number of women who wanted to do a one-minute about Anita Hill, and Rosa waited while seven or eight people went in front of her. Finally, it was her turn and she approached the podium. She began to speak. She called for the Senate to hold off on a vote and to hold hearings regarding the accusations against Clarence Thomas. What Rosa didn't realize, new to the thick morass of parliamentary procedure, was that she had just committed a parliamentary no-no by referring to the Senate by name. What she should have said was "the other body." A couple of Republicans, listening and hoping for a misstep, jumped up and demanded that her words be "taken down," meaning stricken from the record, and as a result she would be banned from speaking on the floor for the rest of the day. At this point, everything came to a halt as the Speaker of the House and the majority leader approached the floor. Rosa was nonplussed and alarmed. "I said to myself at that point, 'DeLauro, something serious is going on here!' "

Speaker Tom Foley then ruled that Rosa could continue her one-minute, having a remaining twenty-eight seconds on the clock. "But those guys got up again; they wanted to deny me my twenty-eight seconds. So there had to be two roll call votes on the floor of the House, one to deal with the words and a second to allow me to go forward. So it was about an hour, an hour-and-ten-minute proceeding, where my colleagues came to the House floor and overwhelmingly voted for me to continue my twenty-eight seconds."

Meanwhile, while Rosa was stuck on the floor, she knew that a group of her colleagues were at that moment planning to storm the Senate in hopes of joining a meeting with the Senate majority leader, George Mitchell. Rosa wanted to accompany them but had to stay on the House floor, holding on to her spot in the well. Barbara Kennelly, a fellow Connecticut Democrat, also wanted very much to be with the group that had gone over to the Senate. But she was in charge of the one-minutes that day and she couldn't get away. "I was there in spirit and I wish to heaven I had been there."

Rosa, who usually talks very quickly because she is a very busy woman with a lot on her plate, stops to pause. She softly chuckles over the inherent irony in the situation. "What the Republicans wanted to do was to cut off debate on the issue. But what they did was to prolong the debate, and this was on national news. They wanted to deny me my right to speak."

Because the Republicans don't have control of the leadership, they know that parliamentary procedure is a very important tool, and they'll use it to death, to an extent that Rosa believes negates the purpose of us all being here in Congress. "The thing you take out of this is that this is a place where we debate everything. This is a place where you debate every single issue and have the opportunity on the floor. This is known as 'the people's house.' But the Republicans wanted to cut off that debate; they wanted to use parliamentary procedure as a way to thwart the ability to speak out."

Nita Lowey was one of the seven Democratic women who were able to get away from the House floor and see what was going on in the Senate. The other six women were Barbara Boxer of California, Patsy Mink of Hawaii, Eleanor Holmes Norton, the delegate from the District of Columbia, Pat Schroeder of Colorado, Louise Slaughter of New York, and Jolene Unsoeld of Washington State. They were ready to give the men what for, and nearly two years later, you can still hear the determination in Nita Lowey's voice when she recalls that day. "We went over to the Senate because we knew they were having a private meeting. We walked up the steps and asked to see George Mitchell and we were stopped right there."

They stood outside the large wood doors and knocked. A pack of reporters had followed the seven congresswomen over to the Senate side and were waiting with cameras and tape recorders, hoping for a real brawl. The senators dispatched a female messenger to deliver a response to the women's request to join them.

"I'm sorry, ma'am, you can't come into this meeting and address the senators," she told the women firmly.

"We're sorry, *ma'am*, but please tell them, 'Either we talk to you or we talk to these reporters.' " The tension was palpable as the women waited and the reporters watched. A few moments later, George Mitchell came out from behind closed doors and explained to the group that they couldn't be permitted to crash the meeting. But the senator, eyeing the bloodthirsty press, ushered the women into a private room and they had their say.

The next day, Wednesday, October, 9, 1991, the *New York Times* ran a photo of the women storming the Senate. Women all over the country read the story and saw the photo, and a collective outrage swept through the land like the plague. Apparently, the women had gotten their message across—loud and clear. The Senate decided to postpone voting on the Thomas nomination in order that they could bring Anita Hill to Washington.

Although Clarence Thomas ultimately won that round, the image of that all-white, all-male panel of the Senate Judiciary Committee was forever branded upon the nation's memory. It had an immediate effect on the politics of that campaign cycle, giving the Year of the Woman a shot of B_{12} in the arm, making her nearly bionic in her appeal.

In fact, there is not a female member whom I've talked to who can't recall where she was during the hearings. Women all over the nation can tell you where they were during the Anita Hill–Clarence Thomas hearings. Ed and I were in Christiana, Pennsylvania, on our way to visit the Metzlers, friends who own a farm there. We were riveted to the radio, and when we arrived at Winding Glenn, the farm, neither of us could tear ourselves from the car. So we just sat there, listening to Anita Hill's testimony.

■ ■ ■

Julie Tippens, at the time a thirty-two-year-old lobbyist for the National Abortion Rights Action League (NARAL), was about to move over to the Women's Campaign Fund (WCF) to become its political director. In politics, timing is everything, and Julie couldn't have timed it better. Her first week on the job coincided with Anita Hill's testimony. Julie says, "There she was, a national visual that told a story we had tried to communicate for years. We saw that her message got through by the overwhelming response to the first piece of direct mail we sent right after her testimony." Julie knew that while the public polls showed that Thomas had a bit of an edge over Hill, women tended to believe her. "And regardless of whether they believed her, they were upset by what they saw in the Senate, by the way she was treated, and they were even more upset that it was a bunch of old white men. A lot of them had never flipped to C-SPAN before. Her testimony captivated America and turned the political tides in a way that few events in history ever have."

Amy Walter was Julie Tippens's assistant political director at WCF at the time. She now works on my staff, as one of my legislative assistants. She remembers just what kind of an effect Anita Hill had on their organization. "We almost doubled our membership with Anita Hill; that's how our membership skyrocketed." All of the major women's fund-raising organizations—EMILY's List, the Women's Campaign Fund, the National Women's Political Caucus, and Wishlist—benefited from the attention on women's issues that the Anita Hill–Clarence Thomas drama engendered. (Wishlist endorses only Republican candidates, EMILY's List endorses pro-choice Democrats, and the other two are bipartisan.)

Jane Danowitz, who was executive director at the Women's Campaign Fund during the 1992 campaign cycle, places a great deal of importance on the Anita Hill–Clarence Thomas hearings and says it was the final straw, the last element in creating the harmonic convergence needed for the Year of the Woman to happen. "I think we were sort of moseying along making these incremental steps, then along came Hill–Thomas. People can talk about reapportionment, abortion rights, the attitude of change . . . but there's no question that we have Anita Hill to thank." Jane recalls the overwhelming effect of the telegenic image of those fourteen white men sitting on that committee. "I think people in Detroit, Des Moines, or Danville saw for the first time that this was extreme, and this country doesn't like the extreme. . . . A sense of fairness arose about the issue of women that we had not seen for a very long time."

"We learned a powerful lesson as the country watched the Thomas–Hill hearings and understood in a very different way how few women there were in top offices. So thousands of men and women took out their checkbooks and wrote millions of dollars," says Ellen Malcolm, who started EMILY's List in 1985. "The Founding Mother," as a *New York Times* profile dubbed her, saw her organization gain major momentum after a "60 Minutes" piece on her and EMILY's List in March of 1992. They got five thousand calls the day after the piece aired, and they had to add several phone lines and hire extra people to answer the calls.

Ironically, even those senators who voted for Thomas's confirmation ended up helping the cause of women, and they did this to pay penance for their misogynist-seeming vote. But they didn't begin to help until their constituents let them know that this was expected of them and that they had better not slip up in a similar fashion in the future.

Anita Hill's experiences before the Senate Judiciary Committee did not make all the women candidates angry. "It didn't make me angry, because I was already angry—angry at the pain and the conditions that my community have been in. So it didn't wake me up," says Nydia Velazquez. Rather than anger, it gave her hope. "I felt very good because all of a sudden this society was talking about things that have been happening but no one wants to deal with because it is not good, it is not easy. These are the kinds of discussions that need to be happening."

■ ■ ■

Elizabeth Furse, a Democrat elected to serve from Oregon's First Congressional District, wanted to come to Washington to make sure that those discussions would begin to happen. Like Nydia, she wasn't surprised by the Senate Judiciary's myopic perception of Anita Hill. "It was not so much a shock to me as it was to many people because I've seen that kind of discrimination—with women, with people of color," says Elizabeth. "So I think I was less shocked than many people were. It was an additional push, but it was not the push that got me into politics."

She felt that if she and enough other women had a presence in Washington, they could begin to get people to listen, not just about sexual harassment but about a whole array of issues that have been on the back burner or haven't even made it to the stove top. "I think we're going to change the focus. That's where the change will come. I'm not sure that we'll change the way business is done. But women's health care will become a very important focus; there's no doubt about it. Because we care about it. We're all vulnerable to breast cancer, for one thing. And we know it. And I imagine that there are a number of women in this place who have had mastectomies. . . . One of the things that I'm hoping to do is to let the women know about the effect of military spending on everything they care about. Women, I think, very quickly get the connection between preserving the environment and preserving health and a future for the children."

The Year of the Woman was when Elizabeth made her first bid for elected office, like mine. But Elizabeth had had plenty of experience as a political activist. "That was her history—her mother and grandmother were both activists. They understood how to go to people and connect with them and that's really what formed Elizabeth," says Amy Walter, who spent a lot of time evaluating the women's campaigns.

Born in Kenya, raised in South Africa, Elizabeth worked with her mother, who was a founder of Black Sash, a women's antiapartheid group in the 1950s. In the 1960s, she was a community organizer in Watts. In the 1970s, she worked with northwestern Indian tribes.

"I think more than anything else for me is that I've been an activist all my life and you can do it in different places. I might go back to being a community activist whenever I decide not to go on here. So this is just another form of community activism for me," Elizabeth affirms in her lilting South African accent.

In 1985, Elizabeth's lifelong commitment to peace came to a head when she founded the Oregon Peace Institute, which promotes nonviolent conflict resolution. It was during this time that she began to realize that coming to Washington might be the only way to get certain things done that she needed to accomplish.

"I was so concerned and upset about the Gulf War, and what I saw was very much a knee-jerk reaction, in my view. I worked very hard on that in the institute; we were very impacted by the Gulf War. And I really felt that need to be here," Elizabeth says, looking around her congressional office with satisfaction. "I wanted to be an influence during that war."

And then Les AuCoin, who had held the House seat for eighteen years, decided to run against Senator Bob Packwood, leaving an open spot in her district. Elizabeth, who was vacationing in Maine, received numerous phone calls from people encouraging her to run. "I drove around Maine a lot and I thought, Yes, this is the right time to bring the issues forward. That's really why I got started. The Gulf War propelled me."

But although Elizabeth was certain about her need to go to Washington, she wasn't as certain she could get elected. "I did not honestly at the beginning think that I would be elected, because I'm a community organizer, because I've worked on some pretty hot issues. I thought I would be branded as a way-out liberal."

Elizabeth had a lot of people rooting for her, however, one of whom was Julie Tippens. "I was damned if she wasn't going to Congress," says Julie adamantly. "She hadn't served in elective office before; she didn't fit the mold of your typical congressional candidate. What the political powers around Washington didn't know yet is that that would prove to be her greatest asset." Julie grew up in Elizabeth's district and she believed in her, heart and soul, and was willing to help her win. "Everything Elizabeth's done in her life has been for bettering other people's lives," Julie says with conviction. Above her head on the bulletin board is a FURSE FOR CONGRESS bumper sticker.

■ ■ ■

Most of the female candidates had already served in elected positions at the state or county level, positioning themselves to make the leap to the federal level when the opportunity appeared. By the time they arrived in Washington, many of them, such as Anna Eshoo, who had served for a decade on the local County Board of Supervisors, knew the game of politics. "Am I newly elected? Yes. However, I don't think the word *freshman* fits me. I just don't think of myself as a freshman," Anna says with an emphatic laugh.

Observes one woman who was very involved in the Democratic women's campaign movement of 1992, "These women are smart; they're not novices. They knew how to raise money and they knew how to get the help they needed. The difference between them and the men is that they started off their campaigns a little more unsure of how to do it exactly. But men get away with that. They encourage men who have been business leaders, whatever, to run for Congress. But to a woman, they say, 'What has she done?' And they answer, 'Well, she's done this and that.' And they say, 'Yeah, but has she done anything political?' Men are automatically given the benefit of the doubt—that they'll pick it up. Women have to prove that they're politically astute enough to handle the campaign. That is incredibly frustrating. But it also brought out an incredible caliber of women."

Most had résumés similar to that of Leslie Byrne, who had served in the Virginia house since 1986 until she ran for an open seat in Congress in 1992. "It was a choice of opportunity. If you look at a lot of us, we ran for open seats. Redistricting created for a lot of women a level playing field, which is one of the favorite clichés around here," says Leslie, rolling her eyes. "There was no incumbent. If you were fairly well established with your own political base, there was no better time to go after a congressional seat, when you had an open seat. They come along only once every ten years and you never know whether you're going to be physically located in a district with an open seat until it happens. I think a number of us chose to run because of that."

The Democratic party was smart in recognizing that not only were the women ready to run but the public was ready for the women. "During the Democratic Convention, the Democratic party wanted to tout the Year of the Woman. Clinton said he wanted to run on her skirttails," remembers Leslie, smiling. And so she joined the other women candidates.

"We were there in the holding room for about four hours waiting for Jesse Jackson to finish his speech!" Leslie got antsy waiting during those four hours and started marching up to other women, trying to find out whether they were similar to her with regard to why they had run. "So I'm walking around and I'm asking people, 'What brought you here?' Here we are in New York City at the Democratic National Convention, running for U.S. Congress, for U.S. Senate, and almost to the person it was, 'I wanted to make my kids' education better'; 'I wanted to save a stand of trees from development'; 'I wanted clean drinking water. . . .' My experience was that they all started out wanting to fix something. It seemed that there was such a strong common thread among us."

Says a female fund-raiser who was there at the convention, "It was very charged. Every single Democratic woman who was running for Congress was up onstage. It was very colorful—just imagine the scene: Clinton and Hillary show up. . . . He knew that by aligning himself with someone who is different, that it was all about change. Think about how much more attractive it is to watch a campaign ad with a woman's face than the same old white guy. . . . I think that people were honestly looking for someone who would not give in to these guys."

"The whole shift from the Cold War to the domestic agenda was helpful to women," says Ellen Malcolm. "Also, voters tend to see women as outsiders, and in an election where they were sick to death of politics as usual, they saw women as candidates who would give a different kind of leadership."

"And with fiscal issues, they trust women much more than they trust men," says Amy Walter. "How many women do you know that have been charged with racketeering or embezzling?" Amy asks rhetorically, holding her hands up, palms open, to the sky. During my campaign, I was approached by an ornery old man who said to me, "Have you ever run for office before?" "No," I responded. "Then you've got my vote," he said.

California congressman Vic Fazio is a strong champion of women in Congress. And as chairman of the Democratic Congressional Campaign Committee, he explains that his support for women isn't only because he's a sensitive nineties kind of guy. "I like to win elections. I'm a very partisan Democrat and I think this is a time when women have a political advantage. In many ways, I've been supportive of women not just because I have an established rapport with them but because I saw their potential and I believe that women could be stronger candidates. It's a very pragmatic position."

The House bank scandal was another reinforcing factor to promote change. A lot of men were getting out, retiring early to avoid ugly and ultimately unsuccessful campaigns. "Again, you had the concept that men can't balance their checkbooks," says Amy Walter. "Women are saying, 'I balance my checkbook every day. That's my job in the family: I pay the bills, I balance the checkbook.' We're trusting [men] to balance our budget and they can't even figure out how much they have in their own checking accounts?"

"That's an important aspect of why we had the Year of the Woman," notes Maryland congressman Steny Hoyer, "a growing trust by the American public, by women in particular, who initially had great trouble dealing with other women in public office. Now that's changed as the generation has changed. And you have a growing generation of younger women who don't have the shibboleth that men are in office and women are at home."

Nita Lowey, who had already served two terms in the House, was thrilled that instead of twenty-eight congresswomen the number would jump to forty-eight. "First of all, I think this is an unusual class," says Nita, one of the senior members on nearly every freshman woman's list of women to look to for advice here in Congress.

"I always feel you don't come here just as a woman. That's an important part of who you are, but you bring with it a whole variety of experience: life experience, academic experience, professional experience. And this time, I think it's very special because many of the women came here with a lot of governmental and political experience." Nita pauses for a moment and then adds, smiling, "And most of us are mothers."

Nita's political fire in the belly started when she was quite young. She was president of her senior class at Bronx High School of Science. Then, during her junior year at Mount Holyoke College, she interned for Senator Hubert Humphrey. Going to an all-women's school reinforced what she had already learned at home, that women could do anything they set their minds to. "I think you are an accumulation of a lot of experiences, and I had parents who really felt that I could be anything I wanted to be and do anything I wanted to do."

But even though politics was thoroughly in her blood by now, it was going to have to wait while she raised her children. "I was in a generation where right after college most of us after a few years got married and had children. Most of us kind of meandered to careers rather than setting a goal and going for it." But all the while, the notion was there that, maybe just maybe, Nita might someday consider running for public office. And when she finally did, many years later, the timing felt right. "Somehow making that decision, opening yourself up, putting yourself on the line, is a very difficult one. And then all the pieces seemed to be in place and it was the right time. . . . I always had the thought, but I wasn't sure I was ever going to do it. Because thinking about it, wanting to do it, and translating that into reality, to action, was quite different."

Nita sees this new generation as being different, more focused, coming to certain realizations much sooner in their lives than the same ones she came to later, in her forties, and she's thrilled to see things change. "I think most of the younger generation now is deciding who they are earlier and what they want to be. I say to them, 'Set that goal and don't worry if there's a little dust on the bench or the paint's chipping. Just set the goal and go for it.' "

Women's involvement in government is just a natural (if not

long overdue) outgrowth of their involvement in every other facet of society. "Everything is a women's issue because women for centuries have had a major role in nurturing and caregiving and preserving the family, and that leads to our involvement in the community," says Nita. "And I think that's why more and more women are running for office today, because people understand that they are committed to family, that they are committed to the community."

Karen Shepherd is the perfect example of just such a woman, someone involved in many different areas of her community. She came to run for office after trying her hand at several different professions. She first taught English at the college level for eight years. As her commitment as a community and political volunteer grew, she made a name for herself, eventually being appointed to the directorship of the Salt Lake County Department of Social Services, holding that position until the county commissioner who had appointed her was defeated. From there, she went on to direct the continuing education program at a small liberal arts college. After three years in this role, she began looking for a bigger challenge. She bought controlling stock in a publishing company and became editor of *Network,* a magazine for Utah women working outside the home. In 1990, she ran for and won a seat in the Utah state senate, where she served for two years.

When Karen decided to run for the open congressional seat in her district, only one woman in the history of Utah had ever served—Reva Zilpha Beck Bosone, elected to the U.S. House of Representatives in 1948. In a state that had sent only one woman to Congress, Karen now found herself running against another woman, Enid Greene. So in the Year of the Woman, Karen didn't even have the advantage of being a female candidate. To make it tougher, she was pro-choice in a state famous for its conservatism. And to top it all off, Karen was not a Mormon, unlike her opponent. Both candidates observed that the only thing they had in common was their gender. "Yes," Karen says, smiling wryly, "that was about it."

But the seat had been held by Democrat Wayne Owens for the past six years (who was relinquishing it to run for the Senate;

he proved unsuccessful in that bid), and so Karen felt that there was a tradition there for Democrats, even though it was a tight swing district.

And there was another difference, one that definitely worked in Karen's favor: She was married, a mother of two children, and in her early fifties; Greene was single, childless, and in her thirties. On the Richter scale of life experiences in a state where family values counted big time, Greene came up short. Karen won the race by four percentage points.

■ ■ ■

The morning after the election, I woke up and squinted at the morning sunlight streaming through the window, yawning at the new day. Then it all came back to me. Sitting up in bed, I blurted out, "Wow! I did it. I really did it. Now I'm going to have to serve." My husband, Ed, looked at me and smiled. Ed, a former congressman himself, had been there. (Ed was serving in Congress when we met; I interviewed him for a story and came home and called my mother. I knew he was the one, from the first time we met. "Mom," I said, "if he calls me, he's a goner." We were married within the year.)

Winning the election, of course, was only the first step. Now I had to figure out how to accomplish all the things that had propelled me forward against all odds. I knew that my stay would be defined by getting on the right committees. I also knew that the Energy and Commerce Committee was where most of the action took place, because between 40 and 50 percent of all legislation passed through it in any given year. And most important, this was where the health-care legislation would land. But they hadn't taken a freshman on this committee since 1983, so I knew that it wasn't going to be easy. I set about doing my homework so I could figure out how to wangle a spot.

In the meantime, there were all sorts of other things to attend to. Tons of activities had been planned for the time between the election and the swearing-in. Orientation week, in December, was a time to get acclimated, to learn about congressional ethics and parliamentary procedure. Then the Democratic freshmen went up to Harvard for some seminars on various issues.

It was clear that the freshmen women needed to come together as a group as soon as possible to state publicly our manifesto. From my twenty-five years as a member of the press, I knew how important it was that we get the word out as quickly as possible and define in the minds of our colleagues and society at large that we were a real force; it was important symbolically for us to agree on something right away. One of the favorite letters I've received since I've been a congresswoman was from a child named Hadley, who signed her letter, "Yours, till Congress agrees." That pretty much summed up how the American public viewed Congress, and I didn't want anyone to think that this new group of women couldn't agree.

So we began to meet. It was in the middle of picking committee assignments and the women seemed preoccupied with that, but I also sensed a subtle reticence to come together as a group. This bothered me. Sometime in the middle of the night, I said to myself, 'I betcha I know how I can get them to think that this is a good idea.' The next day, I called Congresswoman Barbara Kennelly, the only woman in the Democratic leadership, and asked her to come and meet with us.

She stood in front of the group and was impassioned as she talked about her experiences. "Go for it," she told us. She talked about the fact that one of the best friends she'd ever had in her life was Gerry Ferraro. "You will never have these kinds of relationships again, ever. Be cohesive. You're freshmen together only once."

And so, after she left, we were able to hammer out an outline of intent within an hour. Although we were a richly diverse group of women from all walks of life, we agreed that we had to agree on certain fundamental goals.

On Monday, December 7, 1992, at 10:45 A.M., this is the message we delivered at our first official press conference:

> We, the newly elected women of the 103d U.S. Congress, a bipartisan group, recognizing that we share in common our support for certain fundamental legislative

initiatives, believe that to effect the swift enactment of these initiatives into law, we must act in concert.

We understand that this historic moment would not have been possible but for the commitment and dedication of those women in the U.S. House and Senate who have come before us. Indeed, the initiatives for which we, as a class, intend to fight are initiatives that these women have been fighting for in the halls of Congress long before we arrived.

We look forward to working with these women and with the leadership of the House to address the following priorities:

1. Fully Fund Head Start
   The Head Start program was created to ensure that all children enter school ready to learn. We will join efforts to pass legislation guaranteeing that all eligible children are covered by this program.

2. Family and Medical Leave
   We support legislative initiatives that provide for family and medical leave so that no man or woman is placed in the position of having to choose between job and family.

3. Freedom of Choice
   We will support legislative initiatives that codify *Roe* v. *Wade.*

4. Sexual Harassment
   Sexual harassment in the workplace is a form of exploitation and intimidation that is economically enforced by virtue of the professional relationship. We support extension to the U.S. Congress of the present laws that prohibit sexual harassment.

We became such a cohesive unit that when the thirteen officers of the Democratic freshmen group were elected, eleven of them were women or minority representatives. And I submit that it was because we looked like we were together. We would arrive at and depart from meetings together; even if we weren't always 100 percent united, we knew the perception was what mattered. And that was perhaps our first lesson.

When we came to stay, days before the swearing-in ceremony in early January, we had a lottery to pick our offices. Out of 110, my staff picked 97, and we ended up in the back of the Longworth Building, on the fifth floor. There were no imposing views of the nation's Capitol for us. Oh well, there are worse fates. My office is fine, but my staff is squeezed into tiny cubicles with poor ventilation, limited natural light, and drab government-issue furniture. When lobbyists and constituents come to see my legislative assistants, they are forced to meet in the tiny reception area due to the lack of space. But they weather the lack of amenities quite well—in fact, they do it with grace. Most of them worked together on my campaign, and, like a bunch of soldiers in the same infantry, they have shared foxholes and are used to tight quarters.

Speaking of amenities, the decor of Congress is much as one would expect. My colleague Jennifer Dunn, a Republican from Washington State, was disheartened when her two sons, both in their twenties, accompanied her to check out her new digs. "I walked into my office and it looked like the office in *The Distinguished Gentleman*. It was an absolute wreck. The carpet was horrible and torn up, there were no valances, they had just finished painting, and there was no furniture except for this pile of garbage in the front office. It was Saturday night, right before I was going to be sworn in. My sons and I wandered through the building. We ran into a member who said, 'Here's what you do about the furniture. You go around the hallways and if there's furniture out there and it doesn't say "Do not remove," then you can use that furniture.'

"So that's what we did . . . and we ended up with this pretty blue leather furniture, which was just fine. And that was my start in Congress." Jennifer sinks back in the blue leather armchair, musing at the memory of what a neophyte she was regarding the bazaar nature of Congress (pun intended).

"It was really kind of fun. So maybe as a woman my sense of decorating comes in handy," Jennifer adds, laughing.

Finding staff could be an equally interesting experience. Elizabeth Furse and her partial staff, many of whom had worked on her campaign, waded through what seemed like thirty thousand applications. Young men and women, armed with freshly printed résumés, roamed the halls of Congress, sniffing out jobs. One young man arrived on Elizabeth's doorstep as they were setting up camp. He told her that he had worked on Bob Packwood's reelection campaign. He seemed oblivious to the fact that the recent charges of sexual harassment against Packwood might diminish the value of this work experience. She just gazed with steely eyes at the young man. "And I organized fifteen 'Support the Troops' organizations," he continued.

Finally, it was too much for Elizabeth. "Don't you know who I am?" she implored. "I'm a peace activist!"

"But I'm a very good organizer!"

Elizabeth now shakes her head in disbelief at the young man's persistence. "That was sort of a funny thing about people not knowing who you are and not caring."

The day of the swearing-in itself was very moving. It would make even the most jaded and cynical of our citizens feel pride toward their nation if they could be in that room during this ceremony. And this particular ceremony, with all the new female members, was unique. Never before had there been such an array of bright colors: Amidst the sea of red-striped power neckties and dark blue, black, gray, and pinstripe suits, we women stood out like stars on the American flag. And our children were there to support us. When I raised my hand, I looked at my mother in the gallery and thought of how proud my father would have been to be beside her.

"When we were sworn in, there were a lot of kids on the floor. I thought it was a delight," recalls Karan English fondly. "It did sound like an elementary schoolyard, but a lot of noise came from the members. There were kids coughing and crying and young voices and everybody was excited—it was a huge class being sworn in." There was a bit of grumbling from some of the old-timers that perhaps there wasn't as much decorum as usual for an event as solemn and weighty as a congressional swearing-in. When Karan heard of the complaints, she waved them off. "I thought, I couldn't be more proud of all this noise, because it represents all walks of life. Sure, it was disruptive, but it was real life."

Another slice of real life was Carrie Meek, who had the distinction of being the oldest member of the freshman class. Carrie, surrounded by her friends and family who had come from Florida to support her, took time out from the busy congressional carnival of glad-handing and backslapping that had already begun. In the expansive, historic halls of Congress, Carrie's group paused for some private moments of prayer. The occasion brought tears, plenty of tears, tears of joy and gratitude to this grandmother's eyes.

"I always will pray. And I will help people pray. So it's a part of me that I didn't try to suppress when I came here. I let it all hang out. Take me as I am." Carrie stops to let out a low mischievous chuckle. "Beware of me."

■ ■ ■

With one campaign down, there was still what Leslie Byrne calls "campaign number two," committee assignments. Somehow I managed to get the committee assignment I was hoping for, Energy and Commerce, and a seat on the Small Business Committee, as well. Of the twenty-seven Democrats on Energy and Commerce, five of us are freshmen, three of whom are women. The fact that our class is so large, making up almost one-fourth of the Democratic caucus, helped in getting us on.

Other committee slots are even tougher for freshmen to get. Carrie Meek won a highly sought-after position on the Appropriations Committee, the only freshman to do so. And Mel Reynolds, of Illinois, was the only freshman to get on Dan Rostenkowski's Ways and Means Committee. Rostenkowski made no bones about it: He didn't want freshmen on his committee. They could cut their teeth somewhere else. Reynolds got on because he was from Illinois, but that was the only exception Rosty was making.

Leslie Byrne was disappointed to learn this. She had set her heart on Ways and Means. But she switched gears quickly and decided that with northern Virginia's transportation problems and her interest in environmental issues, Public Works and Transportation was the ticket. The Steering and Policy Committee was meeting one night in one of the Speaker's rooms to work on committee assignments. Leslie begged off from several receptions so that she could sit outside the meeting and influence as best she could her chances of getting on the committee. Just outside of the room where they were meeting, there was a row of chairs. She plunked herself down and waited, thinking, If you're going to turn me down for this, you're going to have to look me in the eye while you do it. So every time someone came out to go to the bathroom, Leslie was sitting there eyeing the door. She felt really silly sitting there all alone twiddling her thumbs. When a congressman came out, she'd wave and smile and give him the thumbs-up sign. She talked to the guards to pass the time. At one point, one of the congressmen came out to tell her that it didn't look good, that someone else from the region wanted the spot and that he was going to have to vote for this guy because they were from the same state.

"He doesn't need this seat as much as I do," Leslie said.

"Well, if you can convince him to take another position, I'll vote for you."

Leslie darted to the phone in the guards' office and called the congressman in question, laying her cards on the table. "You know, I need to be on Public Works and Transportation," she told him. "You're in a fairly safe district," she reminded her colleague. "You don't need to prove anything."

He said okay, and Leslie got on the committee. "I was the only person sitting out there. I can say almost with certainty that a couple of committee assignments would have gone differently if people had sat outside of that room."

■ ■ ■

During the State of the Union Address that President Clinton delivered in early February, I remember sitting with my colleagues, looking around at all 435 of us. The women stood out in a truly dramatic fashion, and I thought, My gosh, people are going to turn on the tube tonight and see us and they're going to realize that the rest of the nation has begun to inch itself into this body.

I was sitting next to North Carolina Democrat Martin Lancaster, who was trying to point out somebody on the other side, and he said, "He's the guy with the receding hairline, gray hair." And I said, laughing, "You've eliminated nobody!"

My point is that the people who have always been outside of the system are now beginning to infiltrate it. There aren't nearly enough of us, but we're working on it—all the time. And one of these days, "the guy with the receding hairline" just might be a distinctive description.

CHAPTER TWO

Excuse Me, Miss, but Are You a Member?: The Male Culture of the Capitol

One day, Leslie Byrne and Karan English entered an elevator with some other members. One of them, an older gentleman, eyed the women tentatively.

"It sure is nice to have you ladies here," the congressman announced to the full elevator. Smiling, he added, "It spiffs the place up."

Leslie looked over at Karan, stifling a groan. Then Leslie, who couldn't resist, replied sotto voce, "Yup, chicks in Congress."

■ ■ ■

When we arrived in Washington, we knew it wasn't going to be a tea party. We expected to be challenged on a host of levels. We did not expect to be patronized or to be the victims of irritating and demeaning expressions of sexism. Who would have expected this sort of monkey business? Instead of being confronted with legislative challenges, the first thing we had to worry about was being *recognized* as members of Congress.

Anna Eshoo went to the Pentagon for the swearing-in of Deputy Defense Secretary William Perry. Deputy Secretary Perry lived in Anna's district and she respected him and wanted to show support by attending. At the ceremony, there was a very tall, broad-shouldered officer in full uniform standing beside Anna and he inadvertently bumped into her. He hit Anna so hard, she rocked in her heels, nearly losing her balance. He looked down and Anna thought he was about to apologize.

"All the staff people are over there," the man said, indicating the crowd on the other side.

"With all due respect to you, sir, I'm the assistant secretary's congressperson," Anna informed him.

Maria Cantwell stayed late one night to attend a freshman meeting on congressional reform. When the meeting was over, Maria headed back to her office in Longworth. It was after 9:00 P.M. and her staff had all gone home, but she didn't have her keys with her and the office was locked up for the night. So Maria went downstairs to find a security guard.

"Excuse me," Maria began. "But I'm locked out of my office. Do you know how I can get in?"

"Well, ma'am, if you tell me which member you work for and show me some ID, maybe I'll let you in."

Maria was wearing her little gold pin that indicated she was a member of Congress. "I'm a member," Maria answered evenly. "And I don't have my ID because it's locked in the office."

"Well, go down the hall and talk to my sergeant," instructed the guard officiously. It was clear that he wasn't completely buying her story. Maria shrugged and headed to the sergeant's office. When she returned, the guard was still standing there. They looked at each other. It appeared that in the time she had been away, he had decided that perhaps she was telling the truth.

"You know," he said, somewhat bemused, "they don't make these guys like they used to."

I had a similar experience on the tram that transports members, staff, and visitors back and forth between the Capitol and Rayburn, one of the House office buildings. I was with Louise Slaughter, a Democrat from New York, who has been here since 1987. Louise and I were in the Members Only section when some lobbyists approached the tram, which was about to take off. One of them took a look at us and said, "Oh, it's okay; we can sit here. There are no members here." When we got off, Louise, who sits on the powerful Rules Committee and is universally regarded as a heavy hitter, looked at me and declared in that great southern accent of hers, "Doesn't that just fry you?"

Another time, Maria was on the floor while the House was in session. A member whom Maria didn't know walked up to her and said, "You know, I was going to have you thrown off the floor because I thought you were staff. But then I realized you were a member." How do you respond to something like that? Gee, thanks?

At thirty-five, Maria doesn't fit the central casting image of a congressman. Conversely, her press secretary, Larry West, does. "I have unthinkingly walked through the gate that I'm not supposed to be going through and had nobody question me. I've actually gone back when I realized my mistake and said, 'Sorry, I'm staff.' It's like they see me and wave me through because I'm forty years old and I've got a little gray hair at the temples. They just assume because I'm walking along in a suit, looking like I know where I'm going, that I must be a member."

Elizabeth Furse tells the story of a woman who was walking past a security checkpoint with two male members of Congress. "She was told by a policeman, 'You can't go in there; you have to go through this metal detector,' " says Elizabeth. "And she said to the guard, 'Listen here, you look at my lapel; you don't look at my clothes.' "

These types of incidents may seem trivial in the scheme of things, but they have a cumulative effect and can be extremely annoying. "You think, Isn't it extraordinary—there are only forty-eight of us. It wouldn't take much for every police officer to know who we are," says Elizabeth. Besides that, we all wear our membership pins on our lapels or collars. It wouldn't be so difficult for people to glance there before making assumptions.

Democratic San Diego congresswoman Lynn Schenk tells of a

similar experience. "The Capitol Police, even the women members of the Capitol Police force, it is not their conventional wisdom that women are members of Congress. So when I enter a door that I don't usually enter, this pin is supposed to tell you I'm a member of Congress. But they don't even think to look. So when you go in and there are long lines going through the metal detectors, members of Congress are supposed to be able to go around. I've had more than one say, 'Miss, miss, come back here!' I do, and they say, 'You have to go through the metal detector.' And I say, 'I understand that members don't.' 'Oh, are you a member?' 'What do you think this pin is?' 'Oh, I didn't see it.' 'Why didn't you look?' "

Lynn attended a reception with one of her male aides, whose name tag read CONGRESSWOMAN LYNN SCHENK'S OFFICE. The host, apparently distracted by the hundreds of guests, held out his hand to the aide. "Oh, Congressman Schenk," he said. The aide gently corrected the host by saying, "I'm with Congresswoman Schenk."

"He had the grace to blush," Lynn says, laughing wryly at the memory.

Karen Shepherd says there were at least three times she couldn't get into the parking lot because they didn't believe she was a congresswoman. Twice they asked for her ID. She says, "Once I didn't have it. It was a Monday and we weren't voting, so I didn't bring it. And I didn't have my pin on. I had a congressional plate, though. That should have done it." Finally, after weighing the risks of not letting a member in, the lot attendant relented.

The place itself is laid out inconveniently for us. For instance, the bathroom closest to the House floor for the congresswomen is the Lindy Boggs Room, the ladies' lounge. It is a small sanctuary where we can go between votes; there is a kitchen, a room to take a quick snooze, and a living room–type area. But geographically speaking, it's not as close to the floor as the men's bathroom or the cloakroom—and that can make a difference when you have only a few minutes between votes. The cloakroom is open to both sexes. There are couches with pillows and blankets, a snack bar, big, overstuffed chairs, televisions tuned to C-SPAN, and phones. "The guys just lie around on the couches, with their ties over their eyes," says

Deborah Pryce, flinging an imaginary tie across her face. "And their shoes off and the smoke and the socks and the tuna fish—it doesn't smell very good in there."

Karen Shepherd finds the atmosphere of the cloakroom one of the most blatant expressions of the prevailing male clubbiness. "The image that stands out in my mind that I'll never forget is one of the very first weeks of Congress when we stayed till midnight. I think we were doing Family and Medical Leave and here's John Dingell [chairman of Energy and Commerce], one of the most powerful men of this body—or arguably of either body—sound asleep on a couch, kind of snoring lightly, with his hands crossed under his chin, holding a blanket, like a babe in the woods."

This made a lasting impression on Karen because it underscored for her the disparity in psychic comfort levels between the men and the women; she knew in her gut, without needing to take a survey, that the majority of us would never be comfortable doing that, curling up on a couch and dozing. "We don't have enough power to do it," Karen says. "If we're asleep, we seem, look, and are vulnerable."

Deborah Pryce says, "You don't want anyone to catch you looking like you're not busy and efficient and doing exactly what you're supposed to be doing. Appearances are so important here."

Lynn Schenk is no stranger to male bastions. When she was attending the University of California's San Diego Law School in the late sixties, she fought to get an additional ladies' room installed so that the tiny minority of female students wouldn't have to run up and down three flights of stairs whenever nature called. Things are much different these days. "I have been actively involved with the feminist movement for twenty-five years or more and the progress just in my lifetime has been indescribable," she says. "There's no way to describe to someone of a younger generation what it was like a mere twenty or twenty-five years ago, when it was accepted for a law professor to say to a female student in front of her classmates, 'Why are you here? Why are you taking up the place of a man who is going to have to support his family? Why don't you go learn how to fix a toaster or an iron so you'll be useful to your husband?' Now, that was said to me in all seriousness by a law professor. There is no way to describe the humiliation, the pain as a young person questioning your sense of worth when those things are said. That would never happen today, or if it did happen, that professor would be gone."

Lynn's recollection brought back my own brief encounter with law school. When I was a young woman, I considered going to law school. I was interviewed by the dean of admissions at one of the schools where I was being considered. He said to me, "Look, go and take a good paralegal course. Get yourself into a law firm as a secretary, marry a lawyer, and you'll be just as happy."

"I'm astonished that you would say that to me," I replied, "absolutely astonished."

"I tell most women this," he continued. "The law isn't quite ready for women the way women think that the law is ready for them."

Notes Lynn, "It is no longer acceptable to do those things. There's been a lot of change. But then I come here to the Congress and I find that there is a lot of throwback to twenty-five years ago.

"There still isn't a rest room for the female staffers close to the floor of the House [the Lindy Boggs Room is for members of Congress only, not their staffs]. I had a Republican female staffer come up to me and say, 'Congresswoman, I hope that you and the Democratic and Republican women get together and do something to get us a rest room near the floor of the House. . . .' So here it's 1993 and we're still fighting the bathroom issue.

"But there are still many men who have been here for a very, very long time who have not been buffeted by the winds of change over the past twenty years. . . . It's not that they are mean-spirited or nasty," Lynn submits. "Their attitude is just patronizing. I must say that I feel as if they just don't know what the world has come to."

The members' gym is another place on the Hill that is reluctant to reflect changing times. Karan English enjoys unwinding by shooting hoops. When she tried to play basketball one day, she was told that women have to call in advance. "I refused to do it because it's a members' gym and I shouldn't have to call. But it's not even convenient for me to go to the gym because there's no place for women to dress or take a shower. I have to go to a completely different area, different floor, different facility, so I haven't even joined the gym because they've made it so inconvenient for women to be a part of it. I want to play basketball and I can't go over and play for half an hour and then clean up and go back to work; it's just so inconvenient."

Lynn Woolsey also found the lack of equal access to the courts irritating and said so. So when the women were invited to participate in a nonpartisan game against Georgetown Law School, Lynn figured she'd better put "my body where my mouth is." Lynn signed up and when she arrived to play, she was the only woman who showed. "So here I am, the sixth oldest in the freshman class, and the only woman who played!"

Lynn says that while her performance was honorable, she wasn't exactly Michael Jordan. "I didn't embarrass anybody. I mean, I can play. I wasn't a star. But I could run back and forth. That's the challenge when you're fifty-five," Lynn says, throwing her head back, laughing.

"Now they want me to play baseball." Lynn sighs. And not afraid to let her feminine side show, she says she turned them down. "I don't want to break a fingernail."

Jennifer Dunn is determined to turn the inequity over gym access into an advantage. "If I can't play basketball, maybe I'll push myself a lot harder to do my reading at home at night and to learn about the budget," she rationalizes. Jennifer, at five nine, is a natural for the game and was very disappointed to discover so many barriers to the women sharing the gym.

These types of things happen to us periodically and you can't help letting it get to you sometimes. Someone implied to Anna Eshoo, for instance, that when women got together on the House floor, what they talked about was what they were wearing. "It infuriated me," she said. "We have our hands full, and we have our hands full because there are so few of us here—so few of us that the burden is that much greater."

But Anna is quick to point out that there's no need to let it wear you down. "I possess the exact same thing every other member has, and that is one vote. That vote is just as powerful as the next person's. So when I speak, I speak for 575,000 people."

■ ■ ■

Last summer, the freshman class was invited by the Motion Picture Association of America to a screening. Because the class is so large, we were invited to come in two groups. The first group saw *In the Line of Fire.* Those of us who went the next night saw *Rising Sun,* in which a videotape of a woman being raped is replayed repeatedly.

"It was an appalling choice and all of us felt the same way. We sat there with our colleagues and we were embarrassed," says Karen Shepherd, who was particularly disgusted with the movie. "The worst thing about the experience was that those who invited us were blind to the message the movie sent. The continued lack of consciousness in 1993 about women is shocking."

After the movie was over, there was utter silence and we all just filed out of the MPAA theater and went home. I don't know what the men in the audience were thinking, but the women expressed dismay. "The very next day, we all had to come on to the floor and work alongside men and pretend we don't live in a culture that portrays women in that way. It's very, very difficult," says Karen. But these are issues all women in our society face.

Still, it's hard to know sometimes how much of the alienation comes from being a woman and how much from being a freshman. But it's definitely something that many of us, on some level, are constantly monitoring. "It's always there in terms of walking into a room, sitting in a meeting, always consciously thinking that you have to have your opportunity to be heard," says Democratic California freshman Lucille Roybal-Allard. "And if you don't, you wonder if it's because you're a woman, so you're always observing to see if others are also not being included. You're always trying to weigh the situation to decide whether you need to assert yourself in terms of 'you're not going to ignore me because I'm a woman.' It's always there." Lucille has noticed that in some of the smaller meetings, where perhaps there is less political posturing at work, there is fairness. "If you raise your hand, you get called on; you're not overlooked. And I think there's more of an awareness in a small group because we stand out more and they know that we will make a fuss, that we will come together as a group of women to protest something."

But sometimes it's just getting into the meetings that is the problem. Elizabeth Furse serves on the Armed Services Committee. "I get stopped by people in uniform when I go into briefings that are closed—intelligence briefings, for instance. They just can't believe that I'm going in there. I've given up explaining. I just walk in. And if they're going to make a fuss, they'll be embarrassed."

Anna Eshoo is also on a committee that is predominantly male (they all are, but this one even more so)—Science, Space and Technology—and she sees it as a challenge. "What I'm struck with when I'm in committee hearings is that the room is filled with men, both the experts that come in to testify and the people seated in the hearing room. It's extraordinarily, overwhelmingly male. But it's a great opportunity for me to distinguish myself on the issues that some may not necessarily think of immediately when they think of women legislators."

■ ■ ■

Maria Cantwell points out how diverse our class is, that for the first time, at least among the Democrats, the women and minorities outnumber the white men. She says she feels most comfortable when she is among our freshman colleagues.

Pat Schroeder, the senior woman in the House, has dealt with these issues for more than two decades. "The most refreshing part of all this is for twenty years members here always wanted to be interviewed off the record and talk about me. 'Oh, that flake. What is the matter with her? Why does she have all these causes?' And so now it's really wonderful because there're all these women and they can't say, 'All those flakes. . . .' "

Clearly, Pat's been penalized for speaking her mind and for her grenade-tossing "in your face" style of legislating, as one male colleague characterized it. But we can only hope that as our numbers increase, a lot of these frustrations will simply slip away. Things that are a challenge for us at the moment won't be issues in the years to come. But the way things stand right now, they are issues. The old boys' network is alive and well, which shouldn't come as a huge surprise to us. In fact, Congress has always been a big men's club. Of the 11,363 members who have served in the United States Congress, only 163 have been women.

"Not everybody is a member of that club, the good-old-boy network," says Karan English. "And there are certainly good old boys who can be members of it when it's appropriate and not when it's not appropriate. And there are some good old boys who don't even know they're identified as good old boys, because they really haven't kept up with—God, I hate to use this term—political correctness. But in fact, women can spot 'em in a second."

There are many ways to identify a good old boy. It's become a bit of a sport, in fact. "One way," says Karan, "is some of the language that is used. The men are always referred to as 'congressmen' or 'the Honorable' or 'my esteemed colleague' or 'my good friend.' Then they call the women by their first names."

Lucille also noticed the way language reflects gender tensions. "There is an awareness that things have changed, but they're not sure about it. They say, 'It's really nice to have all these girls here.' And then they say, 'Oh, I guess I'm not supposed to say "girls." ' "

Elizabeth recalls two women asking to speak at a committee hearing. Although the chairman addressed male members who wanted to speak as "the gentleman from . . ." he said to the women, "Well, young lady, what would you want?"

One of the women replied sunnily, "I'll take that as a compliment," but inside she was steaming. After the hearing, she went to the chairman and privately pointed out the inappropriateness of the manner in which he had addressed her.

"Every day you resist getting upset, you resist getting angry, because you don't want to irritate a chairman," says Elizabeth Furse. "So there is a constant thing going on. I think men are just not aware of the strain on women."

And while sometimes it's rudeness that grates, more often it's good manners that exclude you. "The men are polite, but it's often not as colleague to colleague," says Lucille Roybal-Allard. "I'm not even sure that they're that conscious of it. For example, I've noticed that they'll say, 'Hi, Joe,' then talk about such and such an issue. With us, it's more of a polite 'Hello, how are you?'—more of a social kind of thing rather than one professional colleague to another. I guess part of it has to do with the different personalities of the women and how long we've been here. I've noticed with some of the women, especially if they sit on key committees, that there's more of a dialogue that goes on."

The fact that we are sensitive to being treated like second-class citizens doesn't mean we've lost our sense of humor, as our detractors are quick to claim. If someone who has respect for you decides to kid you, that's fine. It's a case-by-case call.

Freshman Democrat Cynthia McKinney's eyes light up mischievously when she recalls being assigned to "whip" a list of men regarding the budget-reconciliation bill. Humor made the task less unpleasant. "I walked up to one member and said that I had been assigned to whip him. He said, 'Oh my God, my prayers have been answered!' " Cynthia laughs long and hard at that memory.

People who are treated like second-class citizens are often more careful of the way they treat the people around them. Some of us, in fact, treat our staffs as extended family. "Right from the beginning, we set the standard that people would care about one another in this office and I think that has really been very important to all of us," says Elizabeth Furse. "Everybody checks out that everybody else is doing all right. It kind of lifts the load a little bit. But are women more careful of their staff? I don't know. I think it's individual. I can't imagine women throwing things at their staff, which I understand some members of Congress do. I think it's just the most horrible behavior that goes on. I mean, these stories that some members' staffs don't get within thirty feet because they throw things when they're angry."

Sexual harassment of female staffers, which has been a problem on the Hill long before we got here, will be tolerated much less readily now that some of the people wielding power are women.

Early on, Elizabeth was alerted by one of her own staff to inappropriate behavior by a senior congressman. It wasn't serious enough to file a complaint, but it put them all on guard. "Now, I have heard stories for years—it may not be true—that young female pages are given a list of whom not to get in an elevator with," says Elizabeth in a cautionary tone. "If it was a page in my office, I would make sure something happened. We're adults here, except the pages. But everyone else here can kick somebody in the ankles, and I would hope they would. But mostly, I would be concerned about pages because they're so young."

■ ■ ■

Fortunately, many of our male colleagues don't hold antiquated attitudes. "There's a certain group of men who were here over time who saw this as a men's club," notes Vic Fazio. "But there aren't very many of them anymore. Many of the men have served with women in other capacities. I would think that most of the people elected here within the last decade have served with women at every other level of government."

Vic is definitely one of those men comfortable working with women, and sexism is not a topic that makes him squirm. Vic is open and warm to his female colleagues and through his work on the choice issue he has made great strides to lessen the congressional gender gap.

Arizonan Democratic freshman Sam Coppersmith jokes, "I'm a guy and they haven't told me where the club is." Sam, who has become a buddy of mine, is another congressman who is completely at ease with women, like many of the men in the freshman class. An attorney, married to an attorney, Sam was president of Planned Parenthood of central and northern Arizona before running for Congress—not exactly the profile of the stereotypical cigar-smoking, backslapping old-time pol.

Yet there are indications that some of the old time–type pols are coming around. "Even some of those who have the image of being the tough old birds . . ." says one congressman, smiling. "Danny

Rostenkowski likes to hang out with some of the women he's compatible with, not all of them, but those that fit his sort of ethnic kind of approach."

The flip side of the men's club is the dutiful spouse club. Until recently, its membership was almost solely dutiful wives. Its increasing male membership faces its own set of problems. Steve Lowey, a successful attorney in New York City and the husband of Congresswoman Nita Lowey, took a leave of absence and worked full-time for four and a half months before Nita was elected to Congress in November of 1988. In that campaign cycle, Nita and Jolene Unsoeld, a Democrat from Washington State, were the only two women added to Congress. Steve was the only new congresswoman's spouse at the 1988 orientation (Jolene is a widow). At the wives' orientation, Steve was given a goody bag with perfume and other female items.

A speaker at the Male Spouses' Orientation Meeting on December 4, 1992, Steve told his compatriots the following: "You are a mere appendage—a prop—sort of like the man in those magazine advertisements for bridal gowns in ladies' magazines—you know, all you see is the back of his head and tuxedo as he dances with the beautiful and radiant bride. . . .

"The ideal role model for us all—indeed, our patron saint—is Denis Thatcher. When I first came to Washington and met Jim Schroeder, he said, 'Welcome to the Denis Thatcher club.' I said, 'What do I have to do to join?' He said, 'Just learn the password.' I said, 'What's that?' He answered, 'Yes, dear.' "

Steve was placed in a backseat position traditionally held by wives. It took some adjusting to. "The hardest thing for me was in making the emotional switch from one hundred percent involvement in Nita's campaign. It was really our campaign. She wouldn't have won without my support. That all changed the moment she was sworn in. From that point on, it was her career. What I began to realize was that the media, her staff, her colleagues, her constituents, interest groups, women's groups around the country care about her, not me. The fact that Nita has a husband is irrelevant—nobody needed me. It wasn't like the campaign. It wasn't easy for me to make the transition to obscurity. I understood the need and I didn't have any hang-ups about it. But her election was a really, really big change in our lives and we both had to adjust."

My husband, Ed Mezvinsky, has had a different experience from that of most of the other husbands because he's got something most congressional spouses don't have: experience as a congressman. I was the congressional spouse.

Ed was a Democratic congressman from Iowa, elected in 1972. He served for four years, losing his third election. As a freshman, he served on the House Judiciary Committee that voted to impeach President Nixon. It was a very tumultuous time in our nation's history, with the Vietnam War winding down and the Nixon administration unraveling. So when I come home now each week with stories from the front, he understands. Every now and then, someone kids him about being a congressional spouse, but Ed just laughs it off. No one is prouder of me than he is; no one gives me better advice. When I first went off to Washington, he said, "Know the rules, and know the people. You really have to understand these rules. These guys stay up nights, the old-timers, and they know the rules." His words came back to me in a rush after the disappointment of the Hyde Amendment, which ultimately was passed because of arcane parliamentary procedural maneuvers on the part of the pro-life members.

So Ed knows whereof he speaks, having been there himself. But I would venture to say that his experience as a congressional spouse is different from what mine was back in the seventies. Back then, wives were just ancillary.

"I can laugh about the experience because I know what it's all about. It is important to show support," says Ed. "But the appendage idea is something we laugh about now, because it's not that way anymore."

Ed's freshman experience began exactly twenty years before mine, so he has an interesting perspective. "I started my first touch on the Hill when I got a call in my senior year in law school, which was 1965, and I ended up coming to Washington to work for Neal Smith, a member from my home district in Iowa. And then I went back and got elected and served with him." Now Ed says to me, "Lo and behold, twenty years later you came. And what do you know? Neal's still here. The place changes, but then again, it doesn't."

■ ■ ■

Vic Fazio sees women legislators, because of their increased numbers, pulling together in a more efficacious way than ever before, and he observes that there are both positive and negative aspects of this. "One thing I think that's occurred this year is that women are here in such numbers that they probably have remained cohesive longer. There's been a consciousness-raising among the women who came together. While these women initially have bonded as a group, it has not been to the exclusion of other men in their class or the other men in the House. Their bonds have served as a bridge that has probably made the transition a little easier and more comfortable."

"Out of the sixty-three Democratic freshmen, thirty-four of us are either women or minorities," notes Leslie Byrne, who, as a freshman whip, also is very aware of the demographics of the freshman class. "When we started to elect class officers, all the women knew one another. We decided among ourselves who we wanted to run for what before we went into the whole class, who would support whom for what. And the men didn't have that cohesion that we had coming into it. So they didn't have the votes, either." The Democratic class freshman president was Eva Clayton, a black woman from North Carolina, and the interim Republican class president was Deborah Pryce.

Leslie says, only half joking, that the white men in the class have a harder time of it. "I think they felt shut out a little bit. But as we work together, I now think we're coming to the point where they know we're not trying to exclude. We're not trying to go it alone. We're trying to pull us together."

■ ■ ■

Leslie Byrne's legislative director had been working on the Hill for ten years when he joined her staff. One of the first days of the new Congress, he happened upon Leslie as she was making a fresh pot of coffee for the office. He literally stopped in his tracks when he saw what she was doing. "I've never seen a congressperson do that," he exclaimed.

"I wanted a cup of coffee and I wasn't going to wait for somebody to make it. Coffee's gone, you make it—for everybody," Leslie replied matter-of-factly.

I believe that many of us bring that kind of down-to-earth quality that will make the institution more friendly and more cohesive. I don't know where it comes from; maybe it's just that we're used to pitching in and running a family. You can see it in the way we relate to our staffs, encouraging a more colleague-to-colleague atmosphere. My office manager, Lynn Miller, was uncomfortable calling me by my first name in the beginning. She had previously worked for an old-time congressman for four years and had called him 'sir,' never by his first name. She was also reticent about coming into my office. My deputy policy director, Amy Sobel, would practically have to drag her into my office when she needed my signature. "I would say, 'Go in there. You need to ask her something; it's not a big deal,' " says Amy.

But the old-guard way works for some women. Vic notes that some of the women who have fit in the best, been the most effective, are those who come off as "a man's woman, one of the boys." One example he gives is Democratic Florida freshman Karen Thurman. "Just where she sits on the floor, who she deals with . . . She's developed a rapport with Rostenkowski. She's clearly been a legislator quite a while and has established ties beyond the coterie of women who came together. Now other women are doing that. It's sometimes a question of self-confidence. Carrie Meek has proven to be very effective in working within the Appropriations process. She's very astute intuitively on a political level."

Nita Lowey also tries to craft her own proverbial silk purse out of her minority status as a woman. "I think because some of the men are used to a more male place, being a woman is almost a benefit.

They know your name; you dress differently; there are fewer of you. All the men tend to look alike, so it's almost a benefit. I've never found it to be a disadvantage."

Corrine Brown doesn't personally feel that women are treated any differently. "I think they treat freshmen all the same, so I can't really say. But I think we did pretty good with first committee assignments; we're very competitive in that area. These are the kinds of things that you can judge it by."

Corrine doesn't feel, as some of the women do in varying degrees, that she has to temper her personality at all or hang her femininity in the closet before she comes to work. "It doesn't have anything to do with what sex you are. You just have to be focused on what you do."

But being focused on what you do doesn't mean having to sublimate your identity, necessarily. "I've been an executive on an all-male corporate executive board and I've been the only woman on a seven-member city council, and I think the worst thing women can do is to think they have to be other than a woman," says Lynn Woolsey. "I mean, I don't go throwing out my sexuality and tease and taunt. There's a big difference. But nobody should be doing that in the business of government."

Like Corrine, Jennifer Dunn doesn't find gender to be a major factor in how she is regarded by her male colleagues. "The first time I walked into one of my meetings, a southern gentleman came up and gave me a kiss on the cheek and said, 'Honey, I'm looking forward to working with you.' He was holding my hand and it was really very cute and charming and courteous—that's really all it was. Someone could come in with the wrong idea and wonder if that sort of thing wasn't overdone. But it's not. I have not run into any sort of negativity from any member yet. They're all different personalities. Some are very tough and abrasive and it makes me amused. Others are wonderful southern gentlemen. Others are calm, cool, and collected. . . . I think they learn to respect you if you show you're going to work hard and you're not going to take something that's given to you because you're a woman. For me, that's the key to it."

Maria Cantwell knows she's got an advantage in that she happens to come from the same state as Speaker of the House Tom Foley. His staff is more accessible to her because of their shared regional concerns and she looks to them occasionally for guidance on legislative issues. That's an advantage most other freshmen don't have, and Maria is grateful for it. But her connection to one of the most powerful people in Congress brings with it its own set of frustrations.

Traditionally, the Speaker chooses which freshmen get on the influential Democratic Steering and Policy Committee, which makes Democratic committee assignments. But with this Congress, new members had to do their own bidding. Maria was one of three freshmen who managed to land a spot. "I worked my tail off for two weeks during freshman orientation to get on Steering and Policy. I got sixty-some votes out of the sixty-five votes from Democrats to be on the committee. And it wasn't because I was from Tom Foley's state. Yet I still have to answer questions from the press who say, 'Oh she got on Steering and Policy because Tom Foley put her there.' "

Elizabeth Furse believes that sexism is there, any way you cut it. But she empathizes with those women who don't or can't acknowledge it. "It may be that people, some people, just develop blinders because it is too painful. They want to get a job done and if they worried about that, it would be too painful."

But ignoring or denying the problem can be problematic. She continues, "I think you do have to let people know, because quite frankly I think a lot of people do say sexist and racist things and truly do not know that's what they are because they don't experience it themselves. Very often, people need to have it brought to their attention."

There are constant reminders to us that we are newcomers, even outsiders, and there are some accommodations that need to be made. For instance, the art around the Capitol barely reflects that women exist—in government or even society at large. Kevin Merida, of the *Washington Post,* wrote last summer, "There is no overall count of art by gender, but only seven of the approximately 190 statues and busts in the Capitol are of women, although the most visible statue, 'Freedom,' is a female form. It has been removed temporarily from its place atop the Capitol dome for restoration."

Everywhere I turn, I see sculptures and paintings depicting white men. When I eat in the members' dining room, I look up and what do I see? George Washington, the father of our country, surrounded by men, staring down at me. Now don't get me wrong, I love old George, but every once in a while I imagine sneaking in there and adding a few women to those walls.

Blanche Lambert is the youngest woman serving in the House. Her opponent in the primary was Congressman Bill Alexander, whom Blanche had worked for in his Washington office in 1983, answering phones and writing letters. So she's observed the congressional men's club as both a staffer and a member.

Blanche feels very comfortable with her male colleagues and, while she acknowledges differences in the way women are treated, she doesn't perceive the clubbiness as a slight. "It's not like you want to crack it. It's not like something you want to conquer or overcome. You want to be a part of it, but you want to be a part of it as a woman. Your strength—as far as I'm concerned, your strength is in your person.

"My grandmother told me one time, a long time ago, 'Honey, you are a southern lady, you're a Christian, and you're a Democrat and don't you ever forget it,' " says Blanche, her southern accent growing momentarily stronger as she echoes her grandmother's words. "So I mean, it's like I have no desire to lose any ladylike qualities—I want to be respected and I feel like I can be. And I don't feel like I have to wear pant suits and smoke cigars to be effective."

When Blanche returned to the Hill for orientation week after winning her race, she ran into some guys who work in the paint shop. They were a friendly bunch and they had always been fond of Blanche, back in the days when she worked for Bill Alexander. The daughter of a farmer, she could really appreciate the tomatoes one of the guys would occasionally offer her from his garden. Blanche laughs when telling this story, obviously getting a kick out of it. When a couple of them ran into Blanche in the hallway, they were very happy to see her. "Where ya been?" they asked. "Who ya workin' for now?"

"Well," Blanche told them, flashing her lovely smile, "I'm actually working for the folks back home!"

■ ■ ■

While there is a sense that women can permeate the men's club, the numbers of women who have done so are remarkably few. While I think we've all made dents in different ways, there's just no question that it's a male bastion and we're still being treated as part of the periphery. To wit: There is only one woman in the leadership, Barbara Kennelly, who is one of the chief deputy whips; in that role, she is responsible for counting and marshaling votes for the Democratic leadership.

Barbara comes from a family of Connecticut politicians—her father was Democratic National Committee chairman during the Kennedy and Johnson years and her husband was Speaker of the House in Connecticut. She underscores how important it is that women don't isolate themselves from men, that the only way to get things accomplished is by working together (and golfing together; Barbara is an avid golfer). "Of course we're going to have our caucus; it would be abnormal if we didn't have a women's caucus. But we've got to be very, very careful that we keep that close relationship with the men, because we still don't have enough members to pass legislation. And I'm watching that very closely right now."

Men like Vic Fazio who take on issues that have traditionally been regarded as women's issues, such as choice, get high marks from Barbara. "Vic's a perfect example of a man who has worked incredibly hard. We all have our own personal things that have happened to us and we put a great deal of ourselves into these decisions. . . . But you don't want to have it put down to being a 'women's issue,' because it isn't; it's a human issue."

Barbara sees a difference in the women who are just coming to Congress now. "They're different; they're a new age. The women in the seventies were our pioneers, really. But there was a lot of 'poor me.' "

Barbara prefers to take a different approach. She feels women can get much more accomplished if their attitude doesn't draw too much attention to their gender. Just do your thing. If people treat you with the respect they give their male colleagues, great; if not, that's their problem.

One of her mentors when she first got here was Louisiana Democratic congresswoman Lindy Boggs. Lindy filled the seat of her husband, Hale Boggs, after he died in a plane crash. "Just watching her taught me so much. She's one of the reasons that I think I got on Ways and Means. That was unusual for me to get on a year after I got here. But it was a good time because we had no women at that time. There was no woman on Budget; there was no woman on Ways and Means. Lindy was on Appropriations. We said, 'We've got to work together,' and so we met with [then Speaker of the House] Tip O'Neill and said, 'We want a woman on Budget; we want a woman on Ways and Means.' "

After that meeting, Lindy went to Barbara and said, "Now make an appointment with Tip alone."

So Barbara did, and following Lindy's advice paid off; she got the coveted seat. "Group action is fine to a point. And then you have to prove yourself," says Barbara, repeating the lesson Lindy taught her.

Lindy, who retired at the end of the last Congress, was a great influence on Barbara. "In so many ways, she taught me patience. Better not to say something than to say something you'll regret later. Her whole manner—I would never be able to emulate it completely, because she was a very special person."

And now, in turn, many of us go to Barbara Kennelly for advice. She is one of our role models, someone we can point to when people ask us if it's possible to shatter the glass ceiling.

In an incident that echoes Lindy's prodding of Barbara to get on Ways and Means, Barbara prodded freshman Carrie Meek. Carrie wanted more than anything to be on the powerful Appropriations Committee. But this would be a rare occurrence, a freshman landing on Appropriations. People told Carrie, "Well, you won't make Appropriations. Why don't you get a second choice?" But Carrie wouldn't do it. She knew the odds were not in her favor, but her mind was made up. She kept talking to the men, letting them know what she wanted. She reminded them that she came from Florida, which had recently lost two veterans on the committee, and that Appropriations needed an African-American woman. Her third point was that she had a decade of experience on Florida's Appropriations Committee.

One day, in the middle of her campaign to get on the committee, she stopped in the ladies' room in the Lindy Boggs Room, where she ran into Barbara Kennelly.

"Carrie," Barbara said, "keep doing what you're doing. But there's one thing that you're leaving out that you should push."

Carrie waited, curious to hear what Barbara had to say.

"That is that you're a senior citizen."

Carrie burst out laughing. It struck her as truly comical, the notion that her advanced years could work as a political feather in her cap. But then, when she stopped laughing, she realized the inherent logic in Barbara's point.

"You're a senior, and there aren't very many people here with your status. You have an age advantage that is an experiential advantage."

Carrie agreed.

"I'll help you," Barbara promised. "I'll speak for you in the Steering and Policy Committee." Generally, someone from the person's state recommends the committee candidate to the group.

After that ladies' room tête-à-tête, Carrie's confidence began to build. She thought to herself, Well now, if Barbara tells me that and she is the only woman in the leadership, I'm really going strong now. And she was. Soon after, she won her spot.

Women also look to some of the men as mentors. Cynthia McKinney is developing what she refers to as "consultative friendships" with some of the male members. "I believe there are some men who are nontraditional in their approach to women on the Hill. That would be refreshing if over time I'm able to establish a real friendship, an advising kind of friendship with some of them."

I only hope that we will all establish those sorts of relationships. As in every other walk of life, men and women need to work together to get the real work accomplished.

Vic believes that our increased numbers here have leavened the institution. "I think we now have perspectives, even ways of saying things that are more reflective of society at large. We are a long way from being an institution that is an exact replica of our population in every sense. We probably never will be. And while I don't want to put a huge burden on forty-eight people, I do think that their numbers and their diversity—they are not a monolith—are really important to the institution's ability to represent a broad cross section of American public opinion."

Florida freshman Republican Tillie Fowler worked as a legislative assistant for Democratic congressman Robert G. Stephens, Jr., back in the late sixties, after finishing law school. She was thrilled at the opportunity, since at that time there weren't very many women in those positions. "There are a lot more women in professional positions now, which is very encouraging. And, of course, there are a lot more congresswomen than there were back then. There were really very few then. So those are some of the good changes that I see. There are a lot more women in responsible positions, both elected and nonelected, and I think that's a real encouraging factor."

And so we've still got some work to do around here to start making this place more representative of the American people, 52 percent of whom are female. We celebrate the small victories and try to let the losses be instructive and pass with humor. A few weeks after Karan and Leslie were in the elevator with that relic of a congressman, Karan was the subject of a favorable *Life* magazine piece, "Ms. English Goes to Washington." We threw her a little magazine-signing party and everybody brought something to eat. Leslie walked in carrying a vegetable platter. After setting it down on the table with the other hors d'oeuvres, her aide placed a sign in front of the dish, saying in bold letters: CHICKS IN CONGRESS CRUDITE.

CHAPTER THREE

Chicks in Congress: What We Bring as Women

When Carolyn Maloney watched as her twenty-three fellow congresswomen marched down the aisle to be sworn in, she felt an electrifying thrill run through her. Imagine, twenty-four women walking down the aisle, not to get married but to be sworn in to the United States Congress.

It was a very satisfying moment for all of us. We felt that our presence would make a real difference, that we could add to the considerable strides such women as Pat Schroeder, Nita Lowey, and Louise Slaughter had made before us. Now maybe, with the added numbers, we could do the work that needed to be done, work that the primarily male-dominated Congress, for one reason or another, had not attended to.

First Lady Hillary Rodham Clinton has been a great source of encouragement for women in Congress, and her dedicated work on health-care reform has brought her to the Hill frequently. On October 5, 1993, she and I sat down to talk about women in government. She said, "I think that women bring their life experience to Congress, in ways that, at least up until now, most men have not.

Women come here knowing what it's like to balance family and work. They come feeling the pull of being both a nurturer and a breadwinner. They have a more hopeful sense of what we can do together to try to support families and children, because they have had to support them in one way or the other in their own life.

"I think back about some of the stories that you and other freshmen women have told me about the worst times of their lives and how somebody was there to help them. Now they're giving back. I believe that any woman who makes it to Congress has to have a certain level of drive and a willingness to put up with a lot. But most of the women are there because they're motivated by something bigger than themselves."

■ ■ ■

Getting the Freedom of Choice Act (FOCA) passed was one of the main things that had propelled Carolyn Maloney forward, that had brought her to this very moment, convinced her that it was necessary even if it meant being away from her husband and two daughters, twelve-year-old Christina and five-year-old Virginia. Carolyn had, in fact, announced her candidacy in 1992 on the day of the Casey decision, a landmark Pennsylvania abortion ruling that upheld the rights of states to set some limits on the availability of abortions—such as allowing Pennsylvania's mandatory twenty-four-hour waiting period to stand. When Carolyn, a member of the New York City Council for ten years, got the news of the Casey decision, she walked out onto the steps of City Hall and declared to the world that she was going to run. Carolyn felt that it was her duty as a female lawmaker to speak up for women, children, and families and that if women didn't speak up for other women, no one else would.

Soon after Carolyn arrived in Washington, that's exactly what she did. On February 3, 1993, she addressed her colleagues. "Mr. Speaker, as a working mother with two children and as the Representative in Congress of tens of thousands of other working parents in New York City, I rise to voice my strong support for the Family and Medical Leave Act.

"As my twelve-year-old daughter might tell you, this bill is a no-brainer. Every industrialized nation in the world has adopted a policy allowing workers time off to care for a new baby or an ill family member. It is ridiculous, and profoundly embarrassing, that we still do not have such a policy. . . ."

The Family and Medical Leave Act, which was to provide three months of unpaid leave for employees, passed. It was one of the first tangible victories for us, the first taste of accomplishment, and Carolyn felt exhilarated to be a part of it, to speak out on the floor about this extremely important issue.

Carolyn, who had started her career as a public school teacher in New York City, quickly moved up through the ranks as an administrator for the Board of Education. She became an aide in the state assembly, then an aide to the minority leader of the state senate, and finally she gained a seat on the New York City Council. Coming to Washington, helping to get policy such as family leave enacted, was all part of the continuum Carolyn saw herself on. "I call it returning to the traditional role of women—cleaning up the mess, cleaning up the House."

■ ■ ■

Anna Eshoo sees a common path among the careers of many women legislators, much like the road Carolyn Maloney took to Washington. "More often than not, women have come to elected positions having had to work up through the ranks. They didn't want trees cut down in their neighborhood, which then became a campaign that took them before their city or town council, which then gave them a broader interest in serving there, and then they ran for local office. Women have always been at the forefront of educational issues. Why? Because we're the first teachers of our children. So we were elected to school boards and from school boards we moved on. And so we come more from the back bench and the more distant places that comprise local government, which I think gives one great experience. It's closer to the home fires."

"I started as PTA president," recalls Nita Lowey. "And the first battle I had, which was a major battle, was to replace a principal, and we won. And then it led to other activities in the community. So whether it's a fight over a streetlight or over a principal or over changing attitudes in the community about pollution or recycling, women often get involved because of issues they care passionately about."

Steve Lowey, who witnessed his wife Nita's political development, reiterates this notion that women come to power in a different manner. "They're doing this for all the right reasons. For Nita, being a congresswoman is not a step up some ladder or a means to some other end. . . . Nita's there because she loves the job. She is absolutely committed to being the best legislator she can be."

Tillie Fowler never envisioned that she would become a congresswoman, but she always had a political fire burning within her. She credits her father, who was in the Georgia legislature for forty-two years, for at least indirectly fanning the flames, if not gathering the kindling and starting it. "I guess I had it in my blood and didn't know it. If someone had asked me if I was going to be in elected office twenty years ago, I wouldn't have said yes. Then when I was on the Jacksonville City Council, I didn't know I was going to be in Congress. And I'm one of those unusual politicians in that I have no long-range goals that I'm trying to reach. I'm a big believer in doing well what you're given to do."

"When I started college, my aptitude tests showed that I should go into politics, real estate, or the stock market. High-pressure salesmanship is what they told me," recalls Pat Danner. "But you know, when you stop to think about it, those jobs weren't available to women at that time, especially not in the small community I came from. Absolutely not. I was Susie Homemaker."

But Susie Homemaker gradually metamorphosed into Susie Activist. "As I became active in the community, I became very involved as a volunteer with the Girl Scouts, the American Red Cross, all those kinds of things. A gentleman who was very active in the Democratic party began to say, 'You have got to run for committeewoman.' And I kept saying, 'No, no, no.' Finally, he convinced me to do it and I won. Two weeks later when the committee met, I was made chairman. I recognized later that it was his hand behind it. And so suddenly, I went from not being involved at all to being chairman of the committee." Pat went on to a ten-year stint in the Missouri senate, only the fourth woman to be sworn in to that body.

Blanche Lambert is of most of these women's daughters' generation, so she didn't experience the same societal pressures and was able, unencumbered, to follow her political inclinations early on. "I think at my age, there's a lot less of a tension problem, whether you're a man or a woman. I have a lot of young women friends who are professionals.

"I'm here because I love my home and I love my family," says Blanche, an Arkansan through and through. "And I felt like things were slipping and wheels were turning and we were getting nowhere, and I wanted to see my home be the best place that I thought it could be. And small towns and rural communities are dying on the vine. If people like me don't stand up and say we want to improve the school systems, the public school systems in rural communities . . ."

Blanche keeps a sepia-toned photograph of her late grandmother on her desk in Washington, a memento that reminds her of all she holds dear. This woman, her mother's mother, is Blanche's idea of a true heroine. "I can see her smiling right now," Blanche says. "She's smiling big time. But I don't really think it would matter to her whether I was a woman or not, but simply that I was doing the best job that I could do and that I was remembering where my roots were, remembering the good things that I was taught—to be fair, to be good, to take care of those who are less fortunate than I am, or to help out where I could help out. She's not smiling because, Oh yeah, there's a woman in there. She's saying, 'Stick to your guns and stick to what you know is right and what you should be doing.' "

"It's an evolutionary process," says Vic Fazio, who is vice-chairman of the Democratic caucus, of the route many of us have taken to get here. "Politics, particularly in the Democratic party, is a process of working your way through the system, where people increasingly move up when they show the ability to perform and develop the skills to campaign and raise money. So most of the women who are in our caucus—and I don't mean to say this is not true of Republicans; I haven't thought about it as much, but my sense is it's more true of Democratic women—have earned their spurs as they've moved through the process. And you'll see more of it."

"I don't know that people understand how savvy women candidates have become," says Ellen Malcolm, of EMILY's List. "Women run for public office because of volunteer work they've done in their communities; they get involved because of their own family and community issues. But the women now are combining personal commitment with becoming really smart political players. They know how to get elected; they know how to make a speech and raise hundreds of thousands of dollars. If you're a voter, a woman candidate is just what you're looking for. They keep in touch on the local level but know how to get things done once they are elected."

Public office is in many cases more of a sacrifice for women than for men, and perhaps this is why the women are so reflective about why we are here. For one thing, many of the congressmen move their families to Washington, thus cutting down on the debilitating effect a legislative schedule has on family life. As far as I know, of the women, only Pat Schroeder has brought her entire family to Washington.

So the majority of us reluctantly leave our families behind, but ironically, many of us are going to Washington *because of* our families. "I am doing this because of my kids," asserts Karan English, who says that life in Washington is lonelier than she had imagined it would be but that she is clear as to why she is doing it. "I ran for public office because I wanted my children to have a better world to live in, and each time I ran for a different office, there was some piece of it that was related to my kids. When I first ran for the legislature, I was so disgusted with the educational system, I said, 'My kids deserve better than this. I want to fix education.' When I ran for the Arizona senate, I thought, You know what, the environmental issues are terrible. My kids deserve better than this. So I ran for the senate. And then when I ran for Congress, I had the same attitude: Women deserve better than this. My daughter deserves to have the same opportunities as men. I'm going to run for Congress."

Karan, who is only the second woman ever sent to Congress by the state of Arizona, feels great pride in having been elected. But the pride is overtaken by an urgent sense of responsibility. "When I speak to college students or women's groups or businesswomen, women have a hope that I haven't seen in my thirteen years in politics. That is an awesome responsibility. I hope that I can live up to it.

"That brings up the next thing, which is scary as hell, and that is the public expectation of not only the freshman class but the women in it. . . . I've always known that women have to be maybe a little more prepared going into what is the traditional male scenario because we can't outyell somebody, because our voices aren't baritone; we can't outmaneuver people just because of our sheer size; and because of our social environment, we've grown up to be kind of forgiving. We aren't necessarily as aggressive as the male gender and we'll be polite about letting them walk right over us at times.

"If we're actually going to succeed, we've got to do our homework, because we've got to elevate the conversation or the debate on an intellectual level, since we're going to lose on the muscular level. Most women realize that if we're going to be successful, if we're going to make our sisters proud, then we have a lot of work to do on three of these fronts: changing the image of Congress; beefing up issues that women should be represented in; and being a part of every decision. And so that's a lot of work, especially when you have to do homework for all of those things, so your competing interests are public relations and putting the women to the front."

But to get to the front, you have to project self-confidence and strong-mindedness—two qualities a good portion of America has not traditionally associated with women. "You have to be forceful and you have to stand firm on issues and ideas that you believe in," says Nita Lowey. "And you have to be willing to get into a fight and to be immovable on those issues. And because women smile a lot and they're so pleasant or are perceived that way, there may be a tendency not to believe that you're going to stand firm and fight to the finish. But they go a couple of rounds and they understand that they don't mess with you."

Pat Schroeder has always been very clear about why she was

here, never worrying about winning popularity contests. "If you come in here and you have beliefs, you ought to lay 'em down. You ought to be out there and you ought to be for something and you shouldn't get caught up in the clubby part of it. That's caused a lot of members to get angry with me. They'd much prefer you come play the 'get along, go along, shut up'—you know, 'don't look silly' and so forth. But that's not why I came, so I haven't done it. And I honestly think people are much happier in this job if they have a clear definition of their core values and what they really are prepared to fight for—and then fight for it."

But Pat concedes it was lonely during the eighties. "In the Reagan era, it was always wonderful," Pat says with sarcasm. "You'd get out there and say, 'Okay, guys, let's go.' And you'd get out there and you'd say, 'Where the hell are they? *Where are they?*' That used to happen all the time. And then they'd bitch and moan, 'You're on TV all the time.' And I'd say, 'You guys could be, too; all you have to do is stand up.' "

Pat tries to foster the kind of atmosphere that will encourage her female colleagues to stand up for themselves and their ideas. "When the women first came, I had some media people come and we did a dinner so they could sit down and talk to them. We've been trying to do everything, trying to fast-forward them. It's wonderful to have an 'old girls' network.' When I came, we really didn't have that. . . . Freshmen can ask questions; seniors can ask questions. There's no rank; there's not that type of ordering."

Rosa DeLauro, who is currently serving her second term, explains why it's so important that the Year of the Woman not be a flash in the pan, that we encourage our sisters, our daughters, our neighbors to consider a life of public service. "This body is very competitive and you've got to build coalitions. We have forty-eight women members, but forty-eight is hardly a majority, particularly when they don't always agree on everything. . . . Is it important that we continue to increase the numbers? I'll give you a couple of specific reasons why I think it's important. When you look at a Budget Committee with only one woman on it—and for a while it was only Louise Slaughter—and when you're looking at money for increased efforts for DES research and women's health, you have only one voice. But now you have women on almost every committee and subcommittee. I'm on a subcommittee of the Appropriations Committee—Labor, Health and Human Services and Education—where previously it was all men. There are now four women: myself, Nita Lowey, Nancy Pelosi, and Helen Bentley, three Democratic women and one Republican. There were no women on this subcommittee before. Therefore, the tone and the agenda get changed in ways that could not have happened before, because you didn't have the critical mass of numbers."

And while 11 percent may not yet be considered a critical mass by most, it is enough to act as a foil, to show that there are alternative ways to play the game, that women bring a different spin to the discipline of lawmaking, that there is a real sense of shared life experiences and common concerns that can be expressed in relative harmony. The fact is that what brings us here is unifying by nature: the collective desire to make this world better for our kids, rather than the individual drive to get ahead personally.

Hillary Clinton agreed with this characterization of what tends to motivate women to serve in public office. "If we woke up tomorrow and in our country violence was ended, all our children were in good schools, women were respected, and there was equal opportunity the kind of world that we've all talked about and had worked hard for—I think most of us would breathe a sigh of relief and go back to doing whatever it was we wanted to do.

"I would love to live in a world where I could walk down any street at any time of day or night, where I could take my daughter anywhere, where I could say good-bye to my daughter in the morning and she could get on a bike with friends and come back at night. The kind of world that a lot of us grew up in and took for granted has been stripped away by all of the troubles and struggles we've faced in this country. And I wouldn't care who got the credit. I wouldn't care who was in the Congress and all that stuff would be irrelevant to me. The women I've talked with and relate to in the Congress want to achieve a better life for ourselves and our families."

According to Blanche Lambert, "When you look at health care and you look at education and you look at budgets, they are issues that traditionally women have had a tremendous amount of input into, whether it's in their family or their community. Even in the pioneer days, women were responsible for teaching and education; they were responsible for the health care of their family; they were responsible usually for the budget, and there's a sense there of responsibility and of living within your means. . . . I think that's a big plus to have a woman's point of view on those issues, those being the most critical issues in our nation. I think men recognize that."

"We can win on issues that matter if we build our numbers and reach out to men who are like-minded in order to create a majority," says Rosa DeLauro. "But in order to get in that position, we need others to join the fight. We are only on the edge of building majority coalitions. The question comes up: Is this a male bastion? Look, there are only forty-eight women. It's not a question; it really isn't."

But despite the fact that we are clearly still a minority, being a congresswoman is a less alienating experience in this Congress than it ever was before. The Year of the Woman took care of that, and this momentum that started in 1992 will entice more women to set their sights on Washington.

Just considering the changes Pat Schroeder has seen during her tenure here is testimony to the fact that the political climate has evolved (somewhat) in regard to issues of gender. Pat's is no longer a lone voice. "It makes you feel better not to have to carry quite so much. You can kind of spread it out," says Pat. "We have task forces we never had before, more enthusiasm. Obviously, I think it's a class where they're not timid about being women, and we've had some senior members who kind of tiptoe around a lot of the issues and don't really want to be too identified. Sometimes it's so refreshing to have a strong core."

We're definitely not a group that shows any timidity about our gender, and that is one of the reasons I am so proud to be a member of this particular class. We're comfortable with our female identities and what we bring to the job. It's the rest of the world (or some of it) that needs to do some catching up. There are people, even as we head toward the twenty-first century, who still don't know what to make of a female politician, who have vague, static images of who we are, why they think we are here, and what they think we are capable (or not capable) of accomplishing.

"I laugh because there're these two versions of women in politics," asserts Leslie Byrne. "One is a very romanticized version: We're caring, loving, warm people with families, Donna Reed next door—you know, Donna Reed goes to Congress. And there's this other version of women in politics, kind of like men in skirts, tough as nails, smoke cigars in the back room with the guys. But between those two versions most of us fall. But the press and everybody else tends to want to pigeonhole you in one of those versions."

Our society is still threatened by a strong woman who has opinions and is driven to try to change things. Whether our role is First Lady, congresswoman, or surgeon, people have a preconceived notion of how a woman should do the job. And if we don't conform, our motives, our loved ones, our moral fiber is questioned. Our professional dedication scares certain people, so our personal lives are attacked.

"People ask, 'Doesn't she care about her family?' or 'Shouldn't she be spending more time with her family?' 'What kind of husband does she have?' 'Could he be a real man if he's married to her?' " says Karen Shepherd, echoing the criticisms she's encountered in her political career. "You know, whatever power I have is coupled with problems. Most of the status that rewards men has a downside for us. For a man, it's pure gravy. 'He's neat, he's fabulous, he's successful, he's dynamic, he's got an adoring family, he's a perfect provider.' Women, on the other hand, are seen as abnormal, neglecting their families, having the 'wrong' priorities, being selfish. These responses become internal kinds of obstacles to overcome. And I think this is one of the reasons it is going to be hard to fill the Congress with women."

But the positive side of this is that while some Americans may not be convinced that we're politically sophisticated or tough enough, they view us as more honest and compassionate than our male counterparts. And these days, honesty and compassion in government count for quite a lot. "There is a growing credibility gap between men and women in the sense that women are perceived to be more trustworthy as candidates and as public officials by a percentage of three or four points," says Steny Hoyer. "They're perceived to be more real in an era that wants real people in public office."

"I don't think there's any question that women generally look at a problem in a different way than men," says Pat Danner. "I know that in my course of years as senator I received many letters from people saying, 'I know you're not my senator, but you're a woman and I think you'll understand.' "

Never was this more poignantly clear to Pat than the time that, years ago, as a state senator, she was invited to a luncheon at a vocational/technical school in her district. She listened to the hardships that some of the women were going through in order to get an education. But the thing that got to her most, that haunted and dogged her into action, was one woman who explained that many of those present that day had had to borrow suitable clothes to attend the function. "She said, 'We needed to wear a dress today and I don't own anything, and I had to borrow this skirt.' " Pat pauses, remembering. "That really kind of takes your breath away."

In the days to come, Pat thought about that woman and the others she had met. She worked for the passage of a displaced homemakers bill in Missouri that allowed tuition-free entrance into vo-tech schools or community colleges for women in this type of situation. When the bill passed, Pat received many letters from the women who would benefit from it. But Pat was still troubled that there were women out there who wanted to work, who were trying to make it and yet didn't have the clothes to appear presentable for a job interview. So she made some calls and organized a drive to collect clothes from professional women in the community.

"We didn't get to become congresswomen by being schmucks," says Leslie Byrne. "But there again, I think that because we came out of the community and because we have different life experiences, because of that, most of us got involved in politics because we wanted to do something, not because we wanted to be somebody."

Last year, Leslie Byrne got the opportunity to travel to Mexico to explore the commonalities of experience with our Mexican counterparts. "Eight women went to Mexico to talk about trade and economics and we met with twenty-five women from the Mexican Congress from all six of their political parties," says Leslie. "It was very focused on jobs and the economy and trade and what it would mean for both our countries, yet with the nuance we bring to it—which is what these words mean to families, what these words mean to our communities. When we talk about eliminating tariffs and open boundaries, what is that going to mean to the electronics manufacturer in my district if he no longer has a job? And what trades are we making for international trade? And are they worth it? I think because we are of the community, we tend to look at things with a community focus, not just with a geopolitical focus, not just with a world economic focus, but taking those things and bringing them right back down from whence we came."

I think this is an extremely important distinction between men and women, regarding why we all are here. Now, of course there are exceptions, and it's dangerous to make generalizations. With that caveat, I'm going to make one. I believe that men and women tend to regard and define power differently. Women see it as a means to an end and men see it as an end. I think it has to do with compassion and nurturing. When you're a mother, you are no longer the center of the universe; your child is. Your focus becomes, What do I need to do for my child today? not What do I need to do for myself?

Hillary Rodham Clinton talks about how this difference can be frustrating for women who are here to get things done, not further their own personal agenda. "I think it rests in a very different set of expectations about human behavior and the possibilities for change in a political system. It is very frustrating when people keep dragging the conversation down to the lowest common denominator, when they forget that there are real people with real problems and real struggles that we're trying to represent. Because we are reminded continually of all the people who need help and those with whom we've worked. And when we see them we are reminded that we are trying to change conditions so that they can help themselves, and other people don't get it at all."

According to Eva Clayton, "Just by our experiences and our expectations, we're expected to perhaps come to a position with a little more caring, a little more nurturing. By men's experiences and society's expectations, they're expected to make quick decisions when they don't have the information, expected to act macho when they're probably trembling in their boots. So in some ways, the world isn't very kind to them, either. They would be better served if they took the time to care and to nurture, and many of them do. They don't want us to know it because it may not seem as manly. And then some of us women are far more dictatorial than our nurturing experiences would indicate. When we need to make hard decisions, we can cut it off."

"I feel this is really an opportunity to make life better for others," says Nita Lowey. "That sounds sort of Pollyanna, but it's true. I really feel it's tremendously rewarding to be able to do something about crime in the streets. And this to me is the greatest job in the world because it gives you the power to really bring about change."

"I'm really interested in results," says Eddie Bernice Johnson, a Democratic first-termer from Texas. "If it means letting someone else take the credit, it's okay if I get results. I've experienced with men that they'll gladly take credit for what you do. I've actually been in a situation where I was standing, getting ready to be interviewed, and a man pushed me out of the way and just got right in front of the camera." She stops to laugh at the ludicrous memory. "You know at this age that you're not going to change them; you give them enough rope and they'll take care of themselves. Because you can rarely fool people back home. Just like people get to know personalities here, people at home know the personalities, too. And so I take comfort in knowing that I don't have anybody up here who votes for me; they're back home. And they're pretty insightful."

"I try to speak only when I have something worthwhile to say. And I feel if I do that, then people will listen to me," says Tillie Fowler. "Because they know if you're up and down speaking all the time, people tune you out. I always had a reputation when I was on the City Council—and I hope now—that I do my homework, that I'm really prepared, that I try to listen to everybody and then make a decision and go forward. Talk about it, be prepared, and be informed—I think that's important, and maybe even more so for women because we get looked at under a microscope."

Leslie Byrne had been approached in the past to run for office, but she had disregarded the suggestion. In retrospect, she thinks it had something to do with a reticence to pursue power. "I think women come to power gradually. I think men chase it. . . . Women don't like the rough-and-tumble of it. I think they're not out to grab power."

But then Leslie had an epiphany when she was testifying before the Board of Supervisors in her northern Virginia community. "I was working in the community. I was in the League of Women Voters and the PTA and the Citizens Association and all of these groups where I wanted to work to make my community better. I was working on a particular issue—to save the watershed from development in order to protect the water supply." Leslie made her case and then listened as the chairman of the board told her that cows caused more pollution than people do.

"Well, you know, Fairfax County hasn't seen a cow in a long time and that wasn't the problem. And it just occurred to me, literally, as I was in this colloquy in front of the boardroom, that it probably would be easier to be on the other side of the dais, making policy instead of trying to convince people."

The pursuit of power is a tricky thing for us. I think that women have been hamstrung by the fact that when girls are growing up, they don't get the same exposure to team sports that boys do. So for the most part, we don't understand team mentality the way men do—viscerally, instinctively. Men, as little boys, get it woven into their very fabric; it seeps into their inchoate bones. They learn that winning is everything, that they must do whatever is necessary to gain and maintain control of the ball.

Hillary Clinton has thought about this a lot. "It's a big struggle as to how much you give in to the game and just play and how much you try to change it. And there are equally good reasons for pursuing each strategy at different points in your life, and depending upon what you're trying to achieve. And I think a lot of it does get back to what you were just saying. Team sports have only recently become widely available to young women. And there is a difference in being raised where you are engaged in solitary activities with only a few people, as most young girls always used to play: pursuing piano or ballet. In team sports where you know you win some and you lose some, you're all in it together. You kind of look at each other's strengths and weaknesses.

"I remember the first time I watched some little girls play softball. They were just stunned that they and their friends might have to be on opposite teams. That's something little boys would relish; that would make the friendship even stronger—to taunt your best friend because he struck out. Girls would be afraid that their best friends would burst into tears. That's a difference in life experience that is beginning to even out. More young girls are engaged in team sports and having those opportunities. But you're right: From a very early age, there are differences in experience that kind of prepare one for different ways of dealing with life later on."

So playing to win is not a part of our experiential development. Power is not something we are taught to crave; it is something we are taught to admire. And we willingly submit to this societal brainwashing, or at least until we realize that our received disaffection for power is directly in conflict with our own good. "It's a maturation process that you come to," Leslie Byrne says. "You don't like the rough-and-tumble, but you understand that that's what comes with political life. Then, as you do it more and more, you say, 'I'm going to give as good as I get. I don't have to take it.' "

Leslie learned in the Virginia general assembly that giving as good as she got meant she would have to command power among her peers. One way to do that was to keep the men on their toes. Occasionally, the men would grow agitated if they spotted a cluster of women on the floor engaged in a seemingly conspiratorial tête-à-tête. "We used to do that in general assembly just to cause trouble. During recess, we'd all go down to the well just to scare them. We weren't talking about anything, but it just made them nervous. It was fun to do," says Leslie, chuckling. But she hastens to add that she's not a troublemaker. "I take joy in my job; I don't take myself seriously at all. I take the work seriously. If you can't have fun at what you're doing, why do it?"

Carrie Meek wasn't intimidated by the fact that as a freshman, a woman, an African-American, and a senior citizen she was in the minority (four times over) on the Appropriations Committee. One day, when she was only a few months on the job, there was a potential crisis of sorts looming above the committee. The word had come down from the leadership that some of the power of the committee was in danger, that they might be forced to give recision powers to the President. So the members convened in a meeting room in the Capitol to discuss their options. "I looked around and there were all these white men, most of them having been here on the average of fifteen or twenty years, and I had just gotten here." Carrie listened as the men talked. Finally, she raised her hand to speak. Her voice, soft and high, must have seemed oddly incongruent with her message. The men looked with mild surprise at this genteel grandmother with the church manners and friendly smile to match.

"I said, 'Well, what are we going to do? I'm used to fighting. It appears to me that many of you are taking this sitting down. I'm not accustomed to that; I'm accustomed to fighting. I can get fifty votes myself to turn this around. How much can the rest of you get?' "

As you can imagine, that fired the men up. "It's just like I took a gas lighter. They were shocked; they were aghast; they were astounded that I would have the nerve to say that to them.

"I seized the opportunity. So I guess they said, 'We're not just dealing with a little old lady from the South; we're dealing with someone who is used to dealing. She's one of the players,' " says Carrie sanguinely. "That's when they began to see me as a player, as someone who could really sit at their table and negotiate with them and go out and get some votes; that's what it's all about. And it wasn't anything that I contrived. It's me; that's the way I do things."

And Carrie sees no conflict in being an effective lawmaker and a woman. "I think that you don't have to have a hairy chest to do well and get out there and work. I believe in kicking ass. I believe in kicking ass and they know it. When you look at me, you would never know that it's there. Because I'm very soft, and I'm very nice and sweet, but if you cross me . . ." says this sixty-seven-year-old grandmother, her voice trailing off.

"The women just have to be able to deal, and deal on their level. There's nothing about our gender that makes us weaker than they are. Nothing! Nothing in my opinion. If God made it so that we could have a baby, bear children, there's nobody stronger than we are. No one! And that intuition that we have and that attunement to social welfare, and to children, and to working mothers, and to parents, and to the downtrodden, that is an edge that I think we have, that the men don't have."

Carrie believes that power is something we can't be shy about going for, that if we sit around waiting for someone to hand it to us, we're going to be disappointed. "I think as [women] begin to push to get more power—and that's what we're doing; we're pushing to get more power, because power isn't anything that people want to give to you all the time—sometimes you have to take it."

Corrine Brown, like Carrie an African-American freshman from Florida, wanted some funds to be appropriated for her district for some specific projects. Instead of going through channels, she went right to the source. She approached Ohio congressman Louis Stokes, chairman of the Appropriations subcommittee for VA, HUD and Independent Agencies. When she told him what she wanted, he replied, "How did you figure out how to get to me?"

"Listen," Corrine told him, "I'm very focused. I know what I'm here for."

He said, "How did you figure it?"

She said, "I know what I'm here for. I want jobs, jobs, jobs, and economic development in my district, and this is what I'm trying to do."

He said, "I don't understand it, but the women from Florida are really focused. All they talk about is money, money, money!"

■ ■ ■

There doesn't seem to be a consensus regarding whether men and women have different styles of legislating. It depends on whom you talk to.

"Women are more cognizant about getting the task done and completed," says Maria Cantwell. "They're less worried about show. Women are less likely to make some bravado speech just to be heard. They want to get the product complete. And so they will forgo the speech to get the final vote or to do whatever. Everybody's got their own way of communicating and their own style, and I guess that I've tried to keep my head down and work. People will recognize the work that you're doing and the fact that you're willing to work with a lot of people and you're not in there for your own interests, that you're willing to share in the responsibility."

Minnesota Democrat Tim Penny, who has had an opportunity to observe his male and female colleagues in Congress for more than a decade now, sees a distinct difference between the sexes regarding what kinds of legislators they make. "First, let me say that I think the women legislators are the better members. To too great an extent, men view politics as a game and we get caught up in the game. Women see it as a service to the country or to the community, and they're more focused on solving the problems. I look at the freshmen legislators, a large number of whom are women, and they're willing to cast tough votes to clean up messes that somebody else created. And it's just attitudinal; it's a perspective on public service that is absolutely needed. But I think there is a gender-related differential, and to the credit of the women members. I think they've got the right attitude about what public service ought to be. And for so many men, it's the partisan posturing and the power struggle and the competitive 'us' against 'them' sort of politics that brings them to work every day. And I think the women are more focused on substantive analysis of the problem at hand, a willingness to look for possible solutions, a willingness to work with others, to find some common ground."

The two obvious categories of legislative styles are the grandstanders and those who work most effectively behind the scenes. "I don't know that there's a big difference there," says one congressman. "There are men who do both and there are women who do both. Pat Schroeder is not a behind-the-scenes player. Pat Schroeder is out there on the cutting edge, in your face, getting exposure, touring the country. For every Pat Schroeder, there is a Henry Hyde on the other side."

"I have always found dealing with men really no problem," says Nita Lowey. "Some of the men are more pleasant than others. There are some men when I first got here who were always willing to talk, to share, to help. There are some women who are willing to talk, to share, to help. There are some women who couldn't take two minutes to stop, and the same with the men because they're so busy with their own agenda. And I've tried to be as helpful as I can because I remember when I first came here not that many people were helpful to me." I can say from personal experience, she is.

"I think our style is highly dependent on very effective communications and very smart politics," says Karen Shepherd. "It seems to me that women have to be able to communicate about ten times better than men in order to get anywhere because they have to overcome all of the obstacles of aggression. We have to be aggressive without looking aggressive. We have to be fierce without looking bitchy. All that means we have to be extraordinary communicators. But this is true of any minority group trying to get in. And so if this were a Congress of women—wouldn't that be fabulous?" Karen asks, breaking into a wide grin. "If it were, it would be hard for men to get in."

Karen is from Utah, a state that is in the lowest quartile of the nation with regard to the number of women in its state legislature. It is at 11 percent. "The federal government, Congress, has just come up to the standard of Utah, which is one of the lowest in the nation. So we doubled the number in Congress; we went from nothing to almost nothing," Karen quips.

Things would certainly be different if the Congress was female-dominated. A lot of our systems would be organized around ourselves and our lives. FOCA would be a reality; Family and Medical Leave would have happened years ago. As it is, there is a camaraderie, a "we're all in it together" quality to the experience that's uplifting. "I do think among ourselves as women we talk more freely about what is going on in our legislative lives," says Leslie Bryne. "If something's not going well, we express it. But if something's not going well with a guy, he finds a way to get even, usually leaving no fingerprints."

This kind of give-and-take discourse happens most frequently when the women's caucus meets. It's a time when we can let down our hair, relax, and say what's on our minds, interrupting one another good-naturedly as you do at the dinner table with your family. This is in sharp contrast to other congressional meetings, where it's stratified; people speak according to seniority and other institutionally imposed constraints.

Deborah Pryce noticed a distinct difference between the men and the women of our class. As interim class president of the Republicans, she tried to lead a meeting of forty-seven Republicans, mostly men, and found it to be a rather frustrating and laborious process. In contrast, when the freshmen women met to form our agenda, it was a drastically different experience. "We pounded out this agenda—boom boom boom—inside of thirty minutes; it was so much more efficient," marvels Deborah. "We were able to come to terms on things without a whole lot of self-serving speech making and ego grandstanding and backslapping."

The old annoying adage "Behind every great man, there stands a woman" may have some truth to it. A lot of us know that to get things done quickly and efficiently sometimes means not getting the same degree of glory that men have traditionally enjoyed.

During budget reconciliation in the spring of 1993, Karen Thurman was very unhappy with the leadership. She felt that the Republicans were really beating up on her party and that the Democrats were letting them get away with it. One day, during a debate over the debt ceiling, she felt particularly frustrated. "I was a first-year member and I was watching people who had been here during the Reagan and Bush years not fighting back, not standing up and saying, 'Well, what about you guys over here?' "

So it got to be about nine o'clock at night and they were discussing pork in the budget. Karen approached her colleague Bill Hefner, a Democrat who had been in Congress nearly twenty years. "Now you're going to tell me these folks never, ever got something in the budget? They never went home with anything?"

Bill, who was at that time chairman of the Military Construction subcommittee of Appropriations, sat there for a moment. "Sure they have," he said.

So Karen said, "Why don't you get up there and tell them?"

The congressman did just that, standing up and approaching the microphone with the proverbial bee in his bonnet that Karen had set loose.

"Don't tell me about this beef jerky stuff!" he said, slamming the Republicans. "Let me tell you about the F-16 or whatever it was that you had, that you wanted. . . ."

Karen just sat there, watching the theater she had engineered. She knew she was in no position to do what he was doing, that she didn't have the standing, the history, the institutional knowledge to challenge the Republicans herself. But she had had the inspiration and it worked. And that was what mattered.

And sometimes, because I believe we do tend to grandstand less, it works in our own favor. Deborah Pryce explains that this is how she got elected interim class president of the Republican freshmen. "I was the least threatening of all the candidates and I was someone who wasn't out to further my own agenda. And that appealed to a lot of the male egos and I ended up in charge of things for a while."

Another difference between the men and women is that I think we tend to be more detail-oriented, while they look at the overall picture. Maybe that comes from running households all these years while simultaneously holding down jobs. We had to be the ones to worry about how to get the kids from school to swimming lessons, how to get dinner on the table, how to pick up the dry cleaning and still put in a full day's work at the office. So we have to be incredibly well organized. Men have always had women around them paying attention to the nuts and bolts.

"I would say that women tend to pay more attention to the details and the personal impact as opposed to the philosophy or the concept of the politics of an issue," says Steny Hoyer. "But that's a simplification, and it's obviously a rule that is disproven by many exceptions."

"Men are more broad-brushed, so they can go into these committee meetings and maybe they just soak it up, and they get it or it doesn't matter that they're just swishing through," says Lynn Woolsey. "I just feel so totally pulled apart when I don't complete something. So what I do is focus on why I'm here and I stay at committee meetings, because it's a learning process for me. I can't just grace the seat for five minutes and leave and think I've gotten something out of it. It's more important that I get something out of it than that I make an appearance."

"What I've tended to see—I wouldn't stereotype women or men—is that women tend to think in a circular rather than linear way, and I think that's where the difference is," says Elizabeth Furse.

Our role as mediator in the home has taught us a thing or two about consensus building. "I've been able to get some very difficult legislation through in the state legislature, and part of that has been attributed to the fact that I don't make it a big public thing," says Lucille Roybal-Allard. "So it makes it easier to work with people and easier to get people to compromise on issues."

Women come with the desire to be more conciliatory; we like to see the people around us happy. We learned it from our mothers, and, yes, we pass it on to our daughters—maybe not consciously, but they absorb our ways.

"I think all of our mothers were mediators," says Lucille. "I think women have to find a balance, because it's also important that the successes—particularly those that women are able to achieve—get attention. Because the experience has been that—and I've heard this from other women—we get the package put together and then our male counterpart ultimately gets the credit for it."

It's a tricky thing, getting things done for the group and looking out for your own interests. If we don't come on strong, we don't command a powerful image, we're not taken as seriously as our male colleagues, and we're just treated as tokens. If we come on too strong, we could be accused of being self-promoters, or worse. "Women often aren't taken very seriously," says Jennifer Dunn.

"Maybe it's because of their speaking style; maybe it's because they haven't been in the working world as long. I know it's very tough to be a woman in politics, and sometimes they're not taken seriously, so I take them seriously. But if the Year of the Woman means that somebody gets elected because she's a woman and not because she's substantive, that's very damaging. In my mind that's as bad as quotas are. I wouldn't want to be 'the woman.' I may be in some of the responsibilities I'm given—a token woman—I don't know. But I'll prove to them I'm substantive."

Tim Penny doesn't need any woman to prove to him that she deserves to be there. He is already completely convinced that women should be on every committee, and not just one or two tokens, but in large numbers. "It makes the institution stronger because it forces us to come at issues in a way that allows for more perspectives to be brought into the room. I think that the 1992 class more than any class in the ten years I've been here really represents a marked difference in the composition of Congress. I've been on the Agriculture Committee since I got here in 1983. A few years ago, Jill Long joined that committee, and she became the first woman to sit on that committee at least since I've been here. Now if you go back in history, there may have been some other women who served on that committee for a period of time. With this last election, we now have a committee that I believe has at least four blacks and four women. And I think even before anyone opens her mouth, it changes the tenor of our committee's work just to have those folks in the room. And then it changes the tone of our debate when they join the discussion, and I think it's going to change the product of our work."

■ ■ ■

In some ways, I feel as if the overriding thing I have in common with my female colleagues is the following: For all the preparation we've had in the trenches of the American workplace, it still at times isn't enough. As a television reporter and a congressional spouse, I thought I'd seen it all and understood how the power chain functions. Many of my colleagues came to the job as skilled lawyers, savvy activists, or brilliant businesswomen, but they, too, faced the same challenges. There's no way for anyone to prepare fully for the U.S. Congress, but for women the challenges sometimes seem double. Maybe it's a function of being a relatively new addition to the system; maybe not.

Whatever it is, in the end all our stellar résumés and impressive pre-Washington political experiences left us only partially prepared for what we were to find on the Hill, and the status quo is only so prepared to reconfigure itself to include us. It's a whole new fight, one in which one has to learn an alien language and different rules in order to be an effective legislator. Few of us are truly winning yet. Sometimes in a brief woman-to-woman glance across a committee room, we look at one another with unmistakable frustration, sometimes amazement. We wonder whether we'll ever be the kind of players we should be. We wonder whether we'll ever change the system so that every kind of voice is heard, no matter whether it comes in bass or soprano. But then another day comes and one of us notches up some small victory—an amendment added to a bill maybe, or just a strong op-ed in a newspaper on a critical issue. And we take a collective deep breath and think that we have a fighting chance . . . and we know we will keep on fighting.

CHAPTER FOUR

Women's Business: How We Approach the Issues

An important thing to know about the women in Congress is that while we share much common ground, we do not speak with one voice. We are forty-eight individuals from all around the country with our own particular experiences and backgrounds that have contributed to who we are, what we believe, and why we have chosen to make this all-consuming journey to Washington and the halls of Congress.

However, our collective female perspective enables us to address certain issues more comprehensively and compassionately than others have through the years. Hillary Clinton is someone who recognizes this and has strong feelings about our presence in Congress. "I can't tell you how wonderful it is to go to meetings and see women there and to know that we share the same kind of life experiences even though the particulars may differ, and that we're involved in what we're doing for largely the same kind of reasons. I think women tend to bring honesty and commitment to politics and to speak with the same kind of clear voices that we do in private in public."

I tell Hillary that she is setting the pace for us, that every time she comes to the Hill and delivers another one of her terrific presentations, we all say, "Yes!"

"I feel the same about you all," she says, laughing. "There is a sense of support that sustains me. One of the very first things I did—going to the women's caucus and talking about health-care issues—was so reinforcing for me. It was wonderful. There had been some thought given as to what the agenda should be," Hillary says, "because there had been task forces developed for caucus members to work on.

"I think we have to keep pushing; I think we can never let up, because there are so many attitudes that still have to be changed."

■ ■ ■

And until those attitudes are changed, we have a lot of work ahead of us. Because there are still so few of us, we don't have the luxury that our male colleagues have of worrying solely about the regional concerns of our districts.

"That is the reason why it has been so important to develop a critical mass of women here, because we would be sharing that burden," says Anna Eshoo. "Because there are issues that we need to tend and carry and be successful on for women and society and the entire nation."

Pat Schroeder, for instance, receives letters and calls from women around the nation who look to her for leadership, who have seen her on the nightly news championing issues that directly relate to them. Over the years, theirs was a language she spoke fluently; hers was a voice that resonated with the concerns, the worries, the hopes for the future that reverberated daily in their own minds.

"What percentage are mothers and wives? It's those kinds of factors in one's background that really give sensitivity to the issues that we work on here," says Nita Lowey. "Child care, the whole issue of choice—women's issues are not compartmentalized. Having an increased number of women who feel passionate about these issues really puts more power behind them."

There is a wide variety of issues that we are working on as a group. "We're trying to make some fundamental changes just in our work environment," says Karan English. "The second area that women are working specifically on is women-related issues, and I hesitate using that term, but people know what I'm talking about. We're talking about child care and mammograms and funding for cervical cancer and things like that that haven't really gotten funded because people who have been in Congress generally don't have those kinds of problems and aren't that aware of them. So we're moving ahead on women's issues."

Steny Hoyer offers a male's perspective on how our presence affects the business at hand. "The fact that we have appreciably increased the number of women has heightened issues of historical concern to women: women's health issues, reproductive rights issues, issues of the working family. Also because you have more women in Congress, there is greater attention to women's issues by men. Just by virtue of their presence, it serves as a reminder and raises the consciousness level on issues of concern to women."

It is because of our own experiences, and those of our mothers, sisters, daughters, and granddaughters, that we have a vested interest in the outcome of gender-specific issues. Only a woman can viscerally know the nightmarish connotations that accompany the word *mastectomy;* only a woman can truly imagine the very personal ramifications of not having the legal right to make her own reproductive choices.

■ ■ ■

In the beginning of the Clinton administration, the women's caucus was invited over to the White House to meet with the President. President Clinton asked senior congresswoman Olympia Snowe whether there were any men in the caucus. Olympia, who is the caucus's Republican cochair, replied, "Men are members, but we don't let them make any of the important decisions."

The President responded, "That's the way it works in my house also."

The Congressional Caucus for Women's Issues was formed in 1977 (as the Congresswomen's Caucus) to address those issues upon which its members could reach agreement. To date, of the forty-eight congresswomen, forty-three of us belong. We forty-three women comprise the executive committee, which makes the policy decisions. An additional 110 congressmen are members, as well as about a dozen senators of both sexes. Our caucus has several task forces, focusing on children, older women, violence, reproductive choices, health, education, and the environment. Nineteen ninety-three, with the influx of pro-choice Democratic women, was the first year the caucus declared itself pro-choice.

Of the three Republican women in the freshman class, only Tillie Fowler belongs to the women's caucus. Deborah Pryce reflects on the sometimes difficult situation of being both a woman and a Republican. "It's a lot lonelier and it's a lot less full of what people refer to as 'women's issues,' " says Deborah, who did not join our caucus because, like other congressional caucuses, it is a Legislative Service Organization (LSO) and its dues are paid out of the funds each member is allotted to run his or her office. "It was a decision I made, and maybe we'll see it wasn't that wise. But I am trying to be perceived as and *be* a reform-minded member."

But Deborah is still involved in and proud of her work on women's issues. "There's a big family bill that I got on, which I thought was important. We're going to draft some legislation on children's issues—soon, I hope. I've been giving a lot of thought, trying to provide incentives, draft bills that would provide incentives for businesses to offer on-site day care, just to make life easier for families. And I think those are the kinds of issues a lot of my constituents expect from me because I am a woman. But that's something I'm very comfortable with, because I'm a mom, too. And I understand how people's lives are really put into turmoil if both parents work. . . ."

But still, the Republican women's agendas are different from those of most of their Democratic colleagues. "I do feel a little bit left out," says Deborah. "For instance, there was a photograph taken of all the women members in the House and Senate on the steps of the Capitol; it was in *USA Today*. Well, I didn't get notice of that and I think that's because I'm not in the caucus. The only way I learned about it was that there was a notice hanging in the ladies' room over in the Capitol. So I was lucky enough—at least I went in there that day and found out about it."

And sometimes being in the minority has repercussions more serious than nearly getting left out of a photo. "The thing I think I didn't realize when I came here was how people in power really play it for all it's worth," says Deborah, "and that the majority does rule, and there is no getting around the fact that those who control the power control the agenda and everything about this place. It's not necessarily a fair process, it's not the right process, but it's how this body is set up to work."

The rules process is something Deborah, as a Republican, finds particularly frustrating. The Rules Committee, which is strongly allied with the House leadership, is where major bills go before they can be considered on the House floor. This committee decides how and if a bill will make it to the floor and which amendments will be permitted.

Deborah says she is pro-choice but believes certain restrictions should be placed on abortion, such as parental notification, and she feels the Rules Committee, which she refers to as "the Black Hole for Good Ideas," will prevent a fair debate of the issue. "As I predicted, the Freedom of Choice Act is going to be coming up, or it should be coming up. But I don't think that they will bring it up until they're certain they have enough votes in the Rules Committee to make it a closed rule. Now, here is an issue that affects fundamentally at least fifty percent of the population, all women. And they want to have a bill that is not fully debated, which has no opportunity to be amended, which is not going to be argued and given full and fair airing in front of the national public, because they don't want it changed from how they write it."

Jennifer Dunn was planning on joining the women's caucus until she learned of its pro-choice stance. "I don't belong to the women's caucus and the reason I don't is that they took a pro-choice position on the abortion issue and I don't think that's a good idea because that means that it's exclusive. And there are some women in Congress who are pro-life. I happen to be pro-choice, but I want to belong to a group that's going to be a network for women, and I have written them and asked them to please reconsider."

While in general there is a great deal of consensus among the women regarding our agenda, our commitment to these issues in no way limits us to them, and we all devote plenty of time and energy to issues not taken up within the caucus. But until we have an overwhelming number of women in the House, say 25 percent, we need a caucus dedicated to issues that have traditionally been overlooked and neglected by men.

"I think the more senior members are trying to get a handle on what this big group thinks," says Maria Cantwell. "Now, if there were only fifteen or twenty of us, they'd probably say, 'Who cares?' But that you're so big and that you might wield some weight is a pretty big thing."

"With twenty-four women coming in, we make those issues more focused," says Eva Clayton. "Forty-eight people cannot put a bill through unless they get other people. You need two hundred and eighteen votes to pass bills, but I think what women do is prick the conscience and give a competitive edge. And I think they sensitize and give confidence to people that it's all right to care. And we also bring to Congress a willingness to stand up and be counted. We may be defeated on some issues."

"Women here are constantly struggling with trying to make this place more family-friendly," says Pat Schroeder. "I think the whole country is going to be a lot better off if we do that. When I hear a Janet Reno say, 'The choice is either we build jails or we build families,' she's absolutely right, but who else would say it?"

"A woman from New York may have a different agenda from a woman from Arkansas," says Nita Lowey. "Yet they are overlapping circles. . . . I'm a part of the New York delegation and there are some interests that we may share and there are others that we may not share. But that's always been true; all women aren't alike. They don't look alike; they don't talk alike. When my first opponent ran against me, he was going to compare me to Bella Abzug; in fact, he tried. . . . I remember one of the jokes of the campaign was, 'You're just Bella Abzug without a hat.' And I looked at him and said,

'You're just Dan Quayle without the good looks.'

"He was going to say that women are all alike. But we're not all alike. But we share agendas—committed to family, to children. Women's issues to many people are just choice issues and child-care issues. If the economy isn't strong, families can't thrive; and if we don't have child care, women can't work; and if we don't have welfare reform, we're not going to build strong families."

"Top priorities of mine include women's issues and choice, child welfare, and accountability in government, including saving taxpayers' money," says Carolyn Maloney. "Medicaid funding for abortion is definitely a goal. I've put in a number of bills on women's issues already. One was the guardianship bill for women who are dying of AIDS—a big problem in New York City. Lots of times, their children are taken away from them, and this bill would allow them to have a guardian so that children in the future would be secure despite the mother's illness. This is the first of the child-welfare bills I introduced."

Carolyn also talks of bills she wants to introduce to improve our nation's patchwork of foster-care systems. "I want to improve the way courts handle foster-care cases by streamlining the system. I also believe the federal government should support permanency planning for children in kinship-care arrangements. I feel strongly that we should require states to hire trained caseworkers. Finally, I would like to expand opportunities for fathers of children in the foster-care system to participate in plans to return their children to a safe and secure home as soon as possible."

Depending on who employs the term *women's issues,* it can be problematic. At times, it is used to pigeonhole us, a sort of semantic ghettoization to keep us in our place. "When Hillary Rodham Clinton came up and spoke, she came to the women's caucus on health care and it was a very substantive and serious meeting, and the next day the *Washington Post* reported it in the Style section," says Elizabeth Furse. "It wouldn't have been in the Style section if she had been to some other caucus." By the newspaper relegating us to the pages of the newspaper that typically deal with celebrities, fashion, and the arts, they are saying implicitly that our concerns are not weighty enough for the front section, reserved for "real politics."

For the first seven months of my term, reporters constantly called me up to ask what it was like to be a woman in Congress. A fair question, but it was practically the only thing they asked, and it began to feel as though they thought this was the only thing I knew about. There is a tendency to assume that our interests are confined to matters of the heart, of the body, and of the soul. But it is true that we are the ones upon whose shoulders it falls to fight such crucial battles as gaining more appropriations for breast cancer research or codifying *Roe* v. *Wade*.

"In my judgment," says Eddie Bernice Johnson, "all issues are women's issues. There are some issues that are women's business. You see, there's not a single issue here in which I'm not interested, and I am a woman. But there are some issues that I figure are my business. And choice is one of those. Mammograms and health care for women—these issues are my business; these are issues that affect me and other women very directly. But all issues, in my judgment, are issues that have no gender per se. I care about what happens in defense of this country; I care about spending; I care about the deficit.

"I've met a lot of women here who don't have what I consider a real woman's perspective. And at the same time, I've met a lot of men who come with some sensitivities to the areas in which women are very concerned. But they're in small numbers as well. Because in most instances, the males' backgrounds have been different from the mainstream backgrounds of most women. Because before we had many women here at all, there were a few sensitive men—and there still are a few, or we wouldn't be able to get anything done. I think that when I look back and realize Ted Kennedy has been there for health care for women before there were any women in the Senate. It's just that there are so few men who have stopped to think about the woman's perspective or had the experience in areas that sensitized them; they didn't come in great supply and we can't assume that every woman will come in the same frame of mind. I have watched facial expressions when choice comes up and I can't even imagine a woman—and I've never had a desire for an abortion and I grew up basically in the Catholic Church—but I cannot even imagine a woman not wanting to have some say over her body. But there are women here who feel that way. . . . And so it doesn't put us all in the same frame of mind, of thinking. I think that probably the more women we get elected, the more likely that those women will be independent thinkers who have determined that they have a right to be."

"When people ask me about women's issues, my answer's always, 'Every issue is a woman's issue,' " says Tillie Fowler. "The economy is a woman's issue; defense is a woman's issue. Please don't pigeonhole just certain issues. We need to address it that way. And I think women have to recognize that more because we do ourselves in if we say, 'These are the only issues that we're interested in,' because we are elected by males and females in our district and it's incumbent upon us to have a broader picture and to see every issue's impact. And maybe as women, we might feel a little more strongly about breast cancer and women's health research and certain things like that, naturally. But overall, we've got to have the bigger picture."

Eddie Bernice Johnson pushed hard to get on the Finance Committee when she was in the Texas state senate. "I didn't want to be left off because I was a woman," she says. "And I didn't want to just deal with Health and Human Services issues. I wanted to deal with the whole of the issues. You can't even deal with those issues unless you can deal with money. So I worked hard when I got on the Finance Committee and I've made myself a part of the finance process and I can look back and see my mark and I'm pleased with that. And I will see my mark here. Because I came to do a job. I didn't come just to say, 'I'm in the Congress.' And that's why I don't have a great love for all of the receptions and flim flam flom. I wish I had more interest in that; I just don't. I know it's helpful, but I really don't. I'm much more comfortable working on things that are going to bring about some hope for the future."

Women have brought attention to issues that over the years have been ignored. "In addition to highlighting them, this year we have numbers that would cause more attention to be given, because I think that's what counts when there are issues before you," says Eddie Bernice. "I know there is quite a difference in the black caucus from other years, and it's been well acknowledged. There are enough numbers frequently to determine whether a major vote will be successful or not. And I think that's where the rubber meets the road, whether or not you've got the numbers to influence what you want to do. I doubt if anyone has brought a new idea here. It's whether or not you've got the numbers to get attention for that idea.

"I think there are many ways in which we do bring perspectives that perhaps are not spoken about. I think a great deal of it has to do with our experiences and background. There are men who have had experiences as social workers and as teachers and who can be equally sensitive about those areas. Generally speaking, however, in these arenas, you find men who have been businessmen or lawyers, and they have that perspective. There are times also that you find women who come here as businesswomen and lawyers, and that is the perspective they bring. When women have been social workers or nurses or day-care workers or some kind of community service center managers, they bring that perspective. And that is probably in least supply of a vantage point in this arena. For this reason, I think that more of that influence is here when women are here, because it's been more their experience. I don't think it really has so much to do with gender. It has more to do with what we've been allowed to do as genders that builds that background."

Karen Shepherd has worked for many years on women's issues, first as an educator, then as a magazine publisher, and finally as a legislator. "The reason I got involved in advocacy at all—in the magazine, for example—was because I believed so strongly that the fate of children is tied to the fate of women, and the fate of children is the determiner of the fate of the country, and ultimately the world. I felt we were neglecting children in a gross and unconscionable way. When I was in the Utah state senate, although I worked on a whole range of issues, I was particularly interested in screening legislation with regard to how it would affect families, and particularly children. I haven't gotten as much opportunity to do that here as I did there because of the committee assignments I have."

But within her committee assignments, Natural Resources and Public Works and Transportation, Karen has gravitated toward environmental issues, which she sees as very tied to the future quality of life. "I think that what drives me—and this is a very key male/female difference—what gets me on the plane every week is the opportunity to make change that will, I hope, make life better for future generations. That's what turns me on. As soon as I feel I'm wasting my time in that regard, I'm not going to be very interested in staying here."

■ ■ ■

It's important, too, that we focus on issues that aren't generally associated with women, because we bring our own spin to them, a spin sorely needed. "Just watching today, we're going to have a vote on the space station and tomorrow the Supercollider," says Deborah Pryce. "To see how women are engaged in that debate has been really great. It's not a woman's thing anymore, as it's very much a territorial thing, and it's also a scientific thing."

"Women have traditionally dealt with health-care issues or social issues or things like that, but there's also a very large need for a woman's point of view in the technical or industrial side of things," says Blanche Lambert, whose overwhelming concerns are agricultural-related because her Arkansan district is largely farmland, and farming has been her family's livelihood for seven generations.

Elizabeth Furse, one of five women on the Armed Services Committee, is thrilled to bring her perspective to the table. "I've sat through many, many briefings when I was the only woman in the room, and I'm very pleased to be there. I'm pleased to be a woman there—not just as an activist—and I know I bring something very important to those meetings. And that's where I think it counts so much. When we can look up and see the Armed Services Committee and half of them are women, we're going to see a different view."

But first, enough women have to be willing to break through the barriers. Some committees are tougher than others for women to infiltrate. "If we can convince the women in Congress that the power is in getting the money out of the Pentagon, then we can convince them to go on those committees and start making shifts," says Elizabeth Furse. "Because this country isn't going to change until we start making that shift. . . .

"It is the place I want to be because I think it's the place where we have to make the greatest change. And the more people like myself who can distinguish real defense and real national security from this excessive spending . . . I'm perfectly in favor of security, but I think that also has to include children and our cities being secure and all those things—they're the priorities. I serve on the subcommittee for conversion, and I chose that because that's where the conversion is going to happen, economic conversion from military to civilian spending."

Cynthia McKinney is of the same mind on matters of defense. She and Maria Cantwell are the only Democratic congresswomen who sit on the Foreign Affairs Committee. "With that committee, it's very important that we never had a Democratic woman's voice being heard on foreign policy issues," says Cynthia. "Now we have two Democratic women who serve on it—although today, mine was the only voice of peace. And I'm concerned that there is some male macho instinct that drives them to military intervention and to military solutions to political problems. If you have an inappropriate military solution, you end up like you did in Vietnam."

Has Cynthia ever discussed gender-related problem solving with her male colleagues? "Oh, I haven't gotten that intimate with these people around here to discuss philosophy with them," she says, laughing.

Clearly, both Cynthia and Elizabeth are pioneering their way through the desolate terrain of no-woman's-land. But each hopes that with time she will have a strong voice on her committee and that she will be joined by her female colleagues. Elizabeth notes that, like all freshmen, regardless of gender, she's got to pay her dues. "I'm so junior that it takes a long time to get down to me. But I have asked questions on a number of occasions. The chairman, Ron Dellums, is so gracious and very egalitarian. So it's wonderful to be there. But we need to change the culture of this place. There's too much of a culture of gung ho and . . . well, sort of 'American' values—which I don't think are American at all. I think the real American values are caring for people and making sure that children get fed, and we've sort of set aside American values for the last perhaps twenty years. And now it's very, very important to get it back again, and I think that that's where the value of getting people of color and women comes in. . . . I'm not saying that white men don't care, but they care in a different way and they're much less likely to be right out there and say the poor matter. You have extraordinary people who do.

"But you know the progressive caucus is now thirty members; that's very large. I think you'll see coalitions of caucuses develop: the Hispanics, the blacks, the progressives. If they came together on a couple of issues—and I think military spending is one of them; I think education is another—that could cause tremendous change in this place."

"Women have just as much to say about deficit reduction, fiscal matters, or foreign policy matters," says Maria Cantwell. "Our perspective may be for certain reasons unique or different from some that are being expressed. And I think that's critical that we voice ourselves on those and that we are heard."

"Women are trying to be a part of every discipline, not just women's issues," says Karan English. "And that's why I can safely use 'women's issues' only in the context that there are social programs that we are relegated to all the time, but in fact we are making a conscious effort to be represented in every discipline. There are women who pay taxes in this country, live in this country, vote in this country, and they should be represented on every single issue. We bring a different perspective. Rightfully so! Not bad, not good, just different. And we deserve to be represented in every discipline, in every decision. And that's where Anita Hill probably made more of an impact. Not whether you agreed or disagreed with her but what you saw on that all-white, male-dominated committee."

"I think that the overriding issue for the 103d Congress, and certainly for me, is that we heal and expand the economy," says Anna Eshoo. "And if there is a group that is more adversely affected in this country today, it's women. No matter which way you slice it, you see single heads of households, women and children. It just continues; it goes on and on."

To underscore to the voters that she had the political and intellectual muscle, as a candidate Anna put out a fifty-eight-page issues booklet called "First Things First." Anna didn't settle for the usual campaign "lite" fare; she wanted to give the constituents something substantive to chew on. "Campaigns have not respected voters' intellect, and I thought that people had a right to know where I was on a whole series of issues. I did seventy-some candidate forums, obviously none of them sponsored by me, but by organizations in the community. And they'd ask, 'What is your prescription for reducing the deficit? And you have sixty seconds or less to answer.' Well, how can you talk about that in that time frame?"

I distributed a similar handbook, "Where I Stand," to constituents because I also felt that the voters weren't being given enough credit. I wanted them to know more about my position on the issues than what they could glean from the endless campaign sound bites. I felt that it was really important for those people who were skeptical of me merely because of my gender. I do believe that old adage, "Women have to work twice as hard to be paid half as much." And to be respected half as much, I might add.

▪ ▪ ▪

When Pat Danner was in the Missouri senate during the Gulf War, she received a phone call from a female constituent. "Senator," the woman said, "I have a real problem. My son is over in Desert Storm; we have his car up on blocks. We've gotten an insurance-premium notice that's astronomical and we don't know what to do. We can't afford to pay it for him, but we know he has to have insurance on his car."

It really started Pat thinking about all the problems that the young men and women overseas were experiencing because of state laws. "Whether it was not being able to sign their tax forms or not being able to apply for their driver's licenses when they came due," says Pat. "So I put in legislation that exempted our Desert Storm people from anything that came due that had to do with state government while they were overseas and gave them an extra six months to file their tax returns when they got back. . . . So that may be something one might think of as more male-oriented legislation, because we usually think of the National Guard as being masculine, although there are a lot of women in it.

"I think the idea is to do the job. And it shouldn't matter a whole lot whether you're male or female, but you do culturally bring a different mind-set to it and the generations do make the difference. There's no question about it. I would not expect my children to have the same mind-set that I have, but to have the same general philosophy." Pat has four children: Her daughters are a businesswoman and a doctor; her sons are a businessman and a state senator—in fact, they were the first mother and son to serve together. "My family is the single-most-important thing in the world to me. It takes precedence over being a congresswoman any day of the week. I feel that if you can't take care of your own family, you can't take care of the family of mankind."

Maria Cantwell talks about the different legislative experience she has had at the state level. Her résumé from her six years in the Washington state legislature is impressive in its variety—the Governor's Growth Strategies Commission, the Legislative Committee on Economic Development, the Joint House and Senate Legislative Transportation Committee. "But I still would say from that experience what matters most to me is helping constituents. I remember there was a woman who was trying to retire early and missed—because of communication with the bureaucracy about the retirement date. She thought she had more time than she had. She came back and said, 'Jeez, can't you help me?' And they said, 'No.' I called them and said, 'Don't you have a review process?' 'Well, we do but . . .' The bottom line is we finally got her the money. . . .

"That's what you're there for; you're there to help people understand their government and to help represent them. I think even after this, that here in Congress, I'll be most excited about people that we've helped."

"I think that to a certain degree we all share one another's issues," says Vic Fazio. "We want women to be on every committee and effective on every issue because there's a perspective they may bring. Not to say that it wasn't there before, but they may bring it or reinforce it. It would be foolish for women to concentrate all their efforts in a few areas that are highly visible. And yet, because women are often elected with the strong support of other women, there is a tendency to want to perform on those issues, to shine on those issues."

Some of the most successful women are those who make a concerted effort to include men in the ongoing conversation regarding "women's issues." Nita Lowey is one such congresswoman; the proof of this is in the fact that she is well liked and well respected by both men and women, although as chairman of the Pro-Choice Task Force, she is particularly committed to women's issues.

Her husband, Steve, explains how she does it. "She has a lot of support from the women's groups, but it's very important that she does not draw a line between women and men. She doesn't turn women's issues against men. She is not antimale; she is not a feminist in the pejorative sense. So even though she is a strong advocate on issues important to women, she does not look upon men as the enemy. On the contrary, she is at ease in the company of men."

Anna Eshoo also believes in this kind of legislating. She points out that men in the House have been instrumental with regard to appropriating funds for breast cancer research, for example. "There are some men in the institution that have been supportive on this—one of them, one of the more powerful members in the House, is John Dingell. You see, there is an art to legislating. Women must know very well where to go to weave things together. That takes, I think, a real sophistication and understanding—and obviously a solid intellect—in knowing how this institution works, who makes it up, and whom you pull together as an ally in order to advance your issue. Or how you enlist new people in the cause—because we don't have enough in terms of women here—to get something through."

"You know, men have also been put into that same box of what they focus on," says Karen Thurman. "We draw the line and we ask women about these things, but men are in the same situation because they're expected to be a certain way and women are expected to be a certain way. The bottom line is we're representative of people. We are representatives. And we're probably very reflective of our districts. We have to be. That's what the House was intended to be from the very beginning, to be the pulse of the public, to be the pulse of the constituencies. So I think that we all have to be aware of those particular issues that are forced by a constituency. And that means that you can't be put into a cubicle or identified or characterized as single-issued."

Blanche Lambert is the kind of woman who, when asked by a reporter from *Roll Call* what magazine she'd most like to grace the cover of, replied, "*Field & Stream,* because I love to go fishing. And it's such a beautiful day, I'd like to be fishing."

Blanche is a congresswoman whose legislative priorities lie more with her rural roots than with her female identity. She is more concerned with being in a minority in terms of representing a rural area than with being a woman in a historically male domain. "There's a difficulty in that your voice is outnumbered. There are fifty-two members of Congress from California. It's hard for us as just four members from Arkansas compared with that. And sometimes it's difficult, and I don't know that being a woman makes it any different."

Actually, the fact that Blanche is a woman might just work in her favor. "It's helpful in the sense that I bring somewhat of a different perspective or a different mix. Some of my colleagues in the rural caucus know that I've walked a rice levee or two, that I've been out scoutin' cotton or I've hung out in the bean fields. But they also know that I was a product of desegregation and that I understand public schools in the South and that I understand the communities and I understand rural health care. I do think that because women are a little bit closer to that, perhaps they have a little bit of a different spin or a little bit of a different outlook."

■ ■ ■

Getting on the right committees is key to making headway on the issues that brought you to Congress in the first place. When it was time to try to get my committee assignments, I decided that Energy and Commerce was where I needed to be because that's where the health care–reform package would end up. The first amendment I got through Energy and Commerce was additional funding for breast and cervical cancer research, and it was just a first step in what I wanted to get accomplished while serving on this vital committee. My number-one priority regarding health-care reform is women's health care, particularly because there are no women on Health and the Environment, the subcommittee that handles health care. I went to Congressman Henry Waxman from day one to make sure that I and the other three women on Energy and Commerce will have a part to play in addressing women's health care and making sure it is dealt with thoroughly.

Subcommittee assignments are also very important. That's where you spend much of your time—listening to witness testimony, hammering out and fine-tuning legislation before it goes to the House floor. I was thrilled to join the Subcommittee on Telecommunications and Finance because it offered me the chance to have a leadership role in shaping both economic policy and the important role the telecommunications industry is going to play in our global economy. The committee deals with highly technical material and, like all members, I have to work hard to keep informed. This means attending as many hearings as possible to absorb as much information as possible. Early on in my term, I was one of the few members to show up at a finance hearing—besides the subcommittee's chairman, Congressman Ed Markey.

Ed smiled, acknowledging my presence, and then passed me a note. I unfolded the piece of paper and read, "Thanks for coming. People join the Subcommittee for Telecommunications and most would rather watch grass grow than sit in on a finance hearing." Ed was part of the reason I showed up and why I tried to attend the meetings regularly. He makes the atmosphere of the meetings pleasant and friendly to newcomers, and he really knows his stuff.

My second subcommittee, Oversight and Investigations, excited me because it meant I could continue to do what I loved most when I was a television reporter—investigating corruption and fraud perpetrated against the consumer and the system. It was the perfect place to be a watchdog against waste, fraud, and mismanagement and to protect taxpayer dollars. John Dingell is the chairman of this subcommittee and he is truly a master at unraveling cover-ups. He loves the quest and, with the help of an extremely able staff, does it better than anyone I've ever seen.

Many of the women are intent on making some progress in the area of congressional reform. Carolyn Maloney is very interested in campaign finance reform. "As a young woman, I was an activist, a volunteer with Common Cause. In fact, in the early seventies as the state issues chair of Common Cause, I wrote with Common Cause the first campaign finance bill ever introduced before the New York state legislature, where it still sits. It never passed. When I was elected to the New York City Council, it was among the first bills that I introduced as a council member, and again they said it was unconstitutional, that there were all these problems with it. It's very hard to pass legislation that in effect makes it more difficult for those who are passing it to be reelected. It wasn't until 1987, after a series of scandals, that the bill was finally passed and signed into law."

Then when Carolyn came to Washington, one of her first roles was that of cochair of the Freshman Task Force on Campaign Finance Reform. "So that was very thrilling for me to have followed a belief from a kid in Common Cause all the way to Congress. . . . I was appointed to the majority leader's Task Force on Campaign Finance Reform, and it was gratifying to be working on the national level on an issue that had been of concern to me from my earliest days as an activist—especially one that would lessen the impact of special interests in government by limiting campaign expenditures. It would also create a more level playing field between incumbents and challengers through partial use of public resources."

California congresswoman Lynn Woolsey is also interested in government reform, and her seat on Government Operations is a perfect place from which to address this concern. "I'm a business person and I'm a business owner. This is the most inefficient place

I've ever been in my life. Part of it is coming to grips with the fact that we're going to have to become a much more high-tech place, and that's going to cost money. And we're going to have to face the public and say we need to spend money to save money—but the paper that goes out of this place, it's criminal. We could be turning on a computer and looking at a letter or the bills that people want us to sign and we could put a message on the machine saying yes or no and save the paper. . . ."

Jennifer Dunn is also reform-minded. "When I came to Congress, I came without a lot of baggage. I'd never been elected before, so I came with an open mind. I have a philosophical direction. I believe that less government is better; I believe that money left in people's pockets is more wisely spent than money put in government's pockets. I believe that government closest to the people is most effective. I believe in personal initiative, and I believe in the individual. And I came to believe that the best solutions are at the local level. So I came to Congress with those beliefs and I also came with the commitment to be a player in the system. I'm not here to enjoy Washington, D.C. I'm not here to waste a few years half-thinking about what I want to accomplish. . . . And so the plan I had in my mind was an aggressive plan. I don't care if I'm a woman or not—there are styles that you pick up over the years. There is training that shows you how to be effective. I've learned all that in my approaches to working with other people, to bring something different to the mix but not to threaten the folks around me, but always to push the envelope."

Jennifer has a seat on the Joint Committee on the Organization of Congress, which is charged with studying and making recommendations on congressional reform. "It was just the perfect thing for me to do because I was state party chairman for years and wondered at the obsolescence of the system. There are only three women on the joint committee and I am the only freshman member. So what happens to me is that I move aggressively with a lot of discipline and also with the knowledge that anything I do as a woman is going to affect people's opinion of other women. So that makes me thoughtful in my approach."

Months after she came to Congress, in May of 1993, Jennifer drafted legislation for a sunshine law much like the one in her home state of Washington. Committees often meet behind closed doors to "mark up" legislation, adding amendments and working on the language of a bill. A sunshine law would open those meetings to the public. "I hope a lot of Democrats will join on," says Jennifer, "because I think it makes a lot of sense to open up this process to people who are paying for it. Why close Ways and Means when you're writing tax policy that's going to affect millions of Americans? And the irony is that we are paying for this process, we as citizens, anyway. So how can Congress say it's a privilege for you to sit in on this process?"

Another example of a freshman woman taking on the powers that be happened just a few weeks later, on May 27, when President Clinton's budget package squeezed through in a 219–213 vote (this was the second of three votes on the budget). Thirty-eight Democrats voted against it (myself included; much more on this later, I promise). In the aftermath, Democrats became divided over whether it was fair that eleven powerful subcommittee chairmen voted against their party, while many freshmen women voted with the party, even though there would be hell to pay back home in their districts from constituents displeased with the package.

"That was a hard vote," says Carrie Meek. "So a lot of people, a lot of us decided that we would vote for it because, number one, it appeared to be the only way the President could get the revenue he needed. . . . So it made us all angry—it infuriated us—for us to step out there and put careers on the line when these men who were committee chairmen didn't."

One of the people this angered most was Leslie Byrne. After the vote, while various Democratic members seethed about their brethren's perceived lack of loyalty to the party, Leslie decided it was a call to arms. She recalls, "There was a discussion among some of the freshmen that here they were first-termers in marginal districts and how come they had to belly up to the bar and these other guys who were sitting pretty didn't. . . ."

A group of congresswomen storms the Senate, in the hopes of joining a meeting with Senate Majority Leader George Mitchell to discuss Anita Hill's accusations against Clarence Thomas. This act eventually contributed to open, internationally televised hearings. (Paul Hosefros/New York Times Pictures)

The freshmen women of the 103d Congressional class. (Tom Wolff)

Hillary Clinton, campaigning with me in Pennsylvania's 13th district.

Press conference in December 1992 at which the freshmen congresswomen presented their bipartisan four-point agenda. From left to right: Anna Eshoo, Lynn Schenk, Cynthia McKinney, Eva Clayton, myself, and Pat Danner. (Laura Patterson/Roll Call)

House Speaker Foley reenacting my swearing-in for my family.

A tearful Carrie Meek in song and prayer with friends after our swearing-in. (Ken Brick)

With Hillary Clinton at the University of Pennsylvania's 1993 graduation, at which Hillary was commencement speaker. (Stuart A. Watson, Wilmington, Del.)

After the Hyde Amendment passed. From left to right: Connie Morella (back), Nita Lowey, Lynn Schenk, Carolyn Maloney, Pat Schroeder, and Maria Cantwell. (Jose Lopez/New York Times Pictures)

President Clinton at the White House with the Congressional Caucus on women's issues. I took the opportunity to deliver books on the environment that were made for the President by the children at my son Andrew's school, Penn Valley Elementary. (White House Office of Photography)

Blanche Lambert signs a baseball for a young fan before the annual congressional baseball game, pitting the Republicans against the Democrats. Blanche, Maria Cantwell, and Ileana Ros-Lehtinen became the first three women in history to play in the annual game, on August 3, 1993.

With Wally Herger catching for the Republicans, Maria Cantwell awaits a pitch at the 1993 congressional baseball game. (Christopher Martin/Roll Call)

Cynthia McKinney jogging with President Clinton. (Reuters/Bettman)

Lynn Woolsey (holding basketball), the first woman to play congressional basketball. (Christopher Martin/Roll Call)

My friends, family, and campaign staff wearing campaign T-shirts.

With President Clinton at the entitlements conference in Bryn Mawr, Pennsylvania, on December 13, 1993. (Bill Cramer)

The freshman class of the 103d Congress.

So Leslie asked her staff to draft a petition to call for a Democratic caucus meeting at which there would be an evaluation of the chairmen and their vote, a group therapy–style bloodletting. "I got it drafted up; I honestly didn't know where it was going. I just knew there were a lot of subterranean feelings floating around. I first showed it to Rostenkowski on the floor. I said, 'Take a look at it.' He read it and said, 'Damn good idea.' I showed it to Bill Ford, chairman of Education and Labor, and he said, 'About time somebody did this.' I thought if I could get some big guns to sign it, then the little guns, the 'Saturday night specials,' would be less hesitant to sign it."

So Leslie and Jolene Unsoeld passed the petition around, working the floor.

"Leslie came to me," remembers Carrie Meek. "She said, 'Carrie, I don't think it's right that they should continue to be chairpeople when they voted against the budget and those of us, freshmen women, just got out there and voted with the budget although it was something that jeopardized us. . . .' "

The day had turned to night and the women needed a dinner break. They headed for the members' dining room in the Capitol. Leslie spotted John Dingell eating dinner with his wife. They showed the petition to him, hoping to get his influential John Hancock to grace the page. John took a look at it. "No, I don't think so," he told them after a minute.

Disappointed, they went to their table. Leslie wasn't interested in trying to pressure anyone into signing anything they didn't believe in. After they finished eating, they returned to the floor of the House. A little while later, Leslie, Jolene, and Louise Slaughter were standing in the aisle, talking among themselves, and John approached them.

"You have that petition?" he asked.

Leslie whipped it out of her purse and gave it to him. He signed it and handed it back to her, saying, "You're doing the right thing."

A few minutes later, John, standing by the well, motioned to Leslie to come over to him. The three women approached him.

"I hope you women never get mad at me," he said.

The women laughed. Imagine, one of the most powerful men in Congress making a comment like that.

As a result of the petition, the caucus met for two and a half hours, in which everyone talked about their responsibilities to the caucus, the country.

"Leslie went to everyone in the Democratic party and she got enough votes to vote to change the rules. . . . It scared them. It scared them," says Carrie.

"People who have been there a long time came over and patted me on the back and said this is the best thing that has happened around here in years," says Leslie. "It was exciting, but it was extraordinarily nerve-racking. In the week interim we had off, there had been a constant barrage of reporters from subcommittee chairmen's hometown papers saying that the chairmen were teed off. They had personalized it not to the eighty-one people who had signed it but to me. I knew that would probably happen, but you sit back and say, 'Is it worth doing?' "

It is, according to Carrie. "What I admired so about Leslie, she had the guts to do that. Not many women would have done that. The point is, the more guts they show, the more viscera they show, the better it's going to be for women. But if they come in and get to the point that they let the men who are in power disembowel them, take away all their strength and their power, then they won't ever get it. But when they take those stands and work hard for them—there are a lot of heroines in this class. We've got a lot of heroines in this class. They're young women and I admire that. I think that's very good."

CHAPTER FIVE

You Can Run but You Can't Hyde: The Hyde Amendment Vote

If the Year of the Woman showed us all how far we have come, the day of the Hyde Amendment vote defined for us in no uncertain terms how much further we had to go. Those members who are uncomfortable with the influx of female legislators will use battles such as the Hyde Amendment as a weapon, a symbolic missile aimed in our direction with the express purpose of sending us running for cover.

There was a lot of soul-searching and Monday-morning quarterbacking after the Hyde Amendment was upheld on June 30, 1993. The amendment, which bans federal funding for poor women's abortions, was modified to make exceptions for cases of rape or incest. But this alteration was not enough for those of us who believe the amendment is discriminatory and that it should be defeated in its entirety.

Yet in the spring of 1993, it was not to be. By a vote of 255–178, the amendment was successfully included in the fiscal 1994 appropriations bill for the departments of Labor, Health and Human Services, and Education.

An abundance of theories quickly became available as to why we had failed to overturn Illinois congressman Henry Hyde's sixteen-year ban on Medicaid funding of abortions. The press, the players on each side of the debate, interested spectators—we all had our own take and were in a hurry afterward to set the record straight, in the interest of posterity, as well as for political face-saving. Everyone's version was slightly different depending on his or her vantage point, and how one interpreted the events of that day became a sort of congressional Rorschach test. The only thing one could count on was that the whole truth was somewhat elusive. The murkiness of the event was intensified by complex parliamentary procedure and a bitter unscripted debate that was perceived by many to be racist and sexist in its tone and content.

My journalistic background instinctively compels me to try to be as objective as possible; however, it is no longer my job simply to record events. As a congresswoman committed to defeating the Hyde Amendment, as well as establishing the codification of *Roe* v. *Wade* through the Freedom of Choice Act, I obviously am not an objective storyteller. Rather, as someone who voted against the Hyde Amendment, I am an active participant, and with that participation comes an agenda. And so what I offer you now is my version of truth as best as I can interpret it. I leave it to you to draw your own conclusions—as I believe it should be in matters as private as choice.

■ ■ ■

Since 1977, Henry Hyde has been successful each year in putting through his amendment preventing federal funds from being used to pay for poor women's abortions. Pro-choice groups around the country, constituents who had sent pro-choice women in record numbers to Congress, and the congresswomen themselves all had what proved to be a false sense of security that things would change in 1993 with a new pro-choice administration.

In addition to a version of the Hyde Amendment passing yet again, the debate itself was perceived by most of the women as a sharp slap in the face. First of all, we felt that we had been bamboozled procedurally because the parliamentarian had given an unfair advantage to our opponents, and secondly, the tone of some of the debaters was at times sexist and racist. I was on the floor that day, watching the debate, outraged. I had drafted a floor statement with the help of my legislative aide Anessa Karney and my press secretary, Jake Tapper, but because of the time limit, I was unable to deliver it. However, I did insert it in the *Congressional Record,* as the rules allow. My statement, in part, read as follows:

> The Hyde Amendment obstructs. The Hyde Amendment impedes. The Hyde Amendment stands in the way of American women and our right to control our own bodies.
>
> The Hyde Amendment only serves to punish low-income women who cannot afford an abortion, often with devastating and tragic results.
>
> Today, we can reverse this gross inequity; today, my fellow Americans, we must overturn the Hyde Amendment.
>
> Next week, the militant and extremist Operation Rescue will come to Philadelphia to once again try and inflict its terrorist tactics upon us, the women of America. . . .

We left the floor that day, not only defeated but feeling as if we had been personally attacked.

The next day, July 1, Pat Schroeder organized a meeting between some of the congresswomen and members of the press in an attempt to clarify what had occurred and why things did not turn out as we had hoped and planned. About ten reporters, ten congresswomen, and several staffers sat in a room in the Rayburn Building and talked about the events of the previous day. The press, used to dealing with traditional politicians who were more concerned with damage control than self-knowledge, clearly weren't ready for what they encountered—a group of women who intended to get to the bottom of what had happened, even if that meant examining a painful and bitter defeat.

"The women sat around and said things like 'We were outmaneuvered,' " recalls Heather Howard, legislative assistant on women's issues to Nita Lowey. Unfortunately, the press interpreted our honesty as vulnerability and wrote stories that had a chiding subtext. Instead of perceiving what they were witnessing as a changing face of power, one in which people were more honest and took legislative losses on a more personal level, the reporters chose to write negative articles characterizing us as overly emotional political neophytes. The media, just like some of our male colleagues, obviously aren't comfortable with change. They just weren't used to the soul-searching, the self-flagellating that they were seeing from these legislators. It was as though the women were speaking a foreign language. "I felt like Deborah Tannen, who analyzes how men and women communicate differently, should have been there to analyze it. She would have loved it," says Heather Howard, chuckling.

Meanwhile, the black women seemed to be the hardest hit by the events of the previous day, and you could feel the reverberations of their emotions across the Capitol on the Senate side. That same day, July 1, Senator Carol Moseley-Braun, the sole African-American in the Senate and one of only seven female senators, withdrew her support for the Freedom of Choice Act (FOCA), stating that the bill "discriminates against young and poor women" and "trades off the rights of some women for the promise of rights for others." This did not bode well for the pro-choice women's agenda. While FOCA is not legislatively connected to the Hyde Amendment, it is intimately linked in the minds of many. The Hyde Amendment was a sort of legislative barometer regarding members' positions on the abortion debate; how they felt about federal funding could very possibly inform how they felt about legalized abortions in general. In addition, how the Hyde Amendment fared in both the House and the Senate could be seen as an augury of how abortion would be dealt with in the upcoming Clinton health-care package.

The next day, Henry Hyde apologized to Cardiss Collins for offensive remarks he had made to her on the House floor during the debate. The apology reportedly came at the prompting of Congressman Kweisi Mfume, the powerful and well-respected leader of the black caucus. Mr. Hyde also had the remarks in question deleted from the official *Congressional Record.* Many felt this was too little too late, a lame acknowledgment that his comments had been totally inappropriate.

In the House, black congresswomen were considering withdrawing their support for FOCA, following Carol Moseley-Braun's lead. On July 13, several black and Hispanic congresswomen met privately to discuss how they might proceed. This division was terribly troubling to the rest of the pro-choice women. No one knew when FOCA would actually make it to the House floor, but when it did, it needed every supporter it could get. Nita Lowey and other white members worked to convince the minority women that a fissure among them would kill any chance we had at getting FOCA passed. Our numbers, compared with those of the men, were so small as it was, we couldn't afford for there to be discord among us. Notwithstanding the political toll it would take, it was personally disturbing to be pitted against other congresswomen. We knew it was of the utmost importance that we not allow the anti-choice forces in the House to create any sort of lasting rift within our ranks.

Meanwhile, back home in Pennsylvania, pro-choice advocates were preparing for Operation Rescue protests at local abortion clinics. On Thursday, July 8, there was a rally at City Hall in Philadelphia. Ellie Smeal, past president of the National Organization of Women and currently the head of the Feminist Majority, myself, and other politicians spoke to the hundreds of people who came out, despite the brutal one-hundred-degree temperature. Our recent loss on the Hyde Amendment only served to buoy my determination and conviction to fight to ensure that *all* women have the right to a safe and legal abortion.

The next two days, I joined clinic defenders in staving off Operation Rescue members at local clinics. Seeing women trying to enter these clinics and being harassed put a real face on the issue. As I stood in front of Planned Parenthood with Ellie Smeal, we spoke of the importance of having women in Congress in numbers that count. Times like these underscored the urgent need for a strong collective female voice in Congress to support the fight of courageous and dedicated women like Ellie Smeal.

After the Hyde Amendment vote there was a series of meetings among the women themselves, and with the leadership to assess what had happened, and, if possible, to clear the air. The pro-choice women were angry and wanted some answers.

On the morning of Wednesday, July 14, a group of women met to discuss what they would say later that day to the Speaker at a scheduled meeting. They talked about the pressing issues on their minds regarding the Hyde Amendment vote. One was the role the parliamentarian had played; it seemed that he had given unfair advantage to those championing the Hyde Amendment. And the Democratic leadership had not done all they could or should have. I felt that we had, in fact, not been treated entirely fairly, that they could have done more, that they had sat by and allowed this to happen—and I wasn't alone. The women who had worked to get the Hyde Amendment quashed were plenty angry with the leadership and didn't plan on going quietly into the night. The other major topic of discussion was the racist and sexist discourse some of the male members had engaged in during the debate that day.

Elizabeth Furse was one of the congresswomen sitting in Tom Foley's office at 2:00 P.M. that day. Elizabeth listened politely to the Speaker, but inside she felt deeply troubled. There was so much she wanted to say, but she refrained from doing so because she thought it would be inappropriate.

While Elizabeth understood the Speaker was in a difficult position, the ramifications of the Hyde Amendment were grave. "I wanted to say, 'As a result of action that we take or didn't take, women are going to die. This is clearly not just any other issue. If there is no federal funding for abortion in the cases of—whatever, whatever the reason—some women will not have the money to get a safe abortion and they will, in fact, get abortions in back alleys because they *will* get the abortion. And so, Mr. Speaker, this isn't just another issue. It is very seldom that we do things in the House that really make a difference to people. People will die as a result of that action.'

"I think he [Tom Foley] felt very badly about what had happened and I think that there's a problem here because he believes he cannot ask people to vote either pro- or anti-choice, and that's right—he can't. Then he feels restrained about throwing his full weight behind what really was a procedural problem. So then it became a substantive problem rather than what it really was, a procedural problem. Mr. Natcher did something really uncalled for and outrageous. He called for the House to rise and spoke against it, and voted against it. That was a procedural vote that shouldn't have been allowed to happen, I think."

But Elizabeth didn't speak up. "I just couldn't. By the time I'd heard all the talk, I just thought, Well, it's not his fault. But I wanted to say that there are very seldom times in this place when it really makes that much of a difference, but this did, and we blew it. It's horrible. And then people intellectualize this whole thing. . . . We're not talking about abortions or not abortions. We're talking about safe or unsafe abortions. But people want to just make it all moral and hide behind that."

One person who did speak up was Cynthia McKinney. Just as she had spoken on the floor during the debate, she did so during the meeting. "We certainly let him have it," Cynthia McKinney later told reporters regarding Tom Foley. "We didn't appreciate the extent to which we had been rolled from the inside."

According to Carrie Meek, "The parliamentarian really committed a historical flaw. He would not allow Cardiss Collins to respond, even on a point of personal privilege at that time. He would not allow it. To me, he took a very cursory approach to the procedures in that the women had already sort of processed this with him. They wanted to know what they could or could not do. The same parliamentarian had given them a lead on how they should proceed. But it angered me just to look at him and to see the body language he portrayed, knowing that he ruled in such a way, which in my opinion was biased. He would not allow Miss Collins to speak, and that may be the worst."

The meeting was rough and very candid, with people airing their grievances. It was clear that palpable, perhaps irreparable damage had been done, and there was no denying it. There were promises from the leadership to try to work and communicate better with the women's caucus in the future. But the ugliness of the Hyde Amendment debate could not be contained; in fact, it seemed to have metastasized throughout the body of Congress.

"It was extraordinarily divisive," says Elizabeth Furse. "You have to understand that the strongly anti-choice—although there were women who supported the Hyde Amendment—the people who took the leadership in this were men. There were definitely, in my belief, racist remarks made. And I think there were sexist remarks, too. So that caused a very emotional response, although anything around the issue of choice is going to be emotional. Especially when people think, Oh, we don't have to fight this—and suddenly here comes Hyde with his cleverly crafted amendment and people felt very betrayed and very taken aback.

"I've not been here that long, but I'm told it was the most acrimonious debate on the House floor that people who had been here for years had seen.

"Some women told me—and they told the group—they felt that they personally were sort of put down by other people saying, 'Why did you bring this up? Get out of our way, out of our face.' I didn't have that; nobody was rude to me. But a lot of women felt that they were really sort of castigated almost."

Besides Henry Hyde's general remarks, and specifically what he said to Cardiss Collins, there was another source of ire contributing to the bloody aftermath. David Obey had shouted "Shut up" at Corrine Brown during the debate and this was interpreted as a sign of outright disrespect for a woman by a man. Many believe David Obey would never have spoken that way to another man.

"He told her, 'You shut up,' in a very, very patronizing manner, a very demanding manner, as if, Who gave you the right to confront me?" remembers Carrie Meek.

"There were several dynamics happening on the floor that day. One was the abortion issue, and the fact that it was being allowed to come to the floor on an appropriations bill; the other issue was the issue of not subtle racism but overt racism in the inferences made by Mr. Hyde. . . . So that made it a bad day for me."

There are those who caution against reading too much gender

and racial politics into it, but I'm not one of them. As I sat there watching the debate, my rage mounted. It was a horrible, embarrassing moment in the history of this body, and I hope one that will never be repeated again.

"Some bad things happened during the Hyde Amendment," says Steny Hoyer. "Henry Hyde made some offensive comments to Mrs. Collins. While he later apologized, many legislators don't think it was a genuine apology and felt that it would not have happened if Hyde was dealing with a man. I tend to disagree. I think Henry Hyde would have tried to demean, not because he's mean-spirited but because he's a tough, tough debater, no matter whom he's debating. And because he feels so very passionate about this issue, he struck back."

Carrie Meek had a different take on it. "He [Henry Hyde] made some very strong racial inferences, and if you had not been subjected to racism in the past, you may not have discerned what he was talking about. . . . It was the condescension; it was the patronizing manner in which he did it, as if he felt he knew more about our black communities than we did. When he addressed his comments to Miss Collins and said, 'You don't know what's going on in your own neighborhood. You should contact some of the black preachers in your neighborhood,' that infuriated me because I knew, there's a man who knows absolutely nothing about our community. But what he was doing, he was using a racist-type behavior to make his point clear—that, I resented. It's not so much that I resented him having a chance to say what he wanted to say—even though I did resent it—but after he did get a chance to debate, to say something, it was with condescension—the reference to the fact that 'You people don't know what's going on in your own neighborhood; ask the preachers what's going on there,' as if there's widespread abortion in the black community. The other one I take issue with is any white male telling me what's going on within my own damn community. I take issue with that because he doesn't know what's going on."

"If you analyze the words, in some people's opinion, what Mr. Hyde said was not racist," says Barbara Kennelly. "But if you just listen to those words, if someone says, 'You people' to me, that's racist. And I love this place, and to have anything that is racist or sexist happen on the floor makes me very, very sad. But it brought us together; it really did. I served on Intelligence with Mr. Hyde and he's a brilliant man and I felt that day, I said, 'I'll tell you what this man is doing. He's separating us as women and you saw'—they had a clipping—'it looked like the water had separated.' All of a sudden, we were all sitting together and the black women gathered and the white women gathered and I said, 'Oh my goodness, he knows what he's doing.' The black women gathered together, which was natural."

But the women knew the water could not remain parted; if it did, it would be playing right into the hands of the enemy. As Karen Shepherd witnessed the debate, she was struck by how Henry Hyde manipulated the scene, dividing the women. "It made it impossible for us to come together in any way—for example, around David Obey's suggestion which everyone would have voted for and would have been a terrific victory. But he sent a racist spear across the House floor and caused harm that required all of us to put up such a barrier of protectiveness that compromise became impossible. I think we'll see this happen again and again, and if we're going to be successful on these issues, I believe we're going to have to talk among ourselves enough to understand how we're being manipulated. We can choose not to allow them to manipulate us if we talk and plan enough."

It was very interesting to me that Karen used the verb *manipulate* in regard to Henry Hyde. This is a verb normally reserved for women, while men are usually depicted as "skillful negotiators" or "clever strategists." Go figure.

In any event, one of the reasons the meetings were called was to mend all the developing fissures—between the men and the women, between the women and the leadership, between the women and the parliamentarian, between the white women and the women of color. "We had four meetings," says Barbara Kennelly. "We had two in the morning and two in the afternoon. . . . It was beautiful to see that we were savvy enough to know that the worst thing we can do is separate. And I think it was sincere."

"I think the meetings have worked to make people, particularly women, aware that they really do have to work together," was the way Elizabeth Furse saw it. "On choice, we pretty well are going to have to be the ones who carry the real promotion, the real strength of the issue."

"July fourteenth was a critical day for the women because they were having their day in court with the leadership, but they were also struggling to hold the women together," says Heather Howard. "I think the women responded well and hung tight and realized the worst thing they could do was be divided. Instead, they went into the meeting with the leadership, united black and white—and their alliances have been stronger ever since."

While the meetings certainly were necessary, serving as an effective salve of damage control, there was only so much healing that could occur. Only time will tell if there are scars that do not fade.

"I still think it was a very serious setback," says Pat Schroeder, reflecting three weeks after the vote. "I think the wonderful thing was having the freshmen women there to reconfirm how sexist this place is. We debate tough issues all the time in this house. But people aren't treated the way the women were treated that day.

"You begin to realize there is a real tension in the body about all the new women and everybody pretty much on the same side. Now people say, 'Well, you didn't get every woman.' No, we got seventy-five percent of them. I mean, really. You'll never get everybody on everything. And we certainly didn't get seventy-five percent of the men, or it wouldn't have gone down. So there was a real marked tension, a real anger, and you begin to think that some of the things people had been saying since the beginning of the year, and you had interpreted as humorous, may not have been so humorous. You know, the guys saying, 'This place looks like a shopping center. Ha ha.' "

Maria Cantwell was stunned by the debate that ensued. "Disappointment, shock, frustration . . . I don't know that you had to be personally involved in the battle. But it was just like somebody slammed you." When asked what the lesson for the women was in this painful episode, Maria responded, "It's time to play hardball."

Maria comes from one of thirteen states that already provides funding for poor women's abortions. So it really felt like a setback for her. "I mean, coming from that to this was just—I mean, I was just shocked. I was surprised that that was what the response was. . . . I was talking to someone who said, 'It should be no surprise to us that men and women communicate differently, but this just showed to me that there is a big valley between us on this—on just this whole issue and what happened and how we responded to it and where we go from here. We're not on the same wavelength, and it's unfortunate, because I think we've got to get there."

"They're having to deal with it much more than they had to in the past," says Pat Schroeder. "The way this body has tended to treat women was kind of once a year or so, say, 'Now, what can we vote for that you little ladies would like? Um, hopefully something that won't cost any money and then you'll all love us forever and you'll come campaign for us and tell them what a great job we do and thank you very much.' Now, not all members, by any means. And when I say these things, somebody says, 'Oh God, there you go demeaning men,' and I don't mean that. There are some who aren't that way at all. But I would say a majority, that's kind of how they want to approach it. Well, all of a sudden, here's this group that isn't going to settle for 'What do you mean, no money?' has a lot of energy, and isn't going to be talked out of taking it to the floor even if they lose. The other thing they say is, 'Oh, you'll lose. You'll lose. You'll look awful.' Well, let's put people on the record. And all these guys who have been saying they were pro-choice are furious because now people are saying, 'Well, you aren't pro-choice. You didn't vote against the Hyde Amendment.' 'Well, I was for allowing abortions for rape and incest; what do you mean I'm not pro-choice?' Well, that's nobody's interpretation of pro-choice except theirs. So they have been able to define themselves as being for these things without really having to be for them. And they're very uncomfortable with it. . . ."

■ ■ ■

Many representatives in the House who identify themselves as pro-choice feel that the issue of federal funding is a separate one from that of choice. Some of them are pro-choice and support federal funding. Others are pro-choice and do not support federal funding. I feel that if it is legal for a woman to get an abortion and she decides to do so, then she should be able to. If she has the will but does not have the money and cannot obtain the money, then there is no choice. And that is why I believe that federal funding and choice are not two separate issues.

Vic Fazio, who is staunchly pro-choice, concedes that most likely this was a loss the women felt more deeply, and rightfully so. But he was in there fighting against the Hyde Amendment and felt disappointed as well. The day after the debate, he was reviewing what had occurred, trying to make sense out of it. "I think yesterday's a good example of where the women who were involved feel more strongly about it. And at the same time may be somewhat frustrated not just in Henry Hyde's traditional role in this whole debate but maybe even on our side, I don't know. Maybe there's a feeling that there are some issues that you really can't understand.

"I think it's clear that the women tend to divide on this issue of choice, but the preponderance of advocates, strong advocates, have been women," says Vic. "In part because the kinds of districts that send them here are more likely to be feeling strongly about the issue on a pro-choice side. For Karen Thurman, who voted with Hyde on funding but is pro-choice, or Pat Danner, who might be similar, they're coming from rural small-town districts where choice was not why they were elected. The fact that she was a woman was probably a net plus, because women are perceived to be less likely to be ethically troubled or you name it. But it's clear that as we get more women here, we will have more division on even the issue of choice. But the preponderance of women who are in our [Democratic] caucus, and even on the Republican side to some degree, who have been elected, come from districts where women have been more politically active and where the issue is normally more likely to attract support—suburban, urban districts—where pro-choice feelings run pretty strong and where it is not only comfortable for women to be out front, it may be essential."

"I voted for the Hyde Amendment because I just have a very conservative district," says Karen Thurman. "When people think of Florida, they don't know the area that I represent at all. Gainesville, the most liberal region, is a small part of the district; the rest of it is very rural in some cases, still left over from some of the Bible Belt, then a lot of urban sprawl."

So Karen voted the way her constituents would want her to, because she felt it was her job to represent their stance. But she feels personally that government ought to stay out of these matters. "I've just always kind of believed that government ought not to be involved in reproduction. It just ought not to be and I've used the example of China. When you allow governments to start to participate in choices for women, then you allow them to take control."

Karen characterized the debate as "awful." "But I was comfortable. You have to understand that I also know who I am, where I am, because I am very pro-choice."

Karen, who is a cosponsor of FOCA, believes that the funding issue and the choice issue are separate. She doesn't see the significance in the Hyde Amendment's passage that others do. "The Fifth District is the second-oldest and second-poorest in Florida," she says. "Quite naturally, the people in the district I represent are more needful of pharmaceutical assistance, long-term care, and women's health services such as mammograms and cervical cancer screenings than they are of abortion services. Frankly, having just voted in the deficit reduction package to hold Medicaid and Medicare funding constant, I couldn't vote to further dilute these dollars.

"I think it's two totally different debates out there, and what's going to be unfortunate about this whole issue is that 'Now you can't bring this to the floor.' It's garbage. I know a lot of people on that floor who voted the way they did who are pro-choice. It isn't the significant vote that people think."

Voting against the Hyde Amendment wasn't necessarily an easy vote for another congresswoman from a rural district, who did so because she felt that she was doing the right thing. She believes that federal funding of abortion is a complicated issue, not one to be taken lightly. "I think that there's a place for it. I think it needs to be structured. Congressman Obey had an amendment that I was prepared to vote for and it wasn't offered, unfortunately. And I think it would have probably codified it. It would have been a little more explanatory and a little more protective."

When another congresswoman characterizes her constituents regarding abortion rights, you can see why the issue is so complex for lawmakers; it is hard to get at what people really believe when it comes down to it. "Well, they think they're pro-life," she says. "But very often you'll find if you take the time to talk to them that they're actually pro-choice as long as they know that there are some reasonable protective parameters.

"I am a definite pro-choice candidate, and I believe that the choice is there because it's not an issue or a decision to be made by the government. . . . And I think it's one that each person individually has to make and they have to consult their own souls and they have got to reach far within themselves to find out what the answer is for them. They look—through the consultation with their doctor and their creator—and whatever their decision is, it's something they have to live with. But if you begin to take away the responsibility of making that decision, then you take away the responsibility to our faith. And when you take away the responsibility to faith, there's nothing left. So I'm by no means pro-abortion. I'm simply a believer that it's just an issue where individuals have to make the decision; it's not something the government can do for you. A lot of people will say to you, 'Well, that's fine; you've got your idea and I've got mine. I can respect there are different ideas, but I don't want my tax dollars going toward something that I might morally disagree with.' And that's difficult when somebody comes at you with that. But you've also got to think that there are other things that people disagree with their tax dollars being spent on, like defense. And if you section out everyone in this nation and give them an opportunity or at least say, 'Okay, well, there's a part of my constituency that disagrees with spending their tax dollars on this,' then you're never going to come to a consensus."

"I voted against the Hyde Amendment," says Karen Shepherd. "I don't believe the federal government should mandate this one way or another. I think there are states, and my state happens to be one of them, that will want to decide. And I will fight for the right for the states to have a strong opinion, a conscience to do that. We give states an option on Title 10, family-planning money, for example. Federal money comes to nonprofit organizations to handle family planning in the state of Utah because the state is absolutely opposed to doing it in the public health clinics. The point is to get access to everyone one way or the other. I don't think we have any business nationally mandating that women without means must be denied access to abortion."

The overriding thing that the Hyde Amendment defined was how muddy the waters are regarding the issue of choice, according to Karan English, who adamantly opposed the Hyde Amendment. "The strategies to defeat choice are so multifaceted and it is such a pure issue that people get caught up in those muddy waters and they can't get a clear picture of what, in fact, the issue is. And because of that, and because we are so new on the block, we have to learn how to clarify; we have to learn how to bring it down to an issue that is understandable to the masses. Women who have been involved with the issue of choice have the picture quite clear. A lot of other people haven't and we hear these arguments: 'I want choice, but only if we don't have to pay for it.' Or 'I want choice, but only in the case of rape or incest.' Or 'I will support choice only when the woman's life is in danger.' None of those statements are in support of choice. The minute people say 'only if' means that they don't believe the fundamental tenet of choice and that it's none of their business. And if we are so insecure that a woman can't make a decision without our help, then we believe too much in government intervention. If we're so insecure that a woman cannot make a decision, it means that we lack respect for women. To me, it couldn't be clearer; it is so fundamental that until we respect a woman totally, we aren't going to give her the right to make those decisions."

While the controversy surrounding the Hyde Amendment debate was perceived to be mainly one of gender politics, Karan English questions this. She says it isn't as clear-cut as the Hill-Thomas hearings, because there were eleven women who voted for the Hyde Amendment. And some of those, like Karen Thurman, consider themselves to be pro-choice. "They got caught up in the argument 'I believe in choice; I just don't believe we should pay for it,' " says Karan English. "That's all a roundabout, fraudulent argument. Right now, we are paying millions of dollars for abortions. It's selective reasoning and they're looking for a way out of it. Whether it's because they have a moral problem with it or it's just politically correct in their district, I don't know."

"I feel fairly confident that the majority of my constituents are pro-choice," says Karan English. "We had a referendum on the ballot the same year I was elected, where there was a clear defeat of the pro-life movement. . . . It was a very clear message that the women were pro-choice—and not just women; the *voters* were pro-choice. But I'll have to say that my district is pretty conservative. And they will get caught up in how could I offer to pay for abortions, when in reality we have again allowed the other side to frame the argument. And that is our failing, that we aren't able to frame the argument first. And that's something we have to learn how to do."

"I think they are going along with a conservative minority," says Elizabeth Furse. "And you have people like Connie Morella, who was working hard to try to stop this Hyde Amendment, people who have got the real credentials, but they could not influence the Debbie Pryces and Jennifer Dunns."

The day after the Hyde Amendment debate, Elizabeth was at the airport, heading home to Oregon. She ran into Jennifer Dunn, who was catching a flight back to Washington State. Jennifer, a pro-choice Republican who voted for the Hyde Amendment, and Elizabeth, a liberal Democrat, are at nearly opposite ends of the political spectrum. The two women stopped to talk briefly.

"Oh, wasn't it surprising how much emotion there was!" Jennifer said of the previous day's events.

Where have you been? Elizabeth mused to herself. Of course it had been emotional—it was one of the most highly charged issues to be debated in the history of Congress.

"You know, like she thought this was amazing. And I had talked to her on the House floor and said to her, 'Jennifer, this is the pro-choice vote.' And she said, 'No, no, no, we've been assured that this amendment won't prevent funding on rape and incest.' Well, that isn't the point. You know, it's pretty amazing that the anti-choice people went further than they've ever been. These people who say they're pro-choice have got to go to the wall on it. They can't just be pro-choice for an election; they have to be really pro-choice."

Kathryn Kolbert, vice president of the Center for Reproductive Law and Policy, is someone who has thought a great deal about this issue. Kathryn, who argued the *Casey* decision before the Pennsylvania Supreme Court, feels very strongly that there is only one issue here. "The point is the women who need assistance, who need the most protection from the system, are low-income and young women. . . . They are most in need of Congress saying we will treat them equally as other women in society. Women with health insurance don't need the government."

Rosa DeLauro, who is both pro-choice and in favor of federal funding, believes they are two separate issues. "I think the Hyde Amendment is essentially an issue of funding. It is not an indication of sentiment on a woman's right to choose or on upholding the constitutional right to privacy or even on the Freedom of Choice Act. Funding and choice are two different issues."

And while she was unhappy that the Hyde Amendment was not shot down, Rosa wasn't exactly surprised. "I think it's impossible at this moment to win the funding issue on the floor of the House. We don't have the votes. You have ninety-eight Democrats who opposed funding. And I would guess that a healthy number of that ninety-eight would vote for the right to choose. That reflects public opinion; that reflects thinking in their districts. So I see the two issues as different and I think it's a mistake to lump them together. I don't believe we can win a funding issue at this time. But I do believe that we can win a vote reaffirming a woman's right to choose. . . . The situation we faced that day was a funding issue, and we lost."

"The political ramifications of this—and it's something I've been concerned about for a while—is that pro-choice people think that because there's a pro-choice President we've got a picnic, and we don't," says Elizabeth Furse. "It's going to be harder. There is a huge anti-choice feeling here and we've just got to get those grass-roots people to be calling."

One freshman also wasn't surprised by what happened. "Just because you've got a new Democratic President and you've got twice as many women doesn't mean that the issue is going to fly through."

This freshman also emphasizes something that many of the other women, in their frustration over the debate itself, didn't give any attention to. That is the fact that the Hyde Amendment was revised to include rape and incest. Despite our rage and frustration over the fact that a version of the Hyde Amendment was passed, some ground was achieved, or at least regained. (At one time, these exemptions were included and then dropped in the early eighties.) A small concession perhaps, but one in the right direction and one in which I take a little comfort at least. "There was some ground that was covered, some ground that was made that hadn't been made previously, and at some point you've got to recognize that you've made some accomplishment," says this freshman. "You may not have reached the goal that you've wanted, which was to defeat the amendment. But you've made some ground and you've got to be thoughtful of that. And that was something that I think was probably forgotten. I think in the excitement, everybody thought, Oh, we've got a Democratic President and he's with us on this and there're more women than there ever have been and we're going to make it happen. Well, it didn't. And I think with the anticipation and the expectation that people had, there was a lot more disappointment than there should have been. We should have been more realistic to begin with; maybe we were going to make some ground. And I also think we were unprepared."

■ ■ ■

Putting aside for a moment the controversy surrounding the nature of the debate, there is the issue of parliamentary procedure. At the disposal of both the Republicans and the Democrats is the parliamentarian and his staff. He is an appointed nonpartisan employee of the House who is available to advise both sides regarding legislative strategy. Because parliamentary procedure is terribly complex and rigid, the parliamentarian plays a crucial role in helping to shape legislation. He is, as it were, a tool to be used by lawmakers. Pro-choice members consulted Parliamentarian William Brown in regard to what their opponents on this issue would do, whether their opponents would be allowed to offer amendments restricting abortion. Because the bill that deals with Medicaid is an appropriations bill, it is typically not allowed to be altered during floor debate. When pro-choice forces approached the parliamentarian, he assured them that no restrictive amendment could be offered. Anti-choice forces, however, discovered a seldom-used precedent that manipulated the very language of the amendment's text, and they consulted with the parliamentarian. When pro-choice members continued their discussions with the parliamentarian, they were not alerted to this precedent and were repeatedly told that their opponents would be restricted from offering any version of the Hyde Amendment.

Nita Lowey, the chair of the Pro-Choice Task Force, felt that the anti-choice forces had engaged in dirty pool. "Because if we knew that there were other opportunities, we would have whipped it. We can count as well as anyone. Even if you don't have the majority of the House, you can do all kinds of things. Instead of the humiliation that took place on the floor, you present your position, you argue your position in the debate, and then you fight another day. But what happened is that we went into that debate thinking the rules of the House were on our side. Instead, we discovered that the rules were not on our side. In most instances, you know whether the rules are on your side and know how to prepare."

But in this instance, that wasn't the case. So now the most productive thing for us to do is to figure out what went wrong and make sure it doesn't happen again in the future. "We were angry, we were humiliated, and the time now as cooler heads prevail is to regroup and to work on a Hyde Amendment in the conference, and work on health-care reform," says Nita. "I'm currently getting signatures for a letter, a second letter, to Hillary Clinton. We sent one before with thirty signatures. This one will reiterate our strong commitment to reproductive health-care services in national health care and request a meeting to discuss it so that we will not be backtracking."

The letter, when it was sent, bore thirty-four signatures and read in part: "The Congressional Caucus for Women's Issues feels strongly that the recent vote on the Hyde Amendment should not deter the administration from its mission to ensure that women receive the full range of reproductive health-care services. This is clearly a different battle from the one over the Hyde Amendment, *and one that we can win with administration support.*"

"Women are not quite there yet," says Karan English, "in several ways. One is that we were outmaneuvered. Partially because of our own failings on total knowledge of the parliamentary procedure—which is really a lot to ask of any special interest, but that's what we're going to need to do; we're going to have to be perfect—and partially because the parliamentarians dropped the ball and weren't entirely prepared for the process that took place, either. And partially because we didn't have the numbers we thought we had. And all those things meant a huge blow. It was a blow."

After the vote on the Hyde Amendment, Elizabeth Furse vowed that she would study parliamentary procedure. "Those who know the rules get to play the hardest. I'm committed to becoming a good parliamentarian," she told the press.

"I think they abandoned us," says Carrie Meek. "I think the leadership saw this as being a situation where they thought, This is something that we can't control; it's gotten out of control, so there's nothing we can do. We just go with the flow."

"Although the parliamentarians are not supposed to tell you the strategy of other people's sides, what seems to have happened is that they did not go far enough to say, 'Here is a possible action plan,' " says Elizabeth. "People seem to feel—in fact I heard one woman say, 'They lied to us.' People feel that it was seriously flawed, what happened. Certainly there are complicated strategies and one of the things that I think everybody is aware of is that the people on Hyde's side knew that this was coming out and that the Speaker and his people and certainly the people in the women's caucus didn't know that it was coming out. In fact, we really thought we were protected, that there were a couple of parliamentary procedures that would prevent that. One, that you don't authorize on an appropriations bill. But they were informed exactly of the language to use to get it through. So it was as if the parliamentarians had almost written it for them."

"I don't think going to the parliamentarian is going to change the outcome of what happened that day," says Maria Cantwell. "I don't care if he says, 'Oh yeah, I should have advised you better.' I don't care. What we need is the ability to stick together and push hard on an issue and say, 'Hey, this is something that we would like to see happen and if it doesn't . . .' I think there's an expectation level there. It's almost like saying, 'This is your issue. And we're sorry you didn't get your issue, but it's your issue.' When that's not the case. It's the party's issue; it's the President's issue, and our leadership should fight for that issue. Now, they cannot guarantee us that every member of our caucus is going to vote for it, but we should treat that like any other issue that the party, that we as Democrats, have coalesced on. We cannot say that this is a 'women's issue' and doesn't have the same status and treatment."

■ ■ ■

The Hyde Amendment is an issue that touches both women's and *men's* lives. And both women and men were involved on both sides of the debate on June 30. The notion that abortion is strictly a "women's issue" was reinforced by the fact that on the day of the debate women stood out more, and it seemed as though it was strictly a battle of the sexes. This is a result of the fact that many more pro-choice women than pro-choice men spoke during the debate.

Nita Lowey thought it was unfortunate that it appeared that only women were fighting a battle that they didn't win. "I'm sorry that that was the perception, because Vic Fazio and Steny Hoyer worked with us. They are a part of the Appropriations Committee and they worked with us. So it really wasn't a male-female thing—people are quick to give the victories to the men when they win. But as Vic and Steny acknowledged, they were part of the defeat and with us on the strategy. In fact, I was very free to admit that I was not an expert on parliamentary procedure. I'm going to be learning it effectively."

It would be a disservice to all to imply that only women care about this issue, or, even worse, that women care only about this issue. "Women are interested in a whole lot of issues and should not be slotted or pegged by either women or men," says Steny Hoyer.

The Hyde Amendment, because of its many layers, is an interesting case study. There is much to be learned from it about race, gender, and politics in general. As time offers the perspective needed for a clearer interpretation, the lessons different people take away from it range from the prosaic and pragmatic to the philosophic.

Barbara Kennelly stresses that "the lesson is, be very careful when you *take* the vote that you've *got* the votes. I grew up in a political family; it was something that my father always said. 'Don't take the vote unless you know what the vote is.' Never call the vote unless you know what the vote is. That's why we whip."

"We still need a majority. We figure it's going to take a couple of hundred years to achieve parity," says Nita Lowey, laughing. "You can have all the force and all the eloquent speeches and all the commitment of the women, but you still need the majority of the vote. So I think clearly the force of the women's caucus to work as a power block is yet to be tested, and I think as we get more comfortable with the power, with our numbers, that we will be able to operate to make a greater impact on a particular piece of legislation."

While not every congresswoman is pro-choice, the majority is, and it really is a defining issue for the women's caucus. "The women's caucus became a pro-choice caucus this year not because it was unanimous but because a majority of women really added to our clout and our power and our ability to influence legislation," asserts Nita.

The one thing everyone involved seems to agree upon is that the

Hyde Amendment debate made a painful and unpleasant imprint on the collective psyche of the 103d Congress of the United States—so painful, in fact, that the official memory, the *Congressional Record,* doesn't accurately reflect what was really said that day. Unlike in real life, members get a second chance, having editing powers over the text of their statements on the House floor. Too bad for some that you can't edit people's memories.

I believe that a variety of factors led to a disappointing outcome, but I am not disheartened. It was just the first round. It underscored the fact that we would need to be wiser in the next go-around, tougher, and perhaps a little less trusting that people would fight fair. But we know we are up for it. After all, most of us got here by beating the odds.

And we are a group that doesn't like to lose and we don't appreciate others trying to frame us within the context of defeat.

Leslie Byrne, as scrappy a fighter as the next guy, perhaps summed it up most honestly. When asked to join some of the other pro-choice women in a picture the *New York Times* was shooting right after the Hyde Amendment vote, she recoiled. "I don't want to be in the picture," Leslie announced. "What's the caption going to say? 'Losers'?"

"I think the women learned something and that is that they could get screwed despite assurance from the leadership," says Kathryn Kolbert. "Sticking together, they have a lot more power, in the same way the freshman class coalition was helpful in making an impact on a body that was hard to make an impact on—with the women members and black and Hispanic caucuses as a base of support. A lot of numbers calls the fight for what it is."

And that fight is one of discrimination. Kathryn perceives the speech that Cynthia McKinney gave on the House floor during the debate as a watershed event in the fight against racism and sexism. "That anger and indignation was a very big shift in how this has been played out in this arena. It was disturbing that we lost, but I don't think it's disturbing that we had the fight. I think we should just build from here."

CHAPTER SIX

Legislating Dignity: Minority Women

The Year of the Woman was memorable not only for the women it brought to Congress but for the diversity of those women. There are not nearly enough minority representatives, but at least there is a beginning and a greater awareness that while the numbers have increased, there is a long way to go to make things as they should be.

Still, this new representation of the nation's population is making its mark on Congress. As I've mentioned earlier, Cynthia McKinney's impassioned remarks during the Hyde Amendment debate forced the powers that be to consider what for so long has been swept under the rug: that a disproportionate number of black citizens are poor and therefore ignored or mistreated by our system. And we're hoping that the promise of this last campaign cycle will continue to gather momentum, inspiring young people from all walks of life to set their sights on Washington.

There are nine black women serving in the House, five of whom are freshmen. In addition, Representative Ileana Ros-Lehtinen, elected in 1989, was the first Hispanic woman and the first Cuban-American to serve in Congress. Nydia Velazquez is the first and only Puerto Rican woman to serve in this body. The members of the black and Hispanic congressional caucuses have rallied together and galvanized both parties and the White House to treat the people they represent with respect and deference. In addition, there is an unspoken alliance between the minorities and the women—a shared understanding that for too long we have all gotten too little of the pie and that if we work together, our numbers will shake up the status quo.

"I think any group that works on common issues has influence," says Eddie Bernice Johnson. "All women are not in the same place on all issues. That will influence those numbers some. For example, in the black caucus, we only have one member who is inclined not to be with the group when we take a stand on certain issues. So that gives us thirty-eight votes. There are more women who are not together than there are blacks, for example. We have more women who are Republicans who tend to vote the party line. And that's what the one black Republican does. . . . The numbers make the difference. Because when the bottom line comes, it's whether or not you can influence the vote outcome. And you can bargain with that, so obviously the more numbers you have that are supporting particular issues, the more successful you will be."

The African-American members have been extremely effective in coming together as a group that wields power. "The black caucus has been very up front about saying, 'You cannot have our vote,' " says Nita Lowey. The fact that of their thirty-nine members, only one, Gary Franks, is a Republican, does make it easier for the caucus to come to a consensus on any given issue. In the women's caucus, we have several Republican members, and some Republican women have chosen not to join for different reasons. And so we lose numbers because of partisan divisions.

It's a complicated issue for many members of Congress who are forced at times to choose one alliance—either a racially, gender-, or party-based one—over others. In the case of Republicans Deborah Pryce and Gary Franks, the choice can be a lonely one.

Deborah, who didn't join the women's caucus, feels uncomfortable in the Lindy Boggs Room, the women's lounge. "I go in there frequently, but I feel a little bit out of place because there are so many Democrats. It's really awful, and nobody makes me feel like that. But I think, Oh gee, here I am, and I'm probably intruding on some kind of political discussion. It's like with Gary Franks—he's the only Republican in the black caucus. I had the feeling that he was going to withdraw from the caucus, because every time something political came up, they had to send him out of the room, and that was all the time. Not that that would make me feel bad, it's just that I know the realities are that they're probably talking and strategizing and here I am within earshot and making them uncomfortable."

Deborah says that because most of her legislative work is done with Republican men, that is ultimately whom she spends most of her time with. "You know if I had a choice who I was going to pal around with, it would be a different answer," says Deborah.

Elizabeth Furse has worked her whole life for peace and racial equality and has thought about these issues a great deal over the years. Elizabeth, who is white, worked alongside her mother, one of the founders of Black Sash. "We all carry a form of oppression. There's nothing as bonding as oppression. And oppression can be very minor and it can be very major. The oppression I faced as a woman isn't anything like the oppression of South African blacks. But oppression—it's that recognition of a kind of shared experience; that is what pulls people together."

But even though we have a bond, there is still an experiential abyss between people of color and white people. "There's that old business, that saying that you can't judge unless you've walked a mile in somebody's moccasins," says Elizabeth. "I don't know what it feels like to be a white male; I don't know what burdens they carry. And so if I said something and some white male said, 'You know, that really offends me,' I'd have to accept that . . . just as I don't think that men understand sexism; they never can and they never will. And if people of color really are the only ones who can understand racism, we can at least empathize. As women, I think we tend to empathize more because we have been put down, too. I think we can empathize, but I don't think we can really understand."

When I hear my colleagues talk of their childhoods and their backgrounds, I compare their experiences with mine and am amazed at how diverse we are and yet how we still manage to find so much common ground. Elizabeth has touched on it exactly—we can empathize, but we can never really understand, not completely, not down to the core of our being. Furthermore, as tough as it was for most of the women to get here, it was that much tougher for the black and Hispanic women. They have not only had to beat the gender odds, but they've also had to struggle against racial barriers that don't exist for white people.

■ ■ ■

Cynthia McKinney explains where her determination to serve came from. "It comes from my dad. He had a drive to change Atlanta and then Georgia, so why not the nation next?"

Cynthia speaks with pride about her father. "He was one of Atlanta's first black policemen and he fought all of the injustices. Many times, he had to fight by himself . . . and eventually he decided, after twenty-one years, after fighting for dignity, he would legislate dignity in the General Assembly of Georgia. And he ran for a house seat and after reapportionment he won."

Her father continues to give her inspiration, particularly in the tough moments that we all face here, those very private moments when we miss our families and ask ourselves whether it is worth it and whether we will really be able to put a dent in business as usual. For Cynthia, it's particularly hard, as she is a single mom who has left her seven-year-old son in her parents' care back in Georgia. When the going gets tough, she thinks about all her dad has worked for. "I figure if anybody can stay in that Georgia house for twenty-one years and still be there fighting today as hard as he was on day one, then that's inspiration enough to withstand these few bumps and bruises that we're having to deal with now and keep the right attitude."

Cynthia, like her father, is a fighter. Her choice of weaponry in the battle against oppression is the written and spoken word. She is both an eloquent speaker and writer. Soon after Cynthia was elected to the Georgia house, she wrote a piece about the genesis of the decision to place the battle flag of the Confederacy on the Georgia state flag and the Georgia house's impending vote on legislation to remove it. "At that time, you had a virtual apartheid system of those after-hour employees who cleaned up and made the building and grounds of the state capitol beautiful for us to work in, and then there were those who placed the next day's legislation in the binders for us on our desks. All of those people who placed that legislation in the binders were white; all of the people who cleaned up were black. And there was something terribly wrong with that statement—with that reality. I took time to get to know those people who cleaned up that state capitol and I understood very clearly that they made life nice for us members of the legislature. And then without one thought about who had prepared that building so meticulously, almost with love, those members would go in there and they would vote against everything that would help those very people who worked and labored so hard in that building. And so my concluding sentence was: 'We don't need to worry about changing the flag of the state of Georgia until we have changed the hearts and minds of the people of the state and of the people who work inside that state capitol.'

"And that's why, of course, when the governor launched his campaign to remove the battle flag of the Confederacy from our state flag in time for the Olympics, it didn't succeed. Because we had not erased those feelings of the propriety of apartheid, those feelings of white superiority. That's not yesterday. That's today in Georgia. And that's why I'm here."

On the Senate side, Carol Moseley-Braun was also elected in the Year of the Woman. While hers is the lone black voice in the Senate, it is a voice hard to ignore. Her message against institutionally endorsed racism rang out over the airways and across the land when she defeated North Carolina Senator Jesse Helms in a Senate battle over the Confederate flag. "The issue," she said then, "is whether or not Americans such as myself who believe in the promise of this country . . . will have to suffer the indignity of being reminded time and time again that at one point in this country's history we were human chattel. We were property. We could be traded, bought and sold."

Corrine Brown explains how being disenfranchised for so long affects her legislative priorities, how her background drives her in different ways from some of the white congresswomen. "One of the things that I think we differ in, a lot of the women are interested in change and campaign reform and different things like that and I'm just interested in pork. I'm a pork-chop congressperson. The people that sent me up here, they've been left out of the system. The system has been for the rich, famous, and well-connected. And I represent a different kind of constituent and so I'm not here on an ideological mission; I'm here for pork. And so I think we think alike on a whole lot of things, but basically I think I'm just really focused on something different. And it may not be as glamorous as some of the things they're interested in, but it's like meat and potatoes for the people who sent me up here."

Carrie Meek, whose grandparents were slaves, whose parents were sharecroppers, and who herself was a domestic worker at one time, remembers her own childhood as one of limitations and restrictions.

The Florida capitol was in her neighborhood, but it was not accessible to her. "Not at that time, not welcome there. It was something that appeared to be, at that time, accepted—by both blacks and whites. And of course I didn't like it. But my mother told me, she said, 'You can't do that; you have to get off the sidewalk when you see whites coming; you can't drink out of the same fountain that they do.' She was telling me that to protect me. . . .

"I've been through a very long struggle; I came up right after the Depression, when we were very poor. My mother had twelve children, but she was a very ingenious person. I think that's where I got my strength. Yes, I got my strength from her. She could take a dress that someone gave her, cut it up, and make dresses for four of us. She was just that resourceful. She taught us not to be afraid of hard work. She encouraged me to stay in school. And because we were very poor, my brothers were dropping out because they didn't like not having what they saw other people have. So she taught us not to be envious of the other girls but to do our very best with what we had. . . .

"And she gave me a strong belief not only in myself but in my femininity and what I could do as a woman. I saw her do it; I saw my mother do it. So I thought, Well now, she didn't have a college education, and she was a very, very strong woman. You will find that a lot in the black community, a whole lot. She just sort of molded us; she was really responsible for my becoming a very strong woman."

After serving in the Florida house for four years and the Florida Senate for ten years, Carrie knew her time had come to run for Congress. "One of the things was deprivation, the fact that we had never been here and that we didn't see anybody here. And we knew that there was a big void. That was one of the big things. And the policy decisions that were made by the men angered most of us. And we knew that as women, had we been here, those things wouldn't have happened. Anita Hill was the thing that really lit the flame." Carrie pauses, reflecting on the hearings. "Oh, it made me angry. There was one of those guys I felt like crushing, the one who thought he was such an irresistible man. Oh, I wanted to gouge his eyes out! Clarence Thomas upset me, but he didn't upset me to the level that some of his supporters did. . . . I was really upset about what happened to Professor Hill. Here was an intelligent, bright woman that they crushed. We've all got to realize that that can happen again to some of us. So we have to be ready for that."

The fact that Carrie is comfortable with herself, that she says and does what she wants, is something she attributes partly to age. Carrie is very self-assured and exudes strength, but she is also extremely warm and nurturing. Some congresswomen hesitate to show their softer qualities, choosing instead to show only their tough side to the world. Though it is not her style, Carrie understands their fear of being misperceived as being weak.

"I think that's a veneer, which I guess they had to put on, having probably been defeated so often," says Carrie. "But because I've always had to struggle . . . I guess I'm sheltered from a lot of that because I've had to fight so far that I'm just used to fighting. I don't have to put my armor on; it's already under there," she says, laughing. That armor she wears like a second skin has put her in good stead, helping her get her highly coveted seat on Appropriations and commanding respect from her male colleagues, who take her very seriously.

It's been a long time coming for Carrie, but she's where she wants to be—in a position to make a difference. She had a strong mother who led her bravely through a racist era, but she didn't have black women in elected positions to look up to. And that is something that stays with her; that is a part of her fabric now, and it compels her to take the time out from her busy schedule to encourage young visitors.

"You know when I get a thrill?" she says. "When some of the little girls come to my office, the little interns. One little girl, I met her in the hall; she came to intern for someone else and she said, 'I just want to take a picture with you.' She said, 'I'm so proud to see a woman like you, a black woman.' She's a little black girl and little tears came to her eyes. And she said, 'Just let me have a picture.' And to see that kind of—I guess the word I want is *admiration,* for me and for the fact that I'm a woman . . . And that one day they'll be here, right? See, ten years ago, or fifteen years ago, she wouldn't have thought she could be here. But now she thinks she can be here, and that is a great part of what I see here, too—when the young come along and they see it can happen."

Eva Clayton reflects on how different the members of our class are and how different paths have led us here. She, like Carrie, hopes that their presence will reaffirm to young women considering their own futures that they can participate and achieve—whether it's in government or not. "Whether we're from southern districts or whether we are minorities or not, women by and large had to struggle to be here. The struggle may be different, defined by our experiences and where we've come from. Now it may be less of a struggle for other women because we're here. It's less of a struggle for us because the other twenty-four were here. So each time it's going to be easier, but it would be the wrong message to give to young people looking at us to say it's going to be easy. They should be prepared for the task at hand."

Both Eva and Carrie see their legislative roles as vehicles for making the world a more equitable place. "There are one or two things that I would like to do, but the major thing I'd like to do is make the world, this country treat everybody the same," says Carrie. "In terms of where I'm coming from, it's a fight for civil rights. . . . So if I'm able to do these two things—improve on the health of women and, number two, help the Haitian refugees—that's what I want to do. But in the meantime, I want to carry back boatloads of money," she adds, smiling widely.

Nydia Velazquez is also first and foremost concerned with her community. "In what sense will this issue have an impact on my community? Should I devote any time and energy? So my position is: My community comes first. For too long, they have been disenfranchised. So whatever I do, I do it in connection with my community, with the needs and concerns of the people I represent. And this is why every Thursday evening I'm going back to my district. First, because I need to be in touch with them, because they really energize me, because I really love it. I love to be surrounded by my community, those people who really gave me a chance and the privilege. . . . I want to learn from my own community, from my own people, so I can be an effective leader here. So I just keep focused. You could be at twenty receptions here and there. But in the end, what is it that you have accomplished as an elected official, as a member of Congress for this nation, and, more importantly, for the people that you represent?"

Nydia says there were many factors that led to her running for her New York seat in 1992. The district was crafted to increase Latino representation in New York City, particularly people of Puerto Rican descent. Her district, which on a map looks like an octopus, covers parts of Queens, Manhattan, and Brooklyn. "I felt that the Puerto Rican Latino community was ready to gain political influence, to elect one of their own," says Nydia. "And I was ready. I felt that I was ready politically. I knew when the discussion was taking place, when the whole redistricting process was happening in New York, that among those Latinos, Puerto Ricans, I was the one with name recognition citywide, particularly in that district that I already represented in the City Council. So I was very much encouraged by women."

And the men? "They, too, were very much supportive . . . they really encouraged me," says Nydia. "You know, in my culture, in the Latino culture, a woman's place is in the home.

"But when it comes to politics in the Puerto Rican community, in New York and Puerto Rico, women are doing much better in terms of being accepted as players in the political arena. I think that men recognized the kind of work that I had done in my community; they respected me. But we had four more Latinos and a very powerful congressman, Steven Solarz, with almost four million dollars. So when community activists, male activists, saw what was happening . . . they knew that they needed a woman with the name recognition to run against Steven Solarz. So that's why they opted to come out really strongly to support me. . . . But the mainstream media, the conventional wisdom in New York, they ruled out this race; they covered this race as Steven Solarz's race. I didn't have any money. The only thing I had was myself."

Once Nydia got here, she used the same single-minded determination that won her the race to gain the respect of her colleagues quickly. She is a small, delicately featured woman who at first glance does not appear to be commanding. But she has a will as resilient as Super Glue, and she says people refer to her as the "Giant Killer."

"I think that I came here with an attitude. My first attitude is that it is up to me to put an end to this attitude of business as usual in the House. And also I have this attitude that I earned this, the right to be here, so I just try to be recognized and I do my work. Whenever there is an issue where I think we should raise concerns to the leadership, I have done it through the Hispanic Congressional Caucus. I have been very much outspoken; I have made it very clear. And because of my criticism and my positions and my attitude, the Speaker agreed to meet with the Hispanic Congressional Caucus on a permanent basis. We joined forces with the Black Congressional

Caucus. Our message was: 'Once and for all, please understand, this Congress is a different Congress and it will remain this way. You have to understand that we are here and you have to deal with us.' We know that 'me by myself' cannot do much. The Hispanic caucus and the black caucus—there is much common ground."

Nydia's unwavering determination seems to be at her very core. She grew up in Puerto Rico, where she was one of nine children. Her father was a sugarcane cutter and the children grew up on the sugar plantations. Her father, who only attended school through the third grade, emphasized to his children the importance of an education. "My father always, before we left home to go to school every morning, he was always praying for us, giving us lessons. 'Remember you are going to school. Remember that we are poor, that when I die I cannot leave you a single penny, that the only thing I can leave you is your education.' So he instilled in me the value of education. And then being a little girl, I knew that education was the key for me to really help my family."

But even getting to school wasn't easy. "I remember one time that the bridge was destroyed by the flood and we had to cross the river. In one arm I was carrying my books and in another I was carrying my shoes, to walk fifty-five minutes to go to school," recalls Nydia. "I think coming from that poverty and being so focused that I wanted to break away from poverty, I knew that I didn't have time to be wasted. So I never went to a dance; I never went to parties; I never did anything but just focus on school."

It is an amazing journey that Nydia has taken to get to Congress. It is not something she takes for granted, and she thinks about it often. "Just now, when I was walking back to my office, it came into my mind—from Puerto Rico to here! You know, this is the center of power! When we talk about the decision-making process, I count myself as an agent who could bring about changes, who could make a difference in this nation!"

In addition to her commitment to the Hispanic caucus, Nydia is also a member of the progressive caucus. "It is a response to the conservative right wing within the Democratic party. When you read in the newspaper about things that are happening in the House, the conservatives asking for more spending cuts, criticizing increasing taxes and all that . . . So we saw the need to create this caucus so that we send a message that we are here, that the President also can count on us. I think the ability that I had to win the campaign, to put a coalition together, that is the kind of ability and skill I am bringing into the House, by working and forging coalitions with other groups. I know that the Hispanics and the Black Congressional Caucus cannot do much by ourselves, but when we add all those numbers, we could cause some trouble in the House. And I just intend to pursue the respect that we deserve as members of Congress by forging coalitions."

There is tremendous pressure on minority women; in addition to doing their job, they have the added stress of having to live up to what people expect of them. "I am very conscious of being the only Mexican-American woman in Congress," says Lucille Roybal-Allard. "I have young Latina women talk to me, not only here in Washington but when I go back to the district, who have so much hope and expectation that it's a tremendous responsibility. It's not only the responsibility of being a woman here but the added responsibility of being a minority. . . ."

Lucille is able to put herself in the shoes of her constituents. She is empathetic, understanding that people need to feel a part of the process. She is troubled by the fact that a bureaucracy as big as the United States government can be a totally alienating force to deal with. Her down-to-earth approach strikes me as inextricably linked to her identity as a woman and as a minority. "My staff and I developed a program in which we try to demystify the political process and help people understand that we are empowered by them and that they have every right to come to our office, to express their concerns and not be afraid to do that. There is a tremendous amount of fear and distrust of government, not only among people in general but particularly in the community that I represent."

Lucille's father, former Congressman Edward Roybal, spent thirty years in the House and before that served four terms on the Los Angeles City Council. Lucille, who is fifty-two, remembers her childhood as the daughter of the first Mexican-American elected to the L.A. City Council in this century. "I grew up with a lot of conflict and contradiction. . . . Here I was growing up in a poor Latino community and then my father gets elected. We weren't accepted by many in the Anglo community. We were faced—my father, my mother, my brother and sister—with tremendous discrimination. We were the first to go into some of the hotels where there would be meetings, and people would stop us at the door and my father would say, 'I'm Councilman Roybal.' And then they would reluctantly let us in and people would stare and whisper. We'd go to places where you never saw a Mexican family go and people would make little comments behind our backs—so that we could hear them."

It was a hard thing for the Roybal children to deal with, being pulled between two separate worlds. "So what happened was, on the one hand I was thrust into an Anglo world where we were not totally accepted. At the same time, we became oddities in our own community, which didn't always understand what we were experiencing. It was real difficult. My dad took on some issues like police brutality—during which time our phones were being tapped. So when we should be telling a young child, 'When you're in trouble you should find a policeman,' we were being told, 'If a policeman stops you, run home . . . don't talk to him,' that kind of thing. There was often conflict and contradiction growing up around the different issues my dad was taking on. It was publicly stated when he first got elected that 'they' were going to have 'that Mexican' within six months. We often felt we had to be the example for our community—we had to be the smartest, and we had to prove that we were not the negative stereotype.

"I've had people say that when they realize I was born in Boyle Heights, they figure if I could do it, they can, too. . . . And sometimes when talking to parents, particularly in the Latino community, the feeling is sometimes that education is wasted on the girls because girls are going to grow up and get married and have children. That's particularly the thinking of Latino fathers. . . . It's interesting when you go to the schools—it's mostly the women who go to the meetings and are the real activists. But I've also noticed that little by little you're seeing more of the husbands attend. It's a whole educational process and there's tremendous pride that these families have when children go to college and eventually graduate. And a lot of families can't afford to send their kids to college. That's the other thing: You're encouraging college on the one hand and on the other hand it's a tremendous financial burden on a lot of these families."

The meetings Lucille has with the children and young adults in her community are perhaps the most resonant for her, the memories that cling to her long after she heads back east for Washington.

One such meeting impressed upon her how vital it was to connect with local youth, when she learned many kids didn't have a clear understanding of government. At one junior high, she was asked, "What's the difference between what you do and what our mayor does?"

"So I talked to them a little bit about it and they had all kinds of questions and I promised that I would be back and that I would take pictures of the White House and the Capitol. I went back with pictures and a lot of the kids asked, 'Can I be what you are someday?' 'How do you do it?' Just the fact that you're stimulating that kind of interest and opening new doors for these kids, that in itself is real exciting to do—letting young people, young women, know that there are options and that they do have choices. It's exciting, because I grew up in two different worlds. There was that very traditional upbringing of the Mexican culture that was being reinforced by what society was saying anyway. For example, I had a father and a mother who recognized the importance of going to college but . . . it was not so much in the sense that you went to college to become a professional; it was more because it made you a better wife. It would put you in a better position to support your husband, who would be a professional. And then in the event that anything happened to your husband, you would have the education to get a good job. That was the thinking when I was growing up back in the fifties."

Nydia Velazquez, too, gets frustrated by this lack of recognition and by those who dare to presume to know who she is and what her struggle stands for. "I think that my entire life has been a life of struggle, and I think that when I listen to all these politicians talking about the pain and the struggle and their commitment, sometimes I ask myself, Do they really know what they mean? Have they felt that? Are they speaking because it sounds good to the listeners? When we talk about poverty . . . well, I could talk about it. And it's not because I saw it. I didn't read it in a solicitation letter; I didn't see it in a photograph. I went through it. We went through it. There were moments in our life growing up in Puerto Rico in the sixties that were very, very painful, when food was not there for us."

Lucille sees the similarities between the way women and minorities are regarded. Problems are overlooked, and then when the oppressed won't take it anymore, when they learn to act, to draw attention to the inequities of the system, they are regarded as troublemakers. "Just like with women," says Lucille. "Most of the work I did in the legislature dealt with environmental issues, domestic violence, or sexual assault. It was an educational process for many of my colleagues. Many times, bills I introduced didn't get out the first year. I would have to provide more information, explain the issues to my colleagues, not so much in the assembly, but in the senate, which is more of an 'old boys' network.' The assembly had the younger men in it; the senate had the older—what you imagine when you think of the old politician. It was often very difficult to change their way of thinking. Most of my bills would die on that side."

Lucille remembers one bill that she worked on regarding divorce, abuse, and custody battles. "Under existing law, in a case involving both a divorce and a child-custody matter, judges would not consider the abusive husband's behavior in awarding custody. If, for example, you were divorcing an abusive husband and were concerned that the violence could be redirected to your daughter, the judge would most likely rule that the domestic-violence charge had nothing to do with the child-custody case.

"The bill that I introduced simply said that the judge had to consider domestic violence in the child-custody case and at least look at it as a possibility. You'd think that we were asking for the world. You know what the fear was? That you can't trust women, you can't trust wives, especially ex-wives. They would just use that charge to get back at their ex-husbands by keeping the children away from them. They didn't express it quite that way, but that was the big concern."

Lucille finally got that bill made into law and she learned that the way to get things done, especially as a woman and as a minority, was to keep working, providing information and not acting in an accusatory or argumentative manner. She says she learned this, in part, from her father, whose legislative style she observed over the years. "I used to get real upset because other members would get credit for things I knew he had worked on so hard. And he always said, 'What's the objective?' I answered, 'It was to help these people.' 'Did we meet that objective?' 'Yes.' And then he'd say, 'Then what's your problem?' And I'd say, 'But Daddy.' This was as a young girl: 'But Daddy!' 'Did these people get the help they needed?' 'Yes.' 'Then you should be happy.' "

As strongly as the women of color feel regarding their racial and ethnic identities or their political parties, their gender is still a terribly compelling component of their total identities. When talking to Carrie Meek about how few women we have here in Congress, I saw her eyes light up mischievously. "I was even happy to see a Republican woman," Carrie declared, remembering the night that Kay Bailey Hutchinson won her Senate seat. "I said, 'I'm so glad you won!' My aide was with me. She said, 'She's a Republican.' I said, 'I don't care. I think she understands my issues better than the men do.' "

CHAPTER SEVEN

For Whom the Bells Toll: Juggling Job and Family

One of the hardest things about being a congresswoman is figuring out how to work really hard, to give it your all, and yet to maintain a life as well. For those of us who are mothers here, it's a particularly tough challenge. It's something I wrestle with personally every day, with a husband and eleven kids in our combined family (we have six still at home). I look to my colleagues, often to the senior female representatives who have raised kids and served in Congress, for guidance. However, it was the advice of one of my male colleagues that most poignantly got the message across.

One afternoon, Congressman Bill Brewster and I were walking from our offices in Longworth over to the Capitol for a vote. We were talking about attendance and Bill said he tried to keep his voting record up at about 90 percent. I was telling him that I had missed two votes the week before because I had gone back to Philadelphia for my son Andrew's graduation from elementary school. "Don't you ever miss those things," Bill said, stopping for a moment.

I just looked at him, his tone was so solemn.

"Spend as much time as you can with your children," he continued. "You don't know how much time you have with them. It's the most important thing in your life. Don't ever miss those years," he said softly. Then he told me that two of his three children, thirteen-year-old Kent and sixteen-year-old Kecia, were killed in a small plane crash on January 31, 1990. It was the day after Bill, at the time a member of the Oklahoma house, had declared his candidacy for the U.S. Congress. He and his wife, Suzie, and their three kids had flown all over the state. Kent and Kecia, much more so than their oldest child, Carol, loved politics; they thought it was just terrific. They had spent every minute they could in the state capitol with their dad.

That day, the family flew around the state in three different small planes. The plane that went down with Kent and Kecia also took with it a local newspaperman and the pilot, who was a close friend of the family's. It took three days to find the wreckage; more than a thousand people joined in the search. "It was the worst thing that ever happened," Bill says simply. For three weeks after the tragedy, Bill and Suzie didn't discuss whether he would go on with the race. Finally, they decided he would.

I could barely respond, I was so moved. What could I possibly say? He was right, of course. My "little" ones were already so big, they would be off to college before I knew it. I thought about how proud Andrew had been when he walked up to receive his diploma, how he looked over at us.

When we got to the Capitol, I took a deep breath and steadied myself, then we went inside to vote.

■ ■ ■

The pace here is unbelievably brisk. It's toughest, obviously, on those members who come from the districts farthest away. Most members are in Washington Tuesdays through Thursdays and back in their districts Fridays through Mondays. People from the western states spend a considerable amount of time flying back and forth, and when they're on the ground, they're adjusting to jet lag.

"Everybody thinks people here are off playing golf or something. I bet if you could add up the sleep deficit in this place, it would be bigger than the national debt," jokes Karen Shepherd. "And moving my body from mile-high elevation to sea level twice a week, spending twelve hours a week on airplanes, is hard. When it's all said and done, I've decided the hardest thing for me is eating right, getting enough sleep, and getting my exercise."

Karen, who's fifty-three, has been a runner for eighteen years and has never given up her running schedule, not while raising two kids or running her own business—until now. "I haven't run for two weeks because I can't do it on sleep deficit. And this altitude change and this jet-lag business, it just grinds my muscles to a halt. I come back just filled with resolutions about paying attention to my health, because I'm not willing to give it up. But it's really, really, really hard. They try to cram all the business of this government into three days. It can't be done, so we're double-scheduled for three days and it's always a conflict here between whether to go to one of the three hearings scheduled at the same time or meet with constituents waiting in the office. It's a pattern. All day, I'm scheduled to be ten places at once until ten o'clock at night, and then I take home an In box to go through before morning so my staff can move forward on their work. After three days of this, I jump on a plane and run home for a day or two of a full schedule in the district. We all feel we have to live like this so constituents feel they have access to us. The problem is that the schedule is so utterly impossible. There's no time in it to have a life."

We're all learning that there are some big adjustments to be made, some calibrating to be done to make it all work. It's hard to know, as freshmen, what has to be done and what doesn't, who's important and what's important.

"I get a schedule with all the hours filled up and I can't even take my clothes to the dry cleaners," says Karen. "In Washington, I can't even go buy a quart of milk so I can put it on my cereal for breakfast." It's the first time in her life that she hasn't had complete control over her own time.

After seven months of go-go-go, I was hobbling toward the finish line, just weeks before the August recess. I thought nothing could stop me. One night, at a reception in the home of Jane Harman, one of my freshman colleagues, I came up against a wall—literally. Okay, actually it was a plate-glass window. When it was time to go, I headed for my car and realized that in my haste I had left my purse behind. I rushed back around the side of the house and smashed nose-first into a plate-glass door. I spent the night in the hospital and had nosebleeds for weeks. Luckily, I didn't break Jane's door. That slowed me down—just a little.

The irony of the place is that while as an institution its ultimate purpose is to make the country a better place to live, to raise children, and to thrive, the people who work here are all running around harried and frustrated, disconnected from their families. "What I think the public is concerned about is that we're an elite body," says Karen Shepherd. "And they attack it from the point of view of parking places and traveling first-class or whatever. I don't think those things are the real issues. What separates us from other people is that this is the most chaotic lifestyle on the face of this earth. There isn't anything we could do to make it worse."

As dismal as all this sounds, Karen is one of the relatively lucky ones. With her kids grown and out of the house, her husband, Vince, sold his business and is able to be with her the majority of the time.

In addition to the crazy pace, living conditions are not all that glamorous, either. Karen and her husband lease a one-bedroom apartment with rented furniture. "It's the same size as the apartment Vince and I lived in thirty years ago, when we got married, except it's twelve times the cost," Karen notes, laughing.

Karen has sympathy for her colleagues whose spouses don't join them. "Everybody in this place is lonely! Their kids are home; their wives or their husbands are at home."

It's particularly lonely for Deborah Pryce, being one of only three Republican women in the freshman class. "I could use some good girlfriends here in Washington. It's a lonely feeling for a woman who doesn't have her family here, too. To think, Well gee, should I call Tillie [Fowler] or should I call Jennifer [Dunn]? You know, I'm starting to develop more male friends, but I'm not at the point where I can call them up and say, 'Do you have dinner plans?'

because that's just touchy. . . . I feel isolated for the very first time ever. Ever."

The summer was particularly hard for her, when her family went on a trip without her. "It was a really stressful time because my whole family, all my sisters, my brother, my parents, my husband and my daughter, and all of my nieces and nephews, were down at Cape Hatteras for two weeks. And there I was in Washington with long voting weeks, so I couldn't even take long weekends," she says, frowning. After a moment, she waves a hand through the air as though surrendering to the implacability of the place. "It's tough," she says squarely. "It's really tough."

I'm sure our male colleagues miss their children as well, but as mothers, I believe we feel the separation more deeply. This is not to say that we shouldn't be here, but perhaps finding creative solutions to the problem—like making the schedules more accessible to family life—falls on our shoulders.

Deborah is one of few women who have very young children. "It's tough for all of us who are away from our children, if they're little. And then I talk to Jennifer, whose children are grown, and it's really nice for her because she has that all behind her. If I could devote myself full-time to nothing but doing this job, it would be a wonderful job—because you just don't have any other concerns. And you don't mind the long hours because you don't have anything else to keep your mind on. But to have to divide yourself does make it pretty hard."

When Deborah is in Washington, she stays in an apartment just a block from her office. Like Karen, she pays a hefty rent for nothing special, apart from its proximity to work. "It's no great shakes. I could have financed my whole college education on one month's rent. . . . I feel like I'm back in college with tie-dyed curtains or something."

Deborah, whose husband, Randy Walker, and three-year-old daughter, Caroline, are back home, finds it very difficult to be separated from them. She's used to being a working mom, having raised Randy's now-grown son from a previous marriage. Before running for Congress, she sat on the Franklin County Municipal

Court for six years, and before that she was a prosecutor. So while she's no stranger to long hours and a demanding schedule, living apart from her family half the time is much more wearing. She gets up at 5:00 A.M. to take the 7:00 A.M. flight back to Washington on Tuesday and normally returns to Ohio on Thursday night. One of the hardest things about this schedule is trying to explain to a three-year-old why Mommy keeps leaving. "I talk to her at night. And last night was the first night she said, 'Mommy, I can't see you.' I said, 'That's right, Caroline, we're on the phone.' " When Deborah talks about being away from Caroline, her voice gets real soft, modulating with emotion. "She's a very bright little girl, so she's a little bit ahead of us even. She's starting to know when Monday night is coming and that I won't be there Tuesday. It's just something intuitive, because she wakes up two or three times."

Deborah says she knows that the occasional pangs of guilt she feels are natural and that she really doesn't need to feel that way. But you do anyway; I know this firsthand. It's an inner demon I have conquered for the most part. Ultimately, you have to tell yourself that guilt is a wasted emotion, that you're doing the best you can, and that it's important that you are both a mom and a congresswoman. Earlier in my career, when I was working at NBC, it was something I struggled with constantly. When I was at work, I felt I should be at home; when I was at home, I felt I should be at work. And I said to myself, Cripe, it's just such a waste of time to do this to myself. I'm doing what I'm doing, and I'm doing the best job I can. I'm a far better mother when I feel fulfilled, when I feel like my whole life is working. And I felt better about the choices I had made.

But try as you might, the doubts do creep back in sometimes. Suddenly, you realize that on some level you're still not completely at peace with it. Like last summer, when my two youngest boys were away, one at camp and the other on a trip—I realized I felt more relaxed because I wasn't constantly worrying about what Marc and Andrew were doing or whether they needed me. Through letters and phone calls, I knew they were both having the time of their lives. It wasn't as if they were at home waiting around, looking at the clock, wondering whether Mom was going to make it home on the last train from Washington on Thursday or Friday night.

And then there's the encouragement you get from other women. I remember one day I was feeling a little bit harried and someone said to me, "You really have proven to all of us that we can do both." That was just about the nicest thing anyone could have said to me that day. It reminded me why I was here.

The fact that you have less time to spend with your family gives you a greater appreciation for the time you do get. "I find that the time with Caroline is so much more important, so much more valuable," says Deborah. "It used to be, 'Here we are together and what are we going to do?' But now I spend a lot of time thinking about what we can do this weekend and how we are going to have fun. It's become a lot more quality time than it ever was before, so I don't think it's all bad. I think there's really some good that's coming out of it. Plus, she's getting to be particularly close with her dad, too."

Deborah gives her husband a lot of credit, as do most of the women who leave spouses behind to cope with the daily challenges of child rearing and maintaining a household. "This is a complete role reversal," she says. "But on the other hand, women have been doing it all their lives. I mean, not all their lives, but forever! But I've always felt that he was very special in his abilities and his willingness to do it."

Karan English believes that husbands are becoming more and more willing to share the load. She really has to rely on her husband, whom she married in July of 1992, just months before the election. They married in the middle of the campaign, both bringing children to the marriage. "He has taken on the father role under very tough circumstances. At the time, it wasn't clear that I would get elected. It could have been the end of my political career or it could have skyrocketed it. And we got married anyway. He knew what he was getting into. We're so high-profile and he's not insulted or intimidated by that. He's confident in himself.

"He took on my family and me and I took on his family and him in the middle of the campaign and it's turned out quite well. He deserves a tremendous amount of credit. It's not just cooking, and he's an excellent cook . . . they do have a little trouble doing the laundry now and then."

But there are some things that even the most devoted husband can't make easier for you, like the hectic traveling. Karan, shortly after beginning to serve her term in Washington, was at home in Arizona for a district work week. She got a call from the White House saying that she was invited to a meeting there with the President about a variety of issues concerning the new administration. "I was quite proud to be asked to go to the White House; there were only two or three other freshmen in the group of about twenty. The meeting was to be at two in the afternoon. So I took a red-eye from Arizona, got in here at eight-thirty in the morning, went to my apartment, and took a shower." Karan, not yet used to the routine of flying back and forth across the country, hadn't slept a wink on the flight. Her aide Bill drove her over to the White House for the meeting, which was to last forty-five minutes but ended up lasting two hours. When she came out, there was Bill waiting for her in his old car, sandwiched in a line of shiny black limos driven by tuxedoed chauffeurs. Her flight was at 4:50 and Bill whisked her off, neither of them actually believing they could make it.

At the airport, Karan ran up to the desk and said, "God, I've got two minutes." And they recognized her because she had been taking that flight regularly for the last month and they hurried her onto the plane without checking her ticket. When the plane landed in Arizona, her staff was nowhere to be found. It was very late at night, so she just got a room at the airport hotel after waiting around the terminal, frustrated and exhausted. "I was ready to fire my entire staff. I said to myself, 'Gosh, I can't believe we've been on the job less than a month. Where was everybody?' And the next day, they said they were there. And I said, 'Well, I was paging you guys.' And they said, 'Well, we were paging you.' Then we looked at the tickets and we realized I had gotten on the wrong flight, the wrong airline!" It turned out that they were in different terminals altogether.

Elizabeth Furse, who, at fifty-seven, doesn't have to worry about small kids back home, still wishes there were more hours in the day to tend to the necessities of life. "Oh my God, laundry! Are we supposed to do that? You mean that pile in the corner of the bathroom? It certainly would be nice to have a wife." She marvels at the emotional and logistical juggling act some of her younger colleagues manage. "I don't know how they do it. Because the guilt factor—you want to work late. . . . That's hard."

Yet even many of us who aren't in our thirties and forties are married to men who are learning to adjust to the way things are changing. I give a lot of credit to my husband, Ed, who comes from a traditional family background. It wasn't expected of him to pitch in and carry some of the load, but he has learned to do what he can, given that he is extremely busy himself. Ed, a former congressman, is a lawyer specializing in international trade. When I decided to run for Congress, I knew we were going to have to incorporate a lot of other people in our lives to make this work. Actually, we had always done this—even when I was a reporter. If I need to pick up the phone and ask someone at home to take one of the younger ones to the dentist for a cleaning, I don't hesitate. I feel very comfortable asking and they feel very comfortable telling me whether they can or can't help out. I knew that if I wanted to make my life work, this was the only way I could do it.

Nita Lowey, who was elected in 1988, says her husband is "absolutely wonderful. There's really a role reversal. He goes to the store on Saturday mornings. He's wonderfully supportive."

Ed also does the grocery shopping. In fact, he's better at it than I am. He practically grew up in a grocery store, because that's the business his father was in. He has always done the shopping, even before I was elected. Ed says, "I always liked it because I know the tricks of the trade, why certain things are on display. . . ." Since I've always been a working mom, things really haven't changed that much around the house—everyone needs to pitch in and help.

Nita's three children are grown, and Steve Lowey is quick to point out that in the early years Nita stayed home to raise the kids. "She was out of the work force from 1962 to 1975. . . . I was trying to build a law practice. I didn't have time to share the chores."

That arrangement was a successful one for Nita and Steve, who figured out how to make it work within the context of the times. But nowadays, with women making great strides to increase their numbers and effectiveness in competitive fields like law and medicine, the old way just doesn't work. It's hard to make partner in a law firm and take thirteen years off to raise the kids.

Ed was raised in an environment where women devoted themselves completely to their families, with no thought to their own needs. "I was brought up where my mother would shine my father's shoes; she would do all those things," Ed recalls, shaking his head at a memory that is so foreign to today's standards. But even though Ed was raised in this atmosphere, he has always encouraged me to do whatever it is I want to do. And he understands the demands on my time and energy because he has been through this exact experience. And because I've been away in Washington so much, he's become even closer to the kids. "I appreciate the family a lot more, this experience has given me that," he notes. "When you're caught up in this pressure cooker, you don't have time; your time is focused on your legislative work. No matter how you intellectually put it in your mind—I've got to spend time with my kids; I've got to do this—how can you when you're locked in here with the votes? The problem with politics is the time that's wasted. You're sitting there waiting to vote. It's a very, very time-consuming process. So that's the hard part; that's the price you pay. So I do some of the chores, but they're no different from what I did before, and I think it gives me a chance, a way of doing things with the family that I may not have had the opportunity to. That part I think is good."

Deborah Pryce and her husband, Randy, adopted Caroline and it was love at first sight when Caroline arrived (on Labor Day!). But both parents knew right from the start that Deborah couldn't handle the daily responsibilities of parenting single-handedly. And Randy didn't want it that way, either. "I mean, she had him wrapped in twenty-four hours; it was just a love affair between Dad and daughter and it has been ever since. He's a truly devoted father and a very hands-on parent—the diapers, the spit-up, nothing has ever bothered Randy."

But even with a great husband and a supportive nearby family network of three sisters and a brother, Deborah knows that there are some things that both she and Caroline are missing out on and there is no way to remedy the situation and still do her job. "I couldn't recommend serving in Congress very strongly to women with small children. And it's no-win. If you stayed in Washington all the time, you'd be criticized, and then you get criticized when you're at home. People say, 'Why aren't you back doing your job?' I think, Isn't my job to be close to you and understand what your needs are and how you want me to represent you?"

Members encourage their families to come to Washington for visits, but it's tricky to work out the logistics of seeing them as we race from vote to committee hearings to meetings with constituents. "I had always said from the beginning that I wanted to have a real family presence both in Washington and in my district," says Deborah. "It's been a lot easier in the district. Spouses are not allowed on the [House] floor and you can't bring your children on the floor if they're under ten or something like that. A lot of people don't even know you have kids."

It's hard to believe this is the same woman whom a male colleague describes as a woman "with a hard veneer." But she's right: Most of our colleagues aren't aware that she's got a little girl back home. Somehow, when you're on the floor debating the BTU energy tax, the subject of motherhood doesn't come up, and we're not always so eager to bring it up.

Privacy is another thing that we have to sacrifice. Deborah realized just how public she had become a few months into the job when she tried to make an appointment back home with her regular hairdresser. He was all booked up and wouldn't be able to fit her in while she was home that week. When she returned to Washington, she decided she had to do something and found someone to cut her hair just that one time. The next day, she was on the House floor doing a one-minute. "Well, my hairdresser happened to see it. And he called my office and said, 'Someone else cut her hair; they butchered her. Tell her to stay off TV until I can fix it!' " Deborah laughs about it now, absently touching her short blond locks. "I can't do anything without the whole world knowing about it. Here's my hairdresser giving me hell because I let someone else cut my hair because I couldn't get in to see him." And then when he does get her in the chair, she's a captive audience while he lobbies her on any number of issues as he holds the scissors to her head.

In fact, most of our constituents don't hesitate to lobby us wherever they find us. Of course, that's our job, but sometimes we need a breather, at least while we're eating. Deborah recalls a recent family dinner at a restaurant back in Ohio. "I was home having dinner with my sister and her kids and my husband and Caroline. I was trying to take Caroline to the salad bar, and trying to take a three-year-old to a salad bar, you know how hard that is to begin with. And here's someone talking about housing issues. It never stops. I was in church on Sunday and those folks are so dear, but . . ." Deborah shrugs, pausing. "You've always got to be on. 'How can I get appointed to this commission?' 'Would you like to come speak to our group sometime?' Every issue under the sun. It's just hard to remain normal anymore, real hard. And I try so hard because of my family; I don't want to always be in the spotlight."

The other side of this is that the women who do have children are often portrayed in a light that their male counterparts with young children are not, their lifestyle decisions scrutinized. Freshman Leslie Byrne notes, "The first thing that people want to ask you is who takes care of the kids. I watched what the press did to Cynthia McKinney, a single mother; CNN and the press did a hit on her. It was a good story and heartfelt and all that kind of stuff, but it showed her wrenching herself from her son all the time, and it was almost marginalizing what she was here for. The story really centered around this poor mom and this kid being broken up instead of on what she was here to do."

This sentiment isn't held exclusively by the press. Some of our colleagues raise the same issue. Steny Hoyer has been serving here since 1982 and has three daughters. Steny, as chairman of the Democratic caucus, is part of the leadership and is considered by most women here to be one of the men more sympathetic to women's issues. "Mothers do have a special relationship with children—particularly the younger the child, the more special the nurturing relationship is. Younger fathers, however, are different from fathers of my generation. In my generation, you just didn't have a consciousness that you stayed home and helped with child rearing. That wasn't your role. The husband's role was to go out and earn money and the wife's role was to stay home and care for the children."

But things have changed and women feel the need to be here as well as to be at home. And families have changed. The Ozzie and Harriet family image of the past is just that: an image of the past. In reality, only about 7 percent of American families have that makeup: Mom stays home, Dad goes to work, and the 2.8 kids go to school. And because single and divorced women these days are often the heads of households, women legislators are usually more tuned in to exactly what these changing demographics mean and how government needs to start understanding as well. The Year of the Woman was all about us recognizing a void in our government that can be filled only by a new perspective, a perspective that until now was told it should be elsewhere.

"It was hard for people like Pat Schroeder to come in," says a former staffer at the Women's Campaign Fund. "She had to fight battles by herself; people would ask her how dare she come to Congress when she had two little kids at home . . . so she's been through a lot more than most of these women will ever see."

Eva Clayton, whose four kids are all grown, points out that even if society has become more accepting of working moms, it's still hard to leave small children at home. "It is tough. You really do have to have a situation at home where you know they're getting the love and attention in your absence. But it's still tough, even when you know they have the best care, because it's not you. You feel neglected; the kid may feel okay. But you feel, Hey, I'm missing something. I'm missing the opportunity to love and to care and to be there."

It's tough on fathers as well. Thirty-eight-year-old Sam Coppersmith has three little kids. Until Sam ran for Congress, he and his wife, Beth, both lawyers, worked together to keep the household running smoothly. "The nice thing is, Beth and I have a relationship where we don't measure who's doing what. We were able to work it so that each of us kind of specialized in areas that we found easier. . . . She does thousands of things better, but I'm a better dishwasher. I give better baths, more thorough; I actually do between the toes and behind the ears."

Sam misses his kids and talks to them every day on the phone while he's in Washington, and they've been out to visit a few weekends. But for the most part, it's like being a bachelor again. "When I'm here, I stay in this two-bedroom apartment. It's a dump, but it's *my* dump. It's big enough that everybody can stay there, because there's a couch that's a sofa bed. So for the first six months, I shared it with my administrative assistant until he moved his family here and rented a house, but that meant for the first six months I was sleeping in a bunk bed. At least nobody was on the top bunk; I had the bottom bunk to myself."

Sam seems a little more sure than many of the women I talked to about whether ultimately it's worth it. "It's such a demanding job, it asks so much of you and, worse, demands so much of your family that if you aren't enjoying it, if you aren't convinced that you're making a difference in some way, then there's no point in putting yourself or, more importantly, your family through it. So I still think I'm making a difference. . . . I don't feel guilty, because the balance is there. Beth jokes with me that when I was in private practice, it would take me twenty minutes to push myself out of bed, and then I got this job and I'm in the shower before she's woken up, and she's the morning person. She can't understand what's going on," he says, laughing, but then grows serious for a moment. "And I'm not going to ask my family to make this kind of sacrifice for a long period of time."

■ ■ ■

The pace is still tough for the lucky few who live in the greater Washington metropolitan area. In fact, sometimes it makes it harder. Leslie Byrne has an easy commute from nearby Annandale, Virginia, but then, of course, so do her constituents. "One congressperson will have one school group a week and I will have five a day," she says. "That kind of differential is because you're close in. You're a local call, and people come in off the street all the time."

The schedule in general drives her crazy, like the rest of us. "I call it being nibbled to death by ducks. You just feel pulled in so many directions and it's not the legislative component. In the general assembly, we dealt with two thousand bills in two months. This is downright leisurely compared to that. It's just that you represent six hundred thousand people and on some days you feel like all of them want to get to you."

It's really hard to organize our calendars because we get the "Vote Schedule" for the month sometimes after we're already into that month. It's impossible to schedule things in advance with any degree of certainty, particularly events back home that your constituents have asked you to attend. The schedule is put together with all the secrecy of Oz, and we lowly freshmen certainly have no sense of who's behind the curtain at the controls. As a result, our scheduling destinies are designed without any consultation with us. "There has to be greater understanding that we would be better members of Congress if we could also have some semblance of family life," says Lynn Schenk. "When there are complaints about Congress members being 'out of touch,' it comes in large measure from the artificial environment in which members conduct their daily business. It is like a never-ending campaign—that's not real life!"

It could just break your heart sometimes. One woman who commutes back and forth to a western state got up at a freshman class meeting early on. We were talking about trying to get the powers that be to change the calendars and make the House schedule more family-friendly. One idea was to be three weeks on and one week off. That way, the weeks would be longer but then so would the breaks, and we would have longer uninterrupted blocks of time to spend back in our districts with our families and our constituents. But for those with the longer commutes, it would make going home for two-day weekends virtually impossible. That particular congresswoman stood up and very movingly declared, "I feel like my kids are becoming orphans."

Anna Eshoo is another of my colleagues who agrees that the scheduling of Congress could use some rethinking. "Right now, there are members who don't want to have Monday as a fully functional day because they want to be en route to the capital."

But the problem is that already there aren't enough days in the week to afford all the hearings. "We have so many things that take place where we're called to vote while we're having a key committee hearing," says Anna. "You can have the Secretary of Health and Human Services or the Secretary of the Interior sitting there testifying before you and the [vote] bell goes off and the whole hearing room clears out. Then by the time you get back, you have to go on to the next one. So I think we could do a better job in the reshaping of it and hopefully it can be more family-friendly. But it's a difficult thing; it's like trying to put socks on an octopus."

Anna was on the San Mateo County Board of Supervisors from 1983–1993, so she's got plenty of experience working with other people trying to get things done in a timely fashion. But she notes that it's going to be awfully tricky coming up with a compromise that makes everybody happy. "Because while that might work for me, there're some younger members who say that that schedule would be a disaster in terms of their families.

"It's up to the members to shape and design a schedule for themselves that will accentuate the most important things, because there's always going to be competition for the time. You have to be a good manager of time. . . . And I think you have to stay very focused. Ask yourself, What is it in two years I want to get done? What is it as an individual member in my district, the Fourteenth District of California, that I want to get done? And every day, you have to remind yourself of what that is."

Our class is trying very hard to get the rest of our colleagues to consider alternatives to make this place more family-friendly as well as better organized. In addition to alleviating some of the pressures on our personal lives, Congress would run more smoothly. As Anna mentioned, committee hearings are often scheduled simultaneously, which means you have to send a staffer to one meeting to take notes while you go to the other.

"Here in Washington, we don't keep up with changing times

and changing requirements," says Lucille Roybal-Allard. "Some things may have worked a long time ago, and now I think they work to the advantage of those who have been here for a long period of time by keeping the new people off balance all the time. I think there needs to be a change. There is a willingness on the part of the leadership to listen and to try to make some changes and some accommodations, because there's no justification for all the confusion. I really believe new people coming in should not try right away to change everything, because new members don't have the perspective of having worked within a particular system. But in the months that I've been here, I've yet to find any justification for the lack of scheduling."

Blanche Lambert echoes Lucille's observations. "People have always said knowledge is a dangerous thing . . . if you have too much knowledge you can be dangerous, so maybe they want to keep us in the dark."

Lucille notes that besides not being family-oriented, the legislative schedule isn't constituent-oriented. "People fly in, particularly from places like California, expecting that they have a scheduled appointment they made weeks in advance—then they get here and they don't see me. And believe me, I hear about it when I get home. It isn't fair to constituents, and it isn't fair to have people fly in to testify and then for us to get up and leave because of a floor vote."

Whether we're trying to carpool our daughters to skating lessons and our sons to Cub Scout meetings or we're trying to see our constituents and to vote simultaneously, it's all a matter of having to split ourselves into two somehow. Lucille sees parallels between the juggling we have done as mothers and the juggling we do here. "But at least when you're being a mom, with all the different things that you have to do, you know that you pick up Johnny at such and such a time and Mary at another time," she says. "As a mom, you can sometimes rearrange things and say, 'No, I have to pick my son up at that time.' Here, you don't have that control at all. So what I've decided to do is just start deciding what my priorities are. I will try to honor my commitments as much as I can. If somebody has come from out of town to see me, I will still go to my committee meeting, but I will have the person brought to the side room off the committee hearing room."

Just then, as Lucille is speaking, her beeper from inside her jacket starts blaring, a rude reminder that there are only ten minutes left to vote. "I swore when I first got here that I wouldn't get one of these," she says, fumbling inside her jacket to turn it off. "But then I almost missed a vote because I was in a room that didn't have the bells and somebody said, 'Aren't you supposed to be voting?' I had five minutes and I ran like crazy."

Running in heels should be a new Olympic sport. I always think of those silly shoe commercials that have a women's basketball team playing in pumps. They should shoot a team of congresswomen sprinting over to the Capitol to vote. I walked around with a pedometer for a week and found that I averaged about five miles a day—in heels, on marble floors. And that was on moderate-to-heavy voting days. Every vote is about a quarter of a mile each way when you are in an office as far from the floor as mine. One senior member said her foot grew an entire size from walking so much her first term.

"I came back from voting and told my staff, 'Order me the beeper,' " says Lucile. "It's a horrible feeling—being afraid that you're missing a vote—if you don't carry it with you all the time, you feel like you're missing something." There's no question around here for whom the bells toll. The answer is always "They toll for thee."

For those who don't have children or husbands waiting for them back in their home districts, it is easier to juggle the various parts of their lives. Jennifer Dunn is divorced and has two grown sons. "They're both in college and so that makes it easier for me. I only have one focus really and that's the work I do in the Congress. So timewise, I can take on a lot more, and I *have* taken on a lot more than almost anybody else just because of that."

But even someone with few demands from her personal life can't be in two places at one time. "I had five breakfasts scheduled the other day," says Jennifer. "At one of them, I had to give a speech, so I was locked into that, but the other four were things I should have attended. If they could all do business more than three days a week, it would help us a lot."

Jennifer flies back to the Northwest every other weekend. The time on the plane is very valuable to her because it gives her five uninterrupted hours to catch up on paperwork. And she's no stranger to juggling, having spent much of her career being pulled in different directions. "It is a lot like being a single mother, where you try to go to two soccer games at the same hour on Saturday morning; I've done a lot of that. You learn how to prioritize; you don't always like it, because here in the Congress everything you're asked to do is of great importance. So you're choosing between things that are most important and more important, and it's very tough."

But Jennifer doesn't have a hard time saying no; she's very disciplined and smart about it. "I can do things quickly. The receptions that you're invited to, for example. One of my baselines is that they must involve somebody from my district, number one. I haven't had a lot of trouble prioritizing. But you do have to get rid of the guilt that comes from wanting to be very conscientious and wanting to be everyplace, because you can't be everyplace. Getting rid of the guilt—I learned that early."

Getting rid of the guilt is one thing, but loneliness is a little tougher to outrun, Jennifer admits. "It's a very lonely city. I don't have family here with me. And I'm not married. So you miss that. On the other hand, if you were, your schedule would be even more difficult, I think. But you need the personalness. And it's hard to find personalness here. That's the one thing that I have felt that I've shorted in my life, and I think it could get to be a problem. But I think most of the men are in families here. Men have their wives do a lot of things. I'm doing double-duty. Any entertaining I do, *I* do, plus all my congressional work."

Jennifer gets a lot of her emotional sustenance by telephone from her two sons. "They're the most important thing to me in my personal life, those two boys, my support group. I talk to them a lot, and they're so proud of me. That makes it worthwhile."

The women whose children are grown definitely seem to be

the ones who are least conflicted about being away from home. But Pat Danner, who has four grown children and seven grandchildren, still finds it painful at times to be away and is distracted by the all-consuming nature of her job. She says it really came to her attention on April 9, when two days after her daughter's birthday she realized that she had missed it. "I had gotten her gift and all those good things, but I had forgotten to telephone her and wish her a happy birthday. And when I did remember, I said that despite what her birthday certificate might show or anyone might have ever told her, she was born on April 9, not April 7!"

Pat has found that her children can be quite resourceful when they want to spend time with their mom. "I was asked to make a contribution for our public television station's auction in Kansas City. So my contribution was to take a couple, a Mr. and Mrs. John Marshall, to lunch at the House dining room in Washington. I was then notified that they would prefer to have lunch in Kansas City.

"I thought, Uh-oh! I've gotten myself set up with no telling who for an hour-and-a-half luncheon and I don't know how this is going to turn out." So Pat went to the lunch, arranging for it to be at a particular restaurant she liked. When she spotted her son, daughter, and daughter-in-law, she was happy to see them but said, "I can't spend any time with you because I'm having lunch with some constituents of mine who have bought this auction luncheon." At this point, her children all started laughing and unrolled a drawing made by the TV station's artist of "Lunch with Pat Danner," and it was clear that they were the "constituents" who had shelled out fifty bucks to have lunch with their congresswoman.

"I was just speechless. There they sat, just laughing. They had a huge box of flowers for me," says Pat, shaking her head in disbelief at the memory. "The restaurant people knew about it; the people in the surrounding booths knew about it."

When Pat's in Washington, though, she gets a chance to be mother hen once again and she speaks of her staff with pride. Of her eight Washington staff members, seven are under thirty. "So I kind of call them my 'kids.' One Sunday, I phoned in here and six of my eight were here working, helping us to get caught up."

Sometimes it's just the little things in life that get short shrift when trying to keep to our schedules. One day, I went to speak to a third-grade class. It's one of my favorite parts of the job, the time I spend actually out in my district meeting people, especially the kids. So one day I was at a school and the kids were asking me all kinds of great questions: "Where did you go on your honeymoon?" "Do you know my mom?" "What are the names of your children?" "How much do you make each day?"

Then one of the little boys asked, "What happens if somebody in Congress does something bad?"

"If it's really bad," I said carefully, trying to be as forthright as possible, "you go to prison."

"When you go to prison—" he continued.

"Do you think we could modify that to *if*?" I interrupted.

Everyone laughed and I thought it was smooth sailing from there. Then this other little boy in the back of the room raised his hand and pointed to my sleeve. He said earnestly, "Why do you have price tags on your clothes?" I looked down and realized that in my haste when getting dressed that morning, I had neglected to cut off the price tag from my sleeve.

And then there's toothpaste. One day, a bunch of the freshmen women were sitting around between votes talking about how frantic their new lives were, how nomadic their existences had become, traveling between home districts and the nation's capital. "You never have time to go to the drugstore to buy anything, so we go at home, which is when you at least have an hour or two to go to the drugstore," observes Tillie Fowler. "So we come back with our suitcases filled with toilet paper, toothpaste, Kleenex—you know, all those basics. A congressman who sits a lot on the plane with me calls me 'the bag lady' because I always have shopping bags. Here there are no places open before eight or after eleven or twelve, so you never can do those basic-living types of things, so you just have to carry them across the country."

Tillie laughs, looking a little sheepish. "I thought I was the only one doing that, you know. Then you find out the others are doing the same thing, so at least you feel better about it."

It's the schizophrenia between your Washington persona and your back-home persona that begins to get to you. You begin to feel as if you're living a sort of *Three Faces of Eve* existence. "There are some things that I have to do that no one can do for me, or no one should do for me," says Lynn Schenk. "I've got to do my own banking. I've got to put gas in my car at home. I've got to do the grocery shopping when I'm home and my recycling, because we don't have curbside recycling in my neighborhood. So those routine chores I used to do throughout the week now have to be done amid a full weekend schedule of activities related to my congressional responsibilities. My constituents expect me to be at community events, giving speeches, making appearances, meeting with them in my district office."

The two-year length of our terms can also be a frustrating component to our experience. Many people feel that by the time you get your sea legs, the ship has returned to port. It's just plain hard to figure it all out and start to be effective while knowing in the back of your mind that you may be leaving in two years.

"It is a little frustrating simply because there's so much to do," notes Blanche Lambert. "And you can spend the first four months getting up to speed, so at that six-month mark it's time to reflect and say, 'Okay, where am I heading and what are the goals that I want to reach?' You come with certain goals and objectives but also think, It's taken me six months to get settled in, and now my mail is up to speed and everything else and I can really focus on things. . . ." And then it's time to fight to hold on to your seat, which takes attention away from your job. Blanche's view of two-year terms has definitely evolved since she got in office.

"People will ask, 'Have you changed your mind about line-item veto?' 'Have you changed your mind about this, that, and the other?' People want to know if you've changed your mind about issues.

"I'm a pretty traditional person, and you know I believe very much in the Constitution and I believe very much that the forefathers really labored over putting it together, making sure that it was strong enough to last but flexible enough to compromise and all that. And I think to myself when you talk about having to amend the Constitution, That's a pretty drastic measure. The only thing I've changed my mind on basically is when I look at the two-year term for a legislator," continues Blanche in her wonderful Arkansas drawl. "In today's terms, it doesn't fit the same way it did two hundred years ago. And the thing I attribute that to the most is the modernization of transportation. You know, those guys two hundred years ago, they loaded up their wagons and they came up here and they stayed three months. And their sole focus was on what they were doing."

As dedicated as Blanche is, it's impossible for her to load up a wagon and camp out here, even though that might be the only way to get out from underneath the perpetual pile of work on her desk. But that's not going to happen. "The thing is, people in my district know I can get home in an hour and forty minutes and they expect me to." And what's more, she wants to be there. Her district is huge, twenty-five counties to be exact. She spends a lot of her time when she's home just driving from one county to the next. And she's got another reason it's important to go back home. She recently got married, just last August, only eight months into her new job. Her husband, an obstetrics and gynecology physician with a subspecialty in reproductive endocrinology, stays home in the South, where he teaches, does research, and maintains his practice. "At a minimum, I'm home three weekends a month," she says. "It didn't make sense for him to move up here."

Before they got married, she explained to her father that she and her fiancé had worked out the mechanics of a commuter marriage. "I said, 'We worked this out.' He said, 'Well, sounds like you worked it all out. Now will it work?' "

Blanche shrugs. If it doesn't work exactly as planned, they'll just reconfigure the plan. "You've got to be flexible. . . . I think for my generation that's a little bit easier because we've had to be. Whereas I know for my parents, who have lived in the same house for the last thirty-three years . . . you know that that kind of flexibility is a different obstacle for them than it is for me."

Clearly, we've got a lot of work ahead of us to make this institution more in concert with our roles as wives and mothers and daughters. The ramifications of this kind of institutional reform carry a greater resonance in female members' lives, I'll grant you that. But the men could benefit from a new zeitgeist as well. Conventional wisdom isn't all that conventional anymore, and it certainly isn't wise.

There is, of course, a broader significance here. If the nation's legislators really begin to take women's lives into account, perhaps that will affect society's regard for women as a whole.

"It has to change in some regard," says Lynn Schenk, "I don't think the women yet have the power to change it because we've only been a group for a short time and in that time we've been pulled in many different directions. We're here to represent our constituents; we're here to be members of Congress, not just women members of Congress. But added to that is a greater responsibility to make this place better for men and women in the future. And you see the younger men who are used to working with women, who have been raised by feminist mothers or married to women who have careers—they want some of the same things. So it's not just for the women; it's for future generations of Congress."

■ ■ ■

When I was trying to decide whether or not to run for Congress, I thought long and hard about how tough it would be on my family, how there would have to be a lot of logistical maneuvering and jury-rigging to make the household run smoothly if I was going to be away so much of the time. I could have convinced myself that it would have been too rough, that things would go to hell in a handbasket if I wasn't around to micromanage it all. I could have focused on the little things, that maybe clothes wouldn't get to the dry cleaners on a regular basis or that the newspapers would stack up in messy piles or that we'd run out of cereal and no one would remember to go to the store. But what it came down to was that this was a decision the whole family was in on, and they were behind me. I knew that it was going to be toughest on Ed, that the tables would be turned and he would be the one left at home to worry about the daily machinations that every home goes through, while I would be the one running off to Washington to try to make a difference. As Lynn Schenk put it, "If the refrigerator's compressor goes out, there's nobody for my husband to rely on, for us to share the load. He has to be the one to be home to let the repairman in."

Ed knew that if I decided to run that ultimately I wouldn't feel I needed his permission. But there was something I did need from him, and that was his blessing. And that he gave me, with grace and with love, as did my terrific children. Recently, when I was back home in the district, I spoke at a synagogue and the audience wrote down questions on cards, which were then collected and given to a moderator. The moderator chose which questions I would answer and one of the ones he rejected was "Don't you think you're neglecting your children?"

I told the moderator that I wanted to answer that question. I thought it was an important issue to address. My response was that I didn't think I was neglecting my children. In fact, I think they're very well-adjusted children and anyone who had ever met them could attest to that. The children know they have been given experiences and opportunities that other children have not been given. My fifteen-year-old son, Marc, had recently been interviewed for a profile about me that ran in the Jewish quarterly *Inside.* "She's been my mom long enough so that she knows what I need, and she knows what she needs," the story quoted him as saying. The thing I thought about afterward was that I would have liked to ask the person whether he or she would have asked the same question if I were a congressman. I think the answer would have been no.

Tillie Fowler says her two teenage daughters were completely supportive, that they really wanted her to run for office. Her husband, as well, was 100 percent behind her. "You've got to be a very secure man to be supportive and happy about your wife being this visible, this active," she says. "There are a lot of men who, while they support women doing these things, feel differently when it's their wife. So I'm very fortunate that my husband has supported me all along."

And like our family, Tillie's sat down and hashed it out. "Before

I ever decided to run, we had a long family discussion, because I would not have run if my family hadn't been behind it. It is too demanding if you don't have a supportive family."

I don't know how many of our male colleagues feel the same way, but I would bet at least some of them do, that to go with a clear conscience you need your family's approval. Because something as public as a decision to run for political office brings with it some incredibly personal consequences. It's hard to make any kind of human relationship work if you're not willing to listen. So I stopped and I listened, and what I heard them say was, "Go for it."

So I got here, and now what remains to be seen is whether it's worth it. "Sure, it's worth it," I tell people when they ask, and I really believe that down to the core of my soul. But I'm a human being, and like everyone else, I have occasional pangs, usually when one of the kids has had a bad day and I wish I was home to try to fix things for him or her.

Anna Eshoo, whose kids are now adults in their mid-twenties, says she's grateful to be serving in Congress at this point in her life. "I think it's very difficult for those who are still raising their families, whether they're men or women, and trying to maintain that. I don't know how they do it, with their spouses and young children. I think it's an enormous burden for them. I don't know how they do it."

When asked whether Anna thinks it's worth it overall, the personal sacrifice, she answers with no hesitation. "I think that our country is worth it, because we're faced with some of the most enormous things that need to be cured, that need to be addressed." Then she smiles wryly, leaning back in her chair, sighing. "I do wish I had a little more quiet time for myself. I've always been very mindful of how precious time is. It's the most precious thing that God gives us, but now I have a renewed appreciation of it."

Deborah Pryce put it poignantly when she said, "I don't know if I've figured out if it's worth it or not. I really want to make it work. I think that what I'm doing now is really important, every bit as important as what I did as a judge. Because I have to be away doesn't mean that I should just chuck it, because I worked hard to get here, and certainly it isn't easy." She sucks in a bit of air and then exhales, thinking over what she's just said. "I think that moms have it worse and they always will, and maybe it will change, but I don't know."

Yet as hard as it is for our kids when we go, I believe they get a lot out of the experience of their mothers being congresswomen. Deborah says, "Every time Caroline hears the news she says, 'Washington! That's where Mommy works!' And when she sees the Capitol she yells, 'Mommy's office!' "

Just behind her, on the windowsill, a photograph shows three-year-old Caroline grinning widely, as though to cheer her mom on. I predict Deborah will decide that it's worth it, and I'd put money on it that when Caroline's old enough to understand, she'll agree.

CHAPTER EIGHT

Shattering the Glass Ceiling: How Far Can We Go?

Figuring how actually to have some influence in this body is a daunting prospect. Very few women have broken through the glass ceiling, but now, as our numbers increase, there is a sense that more and more of us will be tapping at it, creating little imperfections in its smooth, seemingly flawless and impenetrable surface. We look to the senior women, following their lead.

"What I'm mindful of is what they have done," says Anna Eshoo. "Nancy Pelosi—in a Congress serving with a President that was known for foreign policy—was the only member of the House of Representatives really to get into George Bush's face and was enormously successful with her China legislation." Nancy's legislation protected those Chinese students and nationals in the United States whose visas would have otherwise expired, allowing them to stay rather than return to China to face possible government recrimination. "That's an extraordinary accomplishment," says Anna.

"What I would underscore . . . are the advances that they've made on women's health issues. And then the specific role that they played as appropriators . . . chosen to serve on an exclusive committee in the House. That doesn't happen because you wave your bra. They're serious, they know how to do the heavy lifting, and they are trusted by their colleagues and given this gift of having a seat on an exclusive committee."

Nita Lowey is one of those women on the almighty Appropriations Committee whom Anna is referring to, and she is someone I personally look to for guidance. Nita acknowledges that Appropriations is sort of the mother lode of committee appointments and says that may be due in part to the feeling of self-importance among many of the male members on it. When asked whether that feeling is spreading to the women now joining the committee, she thinks about it for a moment before replying. "Only in the sense that it gives you the ability to be more effective because you have the power to persuade and influence the process."

Since her election in 1988, Nita has gradually gained the attention crucial to becoming a prominent and influential member. Completely focused on her work and her agenda, Nita seems oblivious to the admiration she commands from other female members. Yet she has noticed a difference in the way people perceive her since she joined Appropriations. "Generally, they're paying more attention to you, respecting what you have to say," says Nita. "In this institution, politicians understand power, and if you have the ability to affect their pocketbook, it often wins respect."

During the Bush administration, Nita was asked to serve on the Glass Ceiling Commission, which was sponsored by the Department of Labor and chaired by then Labor Secretary Lynn Martin. The glass ceiling phenomenon going on across America in all different sectors was a topic of concern to Nita, something she thought very worthy of her attention.

One day, Nita met someone wearing an interesting-looking piece of jewelry, a pin fashioned from irregular shapes of fused glass, trimmed in gold. "I said, 'I have to have it,' " Nita recalls. Not only did she have to have it but she bought dozens of them for her colleagues, her staffers, and other women among the steady stream of visitors flowing through her office.

Soon the pins were turning up all over the place, women wearing them on their lapels like badges of honor. It turned out that they were the brainchild of California entrepreneur Susan Harris, who had recently left the corporate world. One day, she attended a town meeting and listened to Betty Friedan speak about shattering the glass ceiling. She conceived of the pin right then, imagining what it would look like and how it could act as a small talisman of hope and inspiration for women. But the idea remained just that until months later. Watching the Anita Hill–Clarence Thomas hearings on television, Susan was overcome with emotion and felt stirred to action. She remembered her idea for the pin and began to consider how she might go about making it a reality. About that same time, as fate would have it, Susan met a Laguna Beach artist who worked with glass and she commissioned her to execute the idea. "For me, it represents women being able to choose," says Susan, "whether it be politics, staying home, or the corporate world. It's not just about rising to the top of a male-dominated entity."

One thing led to another, and women all over the country, including Anita Hill, soon began sporting the pins. Susan met Dianne Feinstein early on in her California Senate race and offered the candidate her pins at a reduced rate so that Dianne, in turn, could sell them to supporters at fund-raisers. Dianne took her up on the offer, using the pins to raise thousands of dollars for her Senate race.

The pin has become a symbol of membership in a very *inclusive* club of sorts—women with the common goal of altering the exclusivity of traditionally male enclaves. Where better to increase membership than here in Congress, which is pitifully behind the rest of the country in removing that ceiling?

Nita points out that the lack of females among the leadership is in part a result of the fact that so few women have been here for any length of time. "So many rules of the House are based on seniority, so there are fewer women in leadership because of seniority. That's the prime reason, rather than ability. So then, until the rules evolve and change, it's just going to take longer for women to reach positions of power. But we now have Barbara Kennelly in the leadership, I'm on the Appropriations Committee. Men do understand power. I loved my other committees, Education and Labor and

Merchant Marine and Fisheries, because I was able to work on important pieces of legislation. But I also love Appropriations because, in addition to legislation, you can have important influence on funding decisions, and ultimately that's where the power is."

If you can't master the Capitol Hill game, you won't break through the glass ceiling. "There definitely is a game," says Karan English, nodding her head slowly, knowingly. "I've learned you can't take it personally. I've learned that even if you think you understand the game—and I liken it a little bit to the state legislature, which was sort of like playing checkers—and this is like chess. Well, this is really like three-tiered chess—so not only are you moving in different directions on a horizon but you've got to move up and down three or four levels, too. There are a lot of players and a lot of strategies. And now to start figuring out what they are and whether it matters what they are is the next stage in really being a freshman member—what matters and what doesn't matter."

And what really matters is understanding who's got the leverage and what they do with it and how that may affect what you're trying to accomplish. Without that knowledge, shattering the glass ceiling is just a nice phrase to bandy about. "Being a freshman isn't as much a burden as the lack of knowledge," says Karan. "And I look with relief to a time when I will have acquired some institutional knowledge and experience on things like parliamentary procedure. We've all got these goals, some loftier than others. Those goals are worthless if you can't implement them. Implementation comes with parliamentary procedure, with process, and that is so complex and we're just starting to learn it. In fact, the failure of us to defeat the Hyde Amendment was just that. We were outmaneuvered."

Karan had her own floor show on June 10, 1993. It served as a wake-up call about the way things work around here sometimes. Though painful, it was a learning experience, one she looks back on now with the distance time affords. She was offering her first amendment on the House floor when her Republican colleague Bill Thomas demanded that she explain the amendment. It was to revoke $1.6 million in funds that the House had carried over from 1991 and 1992 and put in the U.S. Treasury.

Some Republicans felt that this amendment was one of three handed to a couple of freshmen Democrats who had been criticized back in their districts for having voted for the President's budget-reconciliation package a few weeks earlier, Bill Thomas among them. Karan became flustered when instead of questioning the merit of the amendment, Thomas went after her personally. Karan didn't know enough parliamentary procedure to head off an attack that *Roll Call* (a Washington-based newspaper that covers Congress) characterized as "cruel."

"He said as a freshman, I have no right running an amendment and how dare I suck up to leadership and beg for some amendment so that I can just make myself look good after I voted for the budget," recalls Karan. "He said, 'This won't help you, and you're in trouble.' "

The little drama continued off the floor when both Karan and Bill Thomas were sent drafts of the *Congressional Record* for editing, as is standard procedure. Because of certain procedural rules, he was the last member to sign off on the revisions before they were returned to the appropriate office. "It was about twelve pages of colloquy and I went over it and did my corrections, and he went over and did his corrections but forgot to hand in one page. It just happened to be the page that had my corrections on it. And so the permanent record won't show the real facts for three years." The permanent bound record, which takes three years to process, reflects all the changes.

Karan filed a complaint with the parliamentarian, stating that the system needed to be revamped to avoid this kind of "mistake" in the future. In return, she received a letter explaining how the "mistake" had occurred and offering assurances that the system had been adjusted to prevent this from happening again. She also received a copy of a memo concerning the oversight.

> Following submission of that Member's revised remarks to the Official Reporters of Debates, another Member on whose time the colloquy occurred and who therefore was entitled to be the last Member to suggest proper revisions,

> obtained the transcript but did not return one page of it to the Official Reporters in a timely fashion, as he was obliged to do. His letter of apology to the revising Member stated that this was the result of staff error in his office. The Official Reporters, not able to contact that Member's office about the missing page due to the lateness of the hour, retranscribed the original unrevised page with the remainder of the transcript and submitted it for printing.

Uh-huh.

"It's a lesson about being a freshman and about being more than prepared. Being prepared isn't enough," stresses Karan. "You have to anticipate everything they're going to throw at you. But it's also learning how not to take it personally. That was a flaw. I was so flabbergasted about what he was saying to me. I was just so amazed that he was attacking me personally, because no one does that. I could hardly believe it. I lost track. Then it took me a long time to get back on track and then by the time I did . . . I remember Patsy Mink—God, she was great. She was the speaker that day and she was chairing the meeting and I looked up at Patsy as I was just struggling—it was probably a matter of thirty seconds, but it felt like about thirty years—to get out the words. My voice was weak and raspy and I was totally humiliated and embarrassed and I looked up at her and she was going like this"—Karan stops to move her hands in an encouraging motion—"just trying to pull the words out of my mouth. Just finish the sentence, Karan, I could just hear her thinking. Just get through it." And Karan did, because Patsy Mink is one of her colleagues for whom she has special regard. "She doesn't know how much she helped me get through it because I was just looking at her. I have very high regard for her; she's an incredibly bright woman, and so principled and so much believes in women. And to have her up there helped me get through probably the most difficult time I've had since I've been here."

Actually, she owes Bill Thomas, too—for giving her a crash course in how to play the game. Not that she wants to play it his way; it's clearly distasteful to her. And she's not going to waste any time nailing him. It's not her style. "I'm friendly to everybody. He owes me an apology. I may or may not accept, depending on how good it is and how long it takes him. But you know, there's one thing I've learned in politics and this is my thirteenth year: 'Don't forget.' I promise you I won't forget that."

Karan often looks to particular colleagues who have distinguished themselves, as well as staffers who have been on Capitol Hill much longer than she. "You start to know who has some parallel philosophies." She points to the ubiquitous television tuned in to C-SPAN. "And you watch a lot of this kind of stuff and you can really draw some conclusions," she says. "Just from what we know is reality and what is perception. Heck, a lot of people on there I don't trust as far as I can throw them. There is some incredibly fraudulent information coming out of that TV set. And I don't trust the people who do that. Because they have other motives and they don't care about what they're doing to hurt the country or what kind of effect they have on the country. Very greedy and cruel people. So it's very easy to narrow down your list of possible role models after watching C-SPAN for a little while," she says wryly.

Barbara Kennelly's position as chief deputy whip, the sixth-highest person in the leadership, is a start, but it is simply not enough. No one should mistakenly believe we will be lulled into accepting this state of affairs. And Barbara is the first to tell you this. "I'm the beginning," she says. "And as you know, I was appointed. I think you're going to see the glass ceiling broken soon as far as elected positions. It's interesting . . . we used to have a position called secretary of the caucus and that just automatically went to a woman. And then there was a move to change it to be called the vice-chair, and I was against that. I felt that the minute you called it vice-chair . . ." Barbara trailed off. I can finish her thought, though. The minute you call it vice-chair and not secretary, the men will want it. "Mary Rose Oakar ran a very tough race for that chairmanship and she lost it; I knew that was going to happen. But today, I wouldn't have opposed it, because I think we've reached that critical mass of number where a woman will be in leadership. I served a number of years when there were nineteen women, and I think we've reached a critical mass now. We certainly want more women, but this bump up to forty-eight is meaningful."

Harriett Woods, president of the National Women's Political Caucus, one of the major fund-raising organizations for women candidates, agrees that we've gone from "tokenism to—not a critical mass yet, but an ability to leverage their individual votes because of their number, their desire to work together. And there's a huge difference between five new women and twenty-four new women. So even if we're only eleven percent, there is a support system that has reinforced this risk taking they were already doing."

While the sense of tokenism was diminished with the Year of the Woman, it is still something that we need to be aware of. It still feels, at times, as though some in the leadership were actually thinking, Okay, we need a woman on this committee. If we put one on here, that'll keep 'em quiet. It's very discouraging. "I see women who have been here for a number of years still not fully on the inside," observes Lynn Schenk. "Yes, they have committee assignments, but I don't believe that they are sitting in the inner sanctum making some of the decisions that need to be made around here."

So we are constantly fighting against being treated like the 11 percent that we are within the Congress, rather than the 52 percent of the population that we represent of the nation. We've got to redefine what the men have thought of as "family" and "women's" issues. We need to remind the male members that these issues are directly related to the women in their lives.

"That's right," Hillary Clinton says, nodding her head in agreement while we talked. "The more unified your voices can be, the more likely you will make an impression. I see it happening. As hard as it may be to believe now, I see a greater sensitivity to many of these issues than just a year ago."

When I ask Hillary for an example of this, she says, "The way the leadership talk now about issues and the way committee members talk about the women on their committee is different. We are heading in the right direction. Even though the number of women in the Senate is still small, the women are respected by their colleagues and are beginning to make a difference."

Pat Schroeder, as chairman of the Research and Technology Subcommittee (part of the Armed Services Committee), has also risen to a position of power. But shattering the glass ceiling has been particularly problematic for Pat because she turned some of her colleagues off with her persistence. They didn't always want to hear what she was saying, even if it happened to be the truth. They wrote her off as strident because it was easier than switching their focus to devote time and energy to "female" issues like family leave and sexual harassment. But now that her issues have become mainstream, her detractors can no longer attempt to write her off as an angry, ineffectual feminist.

Elizabeth Furse, who also sits on the Research and Technology Subcommittee, has had a chance to observe Pat firsthand and gives her a lot of credit for having the courage of her convictions and not worrying about winning popularity contests. "A lot of people say, 'Well, it's how you get on with your colleagues and all that, and you don't want to be a thorn in their sides because . . . it's never going to advance the issues and there's going to be a problem.' "

Thorn or no thorn, Pat made it to subcommittee chairman and Elizabeth believes that being one of a handful of female subcommittee chairs has got to be tough going at times. "I think it's incredibly hard," notes Elizabeth. "I bet you she has to fight twice as hard as any other subcommittee chair for everything she gets, working as she is in that male world of the military. I'm sure they resist her, they go around her, they smile and they think they can outfox her."

Elizabeth talks about the precarious balancing act of moving up through the ranks of Congress, which unavoidably involves playing the game in varying degrees yet somehow staying pure. "In some ways, that is the hardest thing of all. That's why a person like Ron Dellums is so amazing. You know, because he does still get to the issues that he was talking about twenty-five years ago and it's not academic. You have to stay that way. And it can be a very uncomfortable thing. People don't like to be around somebody who always keeps going on." Elizabeth hastens to add that she is not referring to Ron Dellums in this instance, but herself. "I know myself, sometimes my children roll their eyes and say, 'Oh Mother, just drop it now.' You know, they're tired of hearing me talk."

The perception of power is a fascinating thing. "You know, it's always very difficult to ascribe behaviors to things like gender or race or whatever," says Karen Shepherd. "It's obviously a factor and it's also very hard to separate it out from other things. There is an inside power network here. And if you're not in it, you're not in it. And if you are in it, you are in it. And the way that Congress is organized means that the longer you've been here, the more likely you are to be in it. Most women haven't been here a long time, although the women who have are not in it. Pat Schroeder is a subcommittee chair and is powerful there, but I'm not sure she's in the 'inner circle' of committee chairmen, for example, and she's been here since 1972.

"All the women who are influential with leadership have been and are strong advocates for women. Louise Slaughter is certainly an advocate and she is on the powerful Rules Committee. Although again, I know she doesn't feel like she's in the inner circle there. And Barbara Kennelly is certainly an advocate and she is the chief deputy whip and on Ways and Means. Those are the two women who I think are beginning to work inside the network. The rest don't seem to be allowed."

Karen thinks that Barbara Kennelly has definitely broken through the glass ceiling, that she could potentially be Speaker of the House, and that there is hope for others following in her footsteps. "I think Nita Lowey can do it. I think Pat Schroeder may have a better chance at doing it now that so many women are here. She's got the seniority and now we can all help."

Steny Hoyer agrees that while it is slow, there is progress being made. "I think there is a glass ceiling—it's being broken. I mean, clearly, conceptually, in what has been an all-male institution, among males who perceive males to be the leaders and females who perceive the males to be leaders. You know, we sometimes believe that women all of a sudden back in the 1950s or the 1960s decided women ought to be leaders. In fact, they didn't and the polls show they didn't. However, both men and women are becoming more comfortable with women as leaders. You have a woman prime minister in Canada; you have a woman prime minister in Turkey. . . . You had women prime ministers in India and Israel. You've had women leaders all over the world. Really, the United States, in some respects, is late to that. However, Hillary Clinton would not have been accepted thirty years ago in the role she now plays. It's still controversial in some respects, but it's accepted and admired in most respects. In addition, it took a long time for women to obtain the positions where they then were perceived by others to be ready for the next step. And I think you've got women just starting to do that."

Steny believes that being able to work well and comfortably with men is crucial, but women who are able to do so sometimes experience a backlash effect. "In many respects, women who can deal with men are resented by other women—Gerry Ferraro, for instance. There were some women who believed that Gerry Ferraro was not feminist enough, was too much one of the boys, was too much perceived by the men as a 'girl.' The fact of the matter is, if you want to be a successful politician, you better darn well be able to deal with both sexes, all races, and different philosophies, because that's where you find people. We're on to a next generation."

And that next generation is the freshmen women of 1992, whom Harriett Woods gives high marks regarding their individuality and commitment to change. "I can't think of one of them who is following the historic past of silence and riding the coattails of senior congressmen. They're all carving a niche for themselves. So breaking the glass ceiling is not just a matter of numbers but a willingness to behave differently.

"The significance of these women is not the normal notion that we're now going to get to the top of the pyramid. Rather, they are shattering the rituals of the club by their problem-solving approach, their desire to cut through the endless ceremonial dances and get something done for their constituents and the country. I wouldn't want to mislead the public that the ceiling is broken when we still have a Congress that is ninety percent male. The only way it was shattered was in the minds of the voters."

"The women who come here want to roll up their sleeves and solve some of these problems that made them want to run for office," says Congresswoman Jolene Unsoeld, a Democrat from Washington State who was elected in 1988. "I can see increasingly the important role women are playing in getting a piece of legislation through or figuring out how we're going to approach it." Midway through her third term, Jolene can see women getting involved in legislation in a different way. "A couple of years ago, we tackled child-care legislation. We really wanted to make it an early childhood/child-care proposal; we wanted a latchkey program; we wanted to solve the problem for mothers and fathers and their young children and the necessity to work. The legislation got bogged down in a turf war among three committee chairs. The women's caucus was at that time much smaller . . . but the Republican and Democratic women felt we had some unique understanding of this issue, so we volunteered our services to our respective leaderships, and we thought we could hammer out a compromise that would be acceptable to the full House. 'Let us help!' we said. Neither leadership took us up on our offer. And they failed. They thought in terms of hierarchy position and turf and not the issue, or who was best prepared or uniquely qualified to speak about it."

It is not a big surprise that a predominantly male body couldn't figure out how to deal with child care. After all, most of them had their child care all figured out: Their wives stayed home and took care of the children.

Things just aren't copacetic yet, and Jolene's not one for pretending. In fact, her exasperation is apparent. "One of our senior women who occupies a position in the leadership is having constantly to remind the leadership—over and over and over again—that they need women and minority representation; that they should not have a sit-down dinner with some head of state or foreign dignitary without a woman who's part of the leadership; there ought to be a woman and a minority to bring the President into the joint session of Congress. It's not in their subconscious yet. The time will come, though. The time will come."

And after that happens, then not only will the President be escorted to the joint session by a woman but the President may actually *be* a woman. When asked to make a prediction as to when she thinks that could happen, Hillary Clinton says thoughtfully, "Sometime in the next fifteen or twenty years."

CHAPTER NINE

218: The Vote

Looking back on the 1993 session, it seems as if everything led up to the great debate over the President's first budget. And in a way, it did.

Budgets—and especially *the* budget, the federal spending plan crafted annually by the White House and revised by the Congress—are at the core of Washington politics. How much money will this country spend and on what? In recent years, an even more crucial question has dominated budget debates: How do we solve the towering problem of the deficit? Since 1983, our federal debt has increased by $2 trillion, 392 billion—that's about $12,000 per second.

President Clinton had promised he would attack that question in new ways, with new solutions. The first major step he took was a two-parter: reprioritizing the budget and introducing a spending-stimulus package to jump-start the economy with new spending on federal contracts and jobs programs. Businesses in certain economic sectors would have more work, hire more workers, and post more profits. Increased tax revenues—a partial cure for the deficit—would result.

The stimulus package started out with $23 billion in spending when it was submitted in February, and it passed in the House but didn't fare so well in the Senate. The Senate was unable to get sixty votes to cut off a Republican-led filibuster, and thus the stimulus package was killed.

I voted against the stimulus package because, while I knew how important it is to create jobs and energize our flat economy, I also felt that we could not afford to add billions of dollars to our deficit. Just prior to my voting against the stimulus package, I had voted against the Budget Resolution—the first vote in the three-vote annual budget process—and became the only freshman Democrat to vote no on both.

As hard as it was to vote against my party, I felt the budget cuts didn't go far enough, especially in our out-of-control entitlements programs. After studying the budget for countless hours and discussing it in hearing after hearing and meeting after meeting, I saw the inescapable facts: The massive entitlements programs, including Social Security, Medicare and Medicaid, welfare, veterans' benefits, federal pensions, agricultural subsidies, and mandatory student loans, were the greatest drains on the budget, and an essential place to restructure, and not just on the margins. The decisions on how to restructure would not be easy or painless, but the future was hanging in the balance. The interest payments on the nation's debt alone were draining $556 million a day from the U.S. Treasury. We were spending irresponsibly and bankrupting our children, and I knew our class had been elected first and foremost to tackle that problem.

But my freshman colleagues and I soon learned just how sacred entitlements are in contemporary politics, so sacred that you don't even talk about them. The constituencies that support keeping entitlements where they are—powerful lobby groups—apply constant pressure on the Hill not to cut their parts of the budget. But I had looked at the real numbers and knew there was no choice but to address this unpopular subject. The President, who understands the budget as well as anyone in Washington, knew this, too. He talked a lot during the campaign about reining in entitlements as a necessary part of the deficit cure, and I knew he was right.

When the President's budget arrived on the Hill, however, it wasn't the document I had imagined and hoped it would be. There were entitlements cuts—in Medicare payments to hospitals, for example—but they were not nearly as deep as they needed to be. And there were new taxes. The people of my district, whom I knew were as concerned about the deficit as I was, were strongly opposed to higher taxes as a deficit solution. They had told me this time and again, movingly and forcefully. The subject came up with retirees I met at shopping centers, with young professionals who spoke to me after chamber of commerce meetings, with business owners and executives who sat down with me for economic discussions.

They knew whereof they spoke. I had pledged during my campaign that I would try to hold the line on taxes, and now, several months into my term, my reasoning had not changed. History had shown that higher taxes led to higher spending, not lower deficits. In other words, the more money there was in the pot, the more Congress was tempted to come up with new programs on which to spend it.

So when the President's budget—now called an economic plan, because it took in not just spending but new tax policies—came up for its second vote on May 27 (it now had the specifics and was not just a broad outline of spending targets), I voted against it.

We had gotten calls every day—starting ten days out—from the cabinet and the leadership saying they needed my vote. This pressure culminated in a call from the President himself. One afternoon, we were in my office and my press secretary, Jake Tapper, picked up the phone. "It's the President's office," Jake said. I looked skeptically at Jake, who has a wry sense of humor. "I'm not kidding," Jake said emphatically. "I'm not kidding."

That evening the President's economic plan survived, along with his credibility, by a vote of 219–213.

That initial vote was not the last. The plan passed the House by six votes and the Senate was tied, with Vice President Al Gore breaking the tie. But, as always, the two bills were not identical, and a conference committee of the two houses was convened to iron out the differences and produce a final plan that the two houses would vote on and send back to the White House for signature into law.

The conference lasted through July. I steeled myself for the coming debate and decision. Thursday, August 5, the day of the vote, finally came, just before our month-long summer recess. When I woke up that morning, I was a "no," and I intended on still being a "no" when I laid my head back down on the pillow that night. As I dressed for work, I figured it was going to be a long day.

I didn't know the half of it.

■ ■ ■

When I got to the office, my staff reported that we had begun to get occasional calls from our constituents back home. But we hadn't heard a peep from the White House or the Democratic congressional leadership; no one had even suggested that our vote might be needed.

This was in striking contrast to what had happened in the earlier budget vote on May 27. But every indication this time around was that the Democratic caucus had the votes and that I was being counted as a no vote. Even as the day wore on and the vote margin was diminishing, I still received no indication that I would be called upon.

I discussed with staff members what I would do in the unlikely event that the President asked me to switch my vote. I knew if he did call, it would be tough to turn him down. Anyone who says it wouldn't be has never talked to the President of the United States when he's asking you to help him out. I had already done it once when he had called before the first vote. It was going to be harder this time; the stakes for him were higher.

Almost every political analyst recognized at the time that a defeat for Clinton on the budget would cripple his presidency.

The stakes for me were high as well. I knew at the time that changing my vote at the eleventh hour may have been tantamount to political suicide. So the vote would resolve itself into one simple equation and, ultimately, one simple question: Was my political future more important than the agenda that the President had laid out for America during his campaign and that he was seeking to implement over the next four years? While the media has focused upon my request for a conference on entitlements as the "deal" for which I traded my vote, the "deal" for me was, from the very beginning, more of a sacrifice: the political future of one freshman member of Congress for the future of a presidency.

I had told my constituents I opposed higher taxes to achieve deficit reduction. I had voted not once but three times against the President's economic plan, and just hours before the vote I had gone live on local Philadelphia TV to tell my constituents that I remained convinced that this economic plan cut too little and that the tax-to-spending ratios were off.

The idea of an entitlements conference came up in a conversation with my policy director, Ken Smukler. It did not, however, come up in the context of a trade. Rather, it was founded upon the realization that my vote for the President's plan would almost surely be the end of my political future. What could I tell the hundreds of volunteers on my campaign to make them understand that their hard work had not been in vain? What could I tell those who invested their hard-earned money that it had not gone to waste? Most important, what could I tell the thousands of Montgomery County citizens who cast their vote for me in the name of change, that their votes indeed meant something?

The entitlements conference was the answer to these questions: a small but important first step toward addressing the fundamental issues driving our national debt out of control. If the President called and laid his presidency on the line, the "deal" would be done, and the President's economic plan would pass, the political future of a freshman member of Congress would be placed in serious jeopardy. Then, and only then, would I have to answer the questions raised by this vote. Then, and only then, would I be able to tell those who placed their faith in me that it was not all for naught, that we played some small role in finally getting Congress to face up to the mandate of the 1992 election and to place our economic house in order.

But I never believed it would come to that. Certainly there were other members that the Democratic caucus could turn to—members in safer districts, members who weren't freshmen still learning the ropes.

As the day wore on, the tension of the upcoming vote was palpable in the hallways of Congress. The closer it got to the actual vote, the slower time seemed to pass, like when you're on a bad vacation and you just want to go home.

The phones had quieted down after business hours and the office seemed to relax a bit. We ordered Chinese food and settled in for what promised to be a long evening. My legislative aide and budget expert Suzanne Biemiller brought in her yellow Lab puppy, Emma, for a quick visit. Emma bounded around the office as staff members drafted a statement that was to be released immediately after the vote. It explained that I had voted no because the budget didn't go far enough and almost completely ignored entitlements, and it called for an entitlements conference. The more we talked about it and it began to take shape, the more we realized that, regardless of my vote, it should happen in some form, in somebody's district. It was vital that we begin to redirect the conversation toward entitlement spending. However, I knew it wouldn't be an easy sell to most of my colleagues, the administration, and many members of the public who couldn't stomach such an unpopular subject.

My colleague Sam Coppersmith stopped by and we walked down the hall to David Minge's office, where he and his staff were also eating Chinese. David, a freshman Democrat from Minnesota, was one of those members whom the Democratic leadership had been pressuring to switch to a yes vote. But David reiterated over dinner that he just couldn't, that he was an emphatic "no." We sat around and chatted, waiting to be beckoned by the buzzers indicating that time was running out to cast our votes. While we were there, the Vice President called. David explained to him how tough the vote was and that he was a "no." I turned to Sam and said, "Boy, I'm glad they're not calling me."

Around 7:45 P.M., I was called to my office because Roger Altman, the Deputy Secretary of the Department of Treasury, was on the phone from the White House.

Roger asked me if I was a definite "no" and I said that was correct, I was. Then he asked if the President should call me, and I said no, I thought not. There was no point wasting his time on me.

I called home to talk to Ed. Ed, more than anyone else, could understand the pressure on a freshman facing a difficult vote. Ed had empathized with me the first time around in late May when I had been caught between the proverbial rock and a hard place. In late July of 1974, Ed had been the deciding vote on the first article of impeachment. A Democrat, he faced an angry constituency back home in Iowa in his Republican district. They were so upset, they resorted to stoning him. Yes, literally. (People threw pebbles at him in a parade.)

This time around, we both figured the White House had the numbers they needed. But Ed emphasized that if the President called, I had to be prepared. He reminded me that if push came to shove, there were a lot of Democratic good old boys around the place who had been there a long time and wanted to stay there until retirement. I reassured him that I didn't think it would come to my party having to resort to whipping a freshman Democrat in a Republican district. But we talked about the entitlements conference idea for a bit, what it would entail.

One of my aides alerted me that we'd better get going, and I told Ed I'd call later. He wished me luck and reminded me that in this job, in fact in this world, you don't get an opportunity too often to really affect the outcome of people's lives. He said I should just do what I thought was best when the time came.

I hung up and headed over to the Capitol with Ken Smukler, Amy Sobel, my deputy policy director, and Jim Pearthree, my administrative assistant. A few of my other staffers followed soon after, hoping to get a seat in the House gallery to watch the unfolding drama.

But the gallery was packed and they were unable to gain entry. It was a total circus, with staff people lining up to get in as though they had tickets to a U2 concert. I left Ken, Amy, and Jim at the door to the chamber because only members of Congress are allowed onto the floor. Before the vote on the actual budget, there was a procedural vote. After I cast my vote, I walked out into the hall, where Ken and I talked to Vic Fazio. We told him about our idea for the entitlements conference and he said he would run it by the White House.

With the procedural vote out of the way, it was time to return to the floor for the budget vote. When I walked in, I saw two Republicans high-five each other. "It's going down!" one of them excitedly told the other. "They don't have the votes." The conversations of the Democrats also indicated they didn't have the votes.

Just then, Jolene Unsoeld intercepted me. Jolene had been given the task of "whipping" both Pat Williams, a member from Montana, and myself.

"The President is on the phone," she told me quickly. I followed her to the Red Room, a quiet place just off the floor where an open phone line had been set up to the White House. Looking back now, I can barely remember going from the noisy chamber to the eerily quiet Red Room. I've joked since that that's because God protects people who are in bad accidents and those who vote at 218.

I picked up the phone and said hello, then heard his voice, which sounded tired and drained. "What would it take, Marjorie?" the President asked simply.

Oh God, I thought, it's really down to me. I suddenly felt a wave of exhaustion, the kind that can be totally subsuming, like when I went into a twenty-seven-hour labor with my son Marc, including ten hours of walking labor, after having just worked a twelve-hour shift at the television station.

"I gotta tell you, this may mean that I don't come back," I said softly, evenly. Jolene had stepped back, trying to give me a bit of privacy.

"I need your support on this one and I really need it badly. Without your vote, I can't win," said the President. "I think my administration will grind to a halt without the passage of this budget. The entire rest of our agenda depends on getting this behind us. What would it take?"

"We must face up to entitlements," I told him. "An entitlements conference. Not in my district necessarily, but it has to be in *a* community like my district, where people have the same concerns as my constituents and most Americans. It has to be you, members of the cabinet, leaders of the House—both Republicans and Democrats—in a community where people are willing to talk about their fears regarding entitlements, the fears that have prevented us from tackling these issues before.

"I think we're never really going to solve our budget problems until we do that," I added. This from me, the great financial wizard. "I feel a little silly saying this to you, but I think that we are fundamentally not facing up to it," I told the President. "And I think we are not because everybody is so concerned about getting reelected and not really moving the country forward. And I think if I do this, I might not be reelected. But if it means we address the issue of entitlements, which I believe is essential for the future of our children, I will do it. And if it means that this government and your presidency will be able to move forward, which I believe is essential for the future of our country, I will give you my vote.

"So I won't be your one hundred and third, and I won't be your two hundred and nineteenth; I will only be your two hundred and eighteenth vote. If you need me at two hundred and eighteen," I said, pausing, "I'll be there." I knew that only at 218 would the entitlements conversation begin—only then would the eyes of the nation begin to focus on entitlements spending; otherwise, my support of a piece of legislation I didn't like would be meaningless.

I was struggling to maintain my composure and simultaneously trying to register exactly what this would mean to me. I had thought about it only in the abstract up to this point, what I would do if called upon by the President. And now it was happening and it felt like slow motion. It's like when you're taught by your driving instructor what to do if you skid on ice. "Don't fight it; don't turn the wheel away from the direction you're going." But then you get there and the overpowering instinct is to wrest your way out of it. It hit me that if I turned him down, if I let him down, I would personally be cutting a President off at the knees in his first seven months in office. To watch a President who was hamstrung, who was considered by the Washington wags a lame duck for the following forty-one months, would have been unconscionable, not to mention unbearable. I thought of the one overriding message of the voters last year—to break up the gridlock . . . to move forward.

After I hung up, I walked out into the Speaker's lobby and looked at Jolene. She was hanging back, trying not to hover around me, yet concerned I would disappear.

I then talked to Ken and Amy about my conversation with the President and what the staff should be prepared for if I switched my vote. Ken, a fast thinker and a terrific writer, immediately started to compose a new press release in his head. Amy went to call the office to put Jake, Suzanne, and Bradley Edgell, my legislative director, on notice.

Jolene and I stood in the row behind the computer that tabulates the votes. We watched as the leadership kept track of who was voting which way.

In situations like these, when the vote is very close, there will sometimes be a run on vote switching. You can change your vote up until the Speaker bangs the gavel, when the vote becomes closed and you've reached the point of no return. I was standing there observing the scene and I overheard two Democratic congressmen talking, saying that if the vote went down, they were going to switch their votes, and they knew numerous others with the same intention. Then what they would say to the constituents would be, "Listen, the vote went down and I thought I had to support my President by voting yes, but in fact I hated this bill. I want to let you know that I was really a "no." So I switched my vote to no." The President would have gone down in flames. And I stood there and I said to myself, "There are not a lot of profiles in courage here."

It was now a few minutes after 10:00 P.M. and it was becoming crystal-clear that the fate of the President's budget rested on the shoulders of three members: Pat Williams, Ray Thornton, and myself. All evening, there had been a big push to get fifth-term Arkansas congressman Ray Thornton, a Democrat from Bill Clinton's congressional district, to change his vote. Ray, from the President's home state and securely entrenched in a safe district, was a natural candidate to be whipped into a "yes." But Ray wasn't budging.

My colleague Tim Penny, who throughout the whole budget process had been particularly supportive of me, is one of those people who believe Ray should have been handled differently. "I would have gone to Thornton and I would have said, 'How old are you, Ray? Didn't you serve in Congress for ten years back in the seventies? Don't you have a pension from that college you were a president of? What's your problem here? Didn't you vote for this back in May? Don't you represent Arkansas? Where's the President from?'

"I would have shamed him into voting yes," says Tim, emphatically. "I was outraged. That with all the reasons he should have voted yes—there were legitimate arguments as to why he should have been the last vote to get that bill passed. And that should have been the game plan. So to me, it's not so much outrage at Ray Thornton. He's just a symbol, a symbol of the way this place operates. It's like the old eating the young. . . . We're letting somebody who really is in the twilight of his career cast the politically safe votes so that he can come back. How much longer is he going to come back, anyway? He's past retirement age. It just reflected to me that this party leadership is so focused on a short-term win, in terms of passing this bill, that they can't even think about the long-term imperative, which is to build the future of this party on the base provided to us by Democrats, newly elected Democrats."

Meanwhile, Vic Fazio approached me to take my temperature on the status of my vote. "Vic," I said, "if I have to vote for this, we already have a press release ready to go that says I'm a 'no.' Where can we go so we can regroup?"

He left to see whether there was an available office in the Capitol itself. A minute later, he came back and said, "The best place to go would be back at my office." We knew that there was no way I could return to my office once my vote was cast. The phones would be ringing off the hook and the media would be descending on us; we needed a safe haven where we could recraft our statement explaining to constituents what had transpired.

Across the chamber, Tim Penny was watching the unfolding scene with horror. I was to learn later that he was trying to make his way across the floor to me, to tell me I didn't have to put myself at risk like this. Tim, who had been working doggedly to get the package to include more spending cuts, wanted the budget to pass but didn't like the way the leadership was going after freshmen—particularly the way he thought they were going after me. Your first year in this place is hard enough, he thought to himself, a time when you're experiencing shell shock, when you're learning that Congress doesn't always measure up to the idealistic vision you came with.

George Kundanis, the Speaker's aide, intercepted Tim, reassuring him that I wasn't going to be forced to switch my vote. Tim backed off and watched as Ray Thornton walked to the well to vote, carrying voting cards of both colors—red for no and green for yes. Tim assumed Ray had been convinced to vote with the party.

It was now about 10:10 P.M. and the Speaker requested that I come down to the well and cast my vote. Jolene had dispatched one of my female colleagues to get both a green and red card for me. The scoreboard showed the vote was 216–216. Pat Williams and I stood in the well, surrounded by our Democratic peers. Pat, a labor liberal from Montana—where the proposed 4.3-cent-a-gallon gasoline tax was anathema to his constituents, who regularly drove great distances across their sprawling state—looked me squarely in the eye. "I can't do this if you don't do this. We've got to do this together." The bill would go down if only one of us voted for it.

Barbara Kennelly, one of those encircling us, leaned over and said, "You can't let the President down."

I stood there for a moment, letting it all sink in, and then I heard someone whisper in my ear, "We need your vote."

"You've got it," I replied. I gave Pat a "let's do it" nod and we stepped up to cast our votes. It's all a blur to me now, walking down the aisle, being bombarded by Republican men throwing barbs, desperate to stop me in my tracks. They shouted, "Bye-bye, Margie. That's the end; she's gone. Bye-bye, Marjorie."

I was so incensed at the immaturity. I was so angered. Nobody was addressing Pat Williams in this manner, yelling, "Bye-bye, Pat."

Pat and I cast our ballots, then looked to the scoreboard for confirmation of our votes. The President's budget had passed. It was official: 218–216. In our nation's history, there were only two other votes of such importance with this close a margin: The first was the impeachment of Andrew Jackson; the second was the draft.

It would now go on to the Senate. There were cheers from our Democratic colleagues as we left the well and hissing from our Republican counterparts. I knew in my heart I had done the right thing, that this budget, with all its imperfections, was the President's only shot. And I think Pat felt similarly. "I did it not so much for the budget," he later explained to reporters, "as for movement. My vote was to help us set sail again." Many have said since that without this success for the President, we would not have been able to continue the legislative business of the session: health care, the North American Free Trade Agreement (NAFTA), campaign finance reform, and the crime bill.

The fact that I felt okay about my decision did not lessen the two big tasks in front of me: first, to convince my constituents that my vote was an effort to do the right thing—no more, no less; second, to encourage the President that the entitlements issue had to be addressed seriously. However painful a process that would be, it was one that needed to be dealt with immediately.

Jolene very much wanted to get me away from the craziness of the House floor and the press waiting outside. I went back to the Red Room, where many of the Democratic women came in to offer their support. It was a very emotional moment with a lot of hugging and kissing, the women all rallying around. When I look back, it's a bit hazy, but I remember Nita Lowey, Rosa DeLauro, Carrie Meek, and so many others all there, thanking me for helping the budget to pass and concerned with what it would mean for all of us. Karen Shepherd sat down beside me and said, "Thank you for what you did. I for one want you to know that if that piece of legislation had gone down, I'd be finished." Maria Cantwell was very moved and expressed great pride in the freshmen women, many of whom had put themselves on the line. For several of the freshmen women in marginal seats, being number 10 was just as difficult as being number 218.

Jolene had gone through the Republican side of the floor and checked for reporters who might be milling around the doorway.

She came back, reporting that the coast was clear, and I escaped into the elevator, off to meet my staff to work on the press releases and to begin returning what seemed like endless press calls to explain what had just transpired. The first call was to Linda August, my chief of staff, who was back in my district office. She had her work cut out for her, preparing the district office for the onslaught of calls we anticipated.

Finally, hours later, at 2:00 A.M., I went home with Amy. I crashed in her apartment because it was too late to make the trek out to Bethesda, where I stay with my good friend Nancy Chasen when I'm in Washington.

At 4:30 A.M., the phone rang. It was Ed with a message from the "Today" show. I was already scheduled to go on CNN's "Morning Break" and Fox's "Morning News." I knew it was important to get out there and explain why I had switched the vote before the punditocracy started going into overspin. As I got dressed, Amy brought in the *Washington Post* and pointed to the front-page story about the budget and the role I had played in its passage.

"It wasn't a dream," Amy said, rubbing her eyes, handing me the paper. So with only two hours of sleep and major raccoon eyes, I did the morning news circuit.

Meanwhile, back on the Hill, Tim Penny was still furious that I had been persuaded to vote yes. The fact that the vote had played out this way, that it had come down to a freshman, only underscored for Tim that the decision he had settled on recently about his own career was the right one.

And Tim chose that morning, the day after the budget vote, to make his decision public and official. On the House floor, the forty-one-year-old Minnesota congressman announced that after more than ten years serving in the United States House of Representatives he was not going to run for a seventh term in 1994. Many people were quite surprised by Tim's announcement. Tim is well respected by his colleagues, even those who disagree with him, having made a real name for himself as a nose-to-the-grindstone maverick determined to overthrow the beast of deficit spending.

But he was tired of playing the game, particularly in a place where the rules have nothing to do with fair play. And so, on the morning of August 6, he got up, got dressed, and put on one of his favorite ties. It had a floral design, with Mickey Mouse beaming out of the center of each flower. It symbolized to him why he wanted to leave Washington: He wanted his four kids to grow up back home in his beloved state of Minnesota. It was also a commentary on the institution.

■ ■ ■

In the days to come, the reaction to my vote was overwhelming, to say the least. The Republicans were excoriating me, while the Democrats were lionizing me. *USA Today* wrote an editorial suggesting I be added to Mount Rushmore; the *Wall Street Journal* offered me an "Oscar for angst"; local Philadelphia-area papers simultaneously lauded and lambasted me; my colleague Pat Schroeder, back in Colorado to meet with the visiting Pope, declared, "I'm going to ask the Pope to pray for Marjorie Margolies-Mezvinsky." The President and Hillary both called to thank me the next day.

I wasn't comfortable being called a villain or a heroine; that wasn't what this was about. It was about doing what I thought was right.

Looking back on the budget vote, the First Lady said, "What I felt was real pride, because it was a gutsy vote for a lot of people. And it was a vote that put the country first, and put the whole political process on a stronger footing, and the reason a lot of the men gave for voting against it was so transparent, so intellectually empty. And for most women, you know, it was an emotional vote. You told me that a lot of women later went into the Red Room and broke down. I, watching it, felt the same way. So I would have done exactly the same thing. I could not have lived with myself. I don't know how you get up and look in the mirror and live with that kind of intellectual and political dishonesty. For people to say they voted against even though they had voted for it the first time with the BTU tax, because it had a gas tax, when the original version had a seven-cents-a-gallon gas tax as part of the BTU package, that is just beyond my understanding; it is so weak. And I think most women knew what was at stake. I mean, if we hadn't had that vote, we would not have a budget today. It would be after the budget deadline. We would all be sitting there; this country would be going down the tubes. Instead, it was finished. And we could then build. And now we're on the brink of health care; we're dealing with tough issues like crime and violence and NAFTA and a lot of other things that are very difficult. But in the absence of that kind of courage, we wouldn't have gotten there. And I think it also is a vote that most people are not only going to be able to survive but be able to wear as a badge of courage."

■ ■ ■

Meanwhile, my Washington and Pennsylvania offices were overrun with calls from constituents upset with my vote, but, thankfully, also from people calling to voice their support.

We returned to the district to face the music. The days that followed were long. Everywhere I went, I was approached by people who wanted to discuss The Vote—sometimes to argue with me and sometimes to reassure me that they were still behind me. One day, Amy, who has been there for me at every turn since the campaign, suggested we stop by the county fair to defend my 1992 goat-milking championship title. We needed a break, we decided. When we got out of the car, we both put on our sunglasses and laughed. Maybe the glasses would ensure our anonymity.

Amy is the kind of person who gets something done for you before you realize you need her to do something. She's also not big on personal expression. I usually figure out what she's feeling more from what she doesn't say than from what she does. "M," she said, breaking the silence as we walked to the entrance of the fair.

"Yes?"

"I just want you to know I've never been more proud to work for you. You did the right thing, something that will matter for the future of the country and the future of your children and grandchildren."

I looked at her, and couldn't muster a snappy comeback. This whole episode had been an extremely lonely experience and it meant a lot to me. In fact, my entire staff, each person in his or her own way, had let me know each was behind me.

Probably the longest day during the August recess was Saturday the twenty-eighth, when we held two town meetings in our district. They had been scheduled before the vote. We started that morning with an 8:30 meeting at the main district office, going over the presentation I was to give, trying to anticipate what the tenor of the meetings would be. We figured there would be a fair amount of anger, but we also hoped that people would give me the opportunity to explain my decision fully.

As it turned out, we were correct on both counts. From the outset, I laid the ground rules, asking that we all participate in an orderly and constructive manner. The police were on hand outside in case anyone was unduly agitated.

About three hundred people attended the first town meeting; the second drew about half as many. At both meetings, there was standing room only. There were more people at both meetings who opposed my yes vote, but there were also plenty of people supporting me. At each, I gave a twenty-five-minute presentation, with charts to explain the need to address entitlement programs, as well as outlining the projected crisis that would occur if we didn't make the hard calls, saying that this was about our future and that of our children.

At one point, I flashed on a phone conversation I had recently had with my youngest son, Andrew. He had been away at summer camp during The Vote and had seen the newspaper stories and the controversy surrounding my vote. When I talked to him up at camp, he seemed concerned about what he had read. The conversations I had been having all along with him were about how I didn't think the piece of legislation went far enough.

"Mom, what happened to make you change your mind?" he asked.

"It was the right thing to do, Andrew," I said. I told him about the presidency and how important it was for the nation to move ahead. And I also told him we were going to have a big political fight ahead of us. My kids knew better than anybody how hard we had all worked to get this seat. They had been out there on the campaign trail with me, in their MMM T-shirts (I had convinced them that being out on the hustings from morning till night was really a civics lesson and not child abuse).

For me personally, the day's defining moment was when a young man in his late twenties stood up to speak. "When I came here, I was angry with you and didn't like your vote," he said. "But I've listened to what you've had to say and I think I understand why you did what you did."

"You're precisely the person whom I'm talking to today," I answered. "Because it's you and your kids who will be suffering tomorrow if we don't make tough decisions today."

I tried to hang on to whatever sense of humor I had left, and at one town meeting I got a good chuckle when I noticed a woman in the front row sitting next to a man I assume was her husband. The exchange between my constituents and myself had been particularly tense. The woman listened and then during a momentary lull in the debate she leaned over to her husband. "Why does she want this job?" she asked him loudly.

"Finally! A really good question," I quipped.

■ ■ ■

One evening in late September, I ran into Anna Eshoo, whose office is down the hall from mine in Longworth. We were just leaving for the weekend. We looked at each other, both weary from a long week.

As we walked down the long hall toward the elevator, I remembered how she had phoned me back in May, during the first budget vote. Pressured by everyone to vote yes, I had begun to lose sleep over it and had lost my appetite. It had finally gotten to the point where I didn't feel like talking to anyone—I was just plain talked out. One afternoon, my aides told me that Anna was on the phone. I picked it up, expecting more pressure.

"I'm not calling to whip you. I just want to make sure you're okay," Anna said. "How are you feeling? I know there's a lot of pressure on you."

That little phone call meant a lot to me. Someone remembered I was a living, breathing person with a pulse (barely, at that point).

Now, four months later (or, as my press secretary, Jake, refers to it: A.V.E.—after the vote era), we were walking down the hall having a very light conversation. There was a tacit end-of-the-week agreement that we were too tired to talk about anything weighty.

As she stepped onto the elevator, Anna stopped and looked at me. "I think it'll be okay now," she said. "You've passed through the eye of the needle."

Epilogue: Our Legacy to Our Children

When I first arrived back in Washington, I was uncertain what my experience as a congresswoman would be, but at least I wasn't a newcomer to either the city or the Hill. As a reporter, I had run around the halls of the Capitol, tracking down legislators I needed to interview. As a congressional spouse, I had attended many a reception with my husband, seeing another side of things here. I thought after all my exposure, I really understood the place, knew its funny (and not so funny) quirks. But like any large institution, it's a complicated place, rooted in tradition and process and culture, a place you can only truly understand as an insider.

Even though I had my member's pin firmly attached to my lapel, I felt like a stranger in a strange land, and I suspect most other freshmen legislators experienced a similar tentativeness. My overriding desire was somehow to make a difference, a real difference—not the kind you hear politicians talking about ad nauseum, but the kind of difference you see in a person's face when you have somehow made his or her existence on this planet a little easier, a little better.

Those first several months were scary and exciting and sometimes frustrating, but I found solace in an unexpected place—the *Statue of Freedom,* a seven-ton bronze statue. Since 1863, she had been standing atop the Capitol dome. Now she stood in front of the Capitol itself, up on a platform, with scaffolding encasing her. She, too, was no stranger to the Capitol, but like me, she had a new vantage point.

Not long after the twenty-four women of our freshman class came to Washington, *Freedom* had been removed from her perch. Washingtonians and tourists alike gathered in the early-dawn hours to watch as a Skycrane helicopter precariously lifted her down to earth for a rejuvenation. The years she had spent weathering the snow, rain, and sun had taken their toll. She needed a thorough bathing and polishing to remove the corrosion that had built up over the 130 years of her tenure. Each day, she drew crowds of people around her while workmen toiled to make her shine. I walked by her often, noting the progress of her rehabilitation.

Suddenly, after all these years, *Freedom* was getting the attention she was owed. It occurred to me that maybe it was more than a coincidence that the powers that be had decided to recognize her needs in the same year a record number of women were sent to Congress. She had always been there, but now she was having her day in the sun. She became a talisman to me.

■ ■ ■

Many young women look to the female members of Congress as role models. This is an honor for us, and each of us, in our own way, tries to give good counsel. Blanche Lambert, mature and grounded beyond her years, tells girls back home in Arkansas who dream of being congresswomen themselves, "Don't limit yourself in what you want to do by what you think you ought to do. Don't limit yourself—if you have an idea, don't be afraid; if there's an idea of what you want to do or who you want to be, don't be afraid of it; and don't ever think you're limited by the color of your skin or your sex or your age or anything else. Go with it, because I think that's really important to do. If you're interested in politics, the first and foremost thing you have to do is look inside your own heart and your mind and understand what you want and why you want it. Because this is not an easy job. The campaign is not easy, the work is not easy, and you have to know why in your heart you are here."

Anna Eshoo often finds herself meeting young females who look to her with admiration, who want to know what it's really like to be a congresswoman. "I think it's very important to tell people the truth, especially young girls, young women—that running for Congress is not for the faint of heart, nor is the job. This is not just a story about getting here; it's about distinguishing yourself once you get here as well."

While the women here in Congress are a diversely accomplished group, as legislators at the national level we are still finding our way. "I think that collectively as women we will make a difference," says Anna Eshoo. "I can't tell you specifically how. It may very well be on the issue of choice."

We are all too aware of the fact that we can't change things overnight, that we have to pay our dues to command the kind of power that can move mountains (or at least pass bills). "I think that ten years from now, many things will have changed," says Nydia Velazquez. "I know that for me to get the kind of political leverage that will have an impact, a real impact, in my district, I need to be here at least ten years."

■ ■ ■

In the coming election, there's a lot of work to be done to bring more women to Congress and to hold on to the seats we've already won. Some of us, like myself, are in marginal districts. While many of the barriers have been broken down for female candidates, there are still hurdles to overcome. Women have to get themselves out to the polls to vote and they have to learn to pry open their wallets to contribute regularly to organizations like EMILY's List, Wish List, the National Women's Political Caucus, and the Women's Campaign Fund. And most of all, women have to be willing to run. The important thing to remember is the old chestnut we always tell our kids: "It doesn't matter if you win or lose, it's how you play the game." For little girls, I might amend it to: "It doesn't matter if you win or lose, just that you play the game."

My 1992 race was so close, I had composed only a concession speech. When the numbers started to come in—and it was well after midnight when we learned I had actually won by 1,373 votes—I quickly had to cross out *defeat* in about eight places and write in *victory*.

My concession/acceptance speech was in the form of a letter to my youngest child, Andrew. This is what I told him: "Dear Andrew, This is no time for tears. I hope that on the day, this day, when you walk into the voting booth for the very first time in the year 2000 that there will be no more talk of the Year of the Woman or the Year of the Outsider because there will have been lots of us who have changed the face of the body we call Congress."

As the evening wore on and the vote margin began to narrow, I revised my remarks a bit. "Even though we didn't make it over the top, Andrew, this is a form of victory in Montgomery County, and we must look to the future.

"In the year 2000, Andrew, politics as usual will mean that farmers and pharmacists, engineers and architects, fathers and mothers will represent us in Washington in numbers that count. In that year, family issues will not come in vogue a few weeks before the election but will dominate our domestic policy decisions. And on that day, eight years from now, as you walk into the voting booth to cast your first ballot, I hope you will think back to this night and say to yourself, 'Look how far we've come.' " Fortunately, very fortunately, I was able to revise my concession speech—and deliver it as a victory address.

■ ■ ■

I think we have turned a corner and we will never go back. It's never going to be the way it was. This is just the prologue.

THE FRESHMEN WOMEN

Corrine Brown was born November 11, 1946.
Democrat
Florida, Third District: parts of Jacksonville, Orlando, Daytona Beach, and Gainesville
Political career: Florida House, 1983–1993
Committee assignments: Public Works and Transportation; Veterans' Affairs

Leslie Byrne was born October 27, 1946.
Democrat
Virginia, Eleventh District: D.C. suburbs—parts of Fairfax and Prince William counties
Political career: Virginia House, 1986–1992
Committee assignments: Post Office and Civil Service; Public Works and Transportation

Maria Cantwell was born October 13, 1958.
Democrat
Washington, First District: Puget Sound (west and east)—North Seattle suburbs; Kitsap Peninsula
Political career: Washington House, 1987–1993
Committee assignments: Foreign Affairs; Merchant Marine and Fisheries; Public Works and Transportation

Eva Clayton was born September 16, 1934.
Democrat (freshman class president of Democrats)
North Carolina, First District: east—parts of Fayetteville, Rocky Mount, and Greenville
Political career: Sought Democratic nomination for U.S. House in 1968; Warren County Commission, 1983–1992 (chairman)
Committee assignments: Agriculture; Small Business

Pat Danner was born January 13, 1934.
Democrat
Missouri, Sixth District: northwest—St. Joseph
Political career: Missouri Senate, 1983–1993
Committee assignments: Public Works and Transportation; Small Business

Jennifer Dunn was born July 29, 1941.
Republican
Washington, Eighth District: Puget Sound (east)—King County suburbs; Bellevue
Political career: Washington Republican Party chairman, 1980–1992
Committee assignments: House Administration; Joint Committee on the Organization of Congress; Public Works and Transportation; Science, Space and Technology

Karan English was born March 23, 1949.
Democrat
Arizona, Sixth District: Flagstaff; Navajo Reservation
Political career: Coconino County Board of Supervisors, 1981–1987 (chairman 1985–1987); Arizona House, 1987–1991; Arizona Senate, 1991–1993
Committee assignments: Education and Labor; Natural Resources

Anna Eshoo was born December 13, 1942.
Democrat
California, Fourteenth District: southern San Mateo and northern Santa Clara counties
Political career: Democratic National Committee, 1980–1992; San Mateo County Board of Supervisors, 1982–1992; Democratic nominee for U.S. House, 1988
Committee assignments: Merchant Marine and Fisheries; Science, Space and Technology

Tillie Fowler was born December 23, 1942.
Republican
Florida, Fourth District: part of Jacksonville and coastal counties from Georgia border to Daytona Beach
Political career: Jacksonville City Council, 1985–1992
Committee assignments: Armed Services; Merchant Marine and Fisheries

Elizabeth Furse was born October 13, 1936.
Democrat
Oregon, First District: West Portland and suburbs
No former political office: civil rights and peace activist; vineyard owner
Committee assignments: Armed Services; Banking, Finance and Urban Affairs; Merchant Marine and Fisheries

Jane Harman was born June 28, 1945.
Democrat
California, Thirty-sixth District: West Los Angeles County; Manhattan Beach; Torrance
No former political office: lawyer
Committee assignments: Armed Services; Science, Space and Technology

Eddie Bernice Johnson was born December 3, 1935.
Democrat
Texas, Thirtieth District: city of Dallas, about 60 percent; parts of Dallas, Collin, and Tarrant counties
Political career: Texas House, 1972–1977; Texas Senate, 1987–1993
Committee assignments: Public Works and Transportation; Science, Space and Technology

Blanche Lambert was born September 30, 1960.
Democrat
Arkansas, First District: northeast—Jonesboro; West Memphis
No former political office: former lobbyist and congressional aide
Committee assignments: Agriculture; Energy and Commerce; Merchant Marine and Fisheries

Carolyn Maloney was born February 19, 1948.
Democrat
New York, Fourteenth District: East Side of Manhattan; parts of Brooklyn and Queens—Greenpoint and Astoria
Political career: New York City Council, 1982–1993
Committee assignments: Banking, Finance and Urban Affairs; Government Operations

Marjorie Margolies-Mezvinsky was born June 21, 1942.
Democrat
Pennsylvania, Thirteenth District: northwest Philadelphia suburbs
No former political office: television journalist
Committee assignments: Energy and Commerce; Government Operations; Small Business

Cynthia McKinney was born March 17, 1955.
Democrat
Georgia, Eleventh District: east central—Atlanta suburbs; parts of Augusta and Savannah
Political career: Democratic candidate for Georgia House, 1986; Georgia House, 1989–1992
Committee assignments: Agriculture; Foreign Affairs

Carrie Meek was born April 29, 1926.
Democrat
Florida, Seventeenth District: southeast—north Dade County; part of Miami
Political career: Florida House, 1979–1983; Florida Senate, 1983–1993
Committee assignment: Appropriations

Deborah Pryce was born July 29, 1951.
Republican
Ohio, Fifteenth District: central—western Columbus and suburbs
Political career: Franklin County Municipal Court Judge, 1985–1992
Committee assignments: Banking, Finance and Urban Affairs; Government Operations
Interim class president for Republican freshmen members; policy director of the freshman class

Lucille Roybal-Allard was born June 12, 1941.
Democrat
California, Thirty-third District: east central Los Angeles; Pasadena
Political career: California assembly, 1987–1992
Committee assignments: Banking, Finance and Urban Affairs; Small Business

Lynn Schenk was born January 5, 1945.
Democrat
California, Forty-ninth District: San Diego; Coronado; Imperial Beach
Political career: California Secretary of Business, Transportation and Housing, 1980–1983; San Diego Unified Port commissioner, 1990–1993
Committee assignments: Energy and Commerce; Merchant Marine and Fisheries

Karen Shepherd was born July 5, 1940.
Democrat
Utah, Second District: central—parts of Salt Lake City
Political career: Utah senate, 1991–1993
Committee assignments: Natural Resources; Public Works and Transportation

Karen Thurman was born January 12, 1951.
Democrat
Florida, Fifth District: northern part of West Coast—parts of Alachua and Pasco counties; Hernando, Citrus, Sumter, Marion, Levy, Dixie, and Gilchrist counties; parts of Gainesville
Political career: Dunnellon City Council, 1975–1983; mayor of Dunnellon, 1979–1981; Florida senate, 1983–1993
Committee assignments: Agriculture; Government Operations

Nydia Velazquez was born March 22, 1953.
Democrat (first and only Puerto Rican woman elected to Congress)
New York, Twelfth District: Lower East Side Manhattan; parts of Brooklyn and Queens
Political career: New York City Council, 1984–1986
Committee assignments: Banking, Finance and Urban Affairs; Small Business

Lynn Woolsey was born November 3, 1937.
Democrat
California, Sixth District: Marin and Sonoma counties
Political career: Petaluma City Council, 1984–1992
Committee assignments: Budget; Education and Labor; Government Operations